CLASSIC WALKS IN
Wales

Teithian Cerdded Clasurol yng Nghymru

by Steve Ashton

FRASER STEWART BOOKS

Dedication
This book is dedicated to J. Norman Ashton,
who, though he may have had better things
to do, accompanied me in spirit on all these
walks.

First published by Oxford Illustrated Press Limited,
Haynes Publishing Group.

This edition published 1995
by The Promotional Reprint Company Limited,
Deacon House, 65 Old Church Street,
London SW3 5BS

ISBN 1 85648 210 3

Printed in Malaysia

Contents

Preface 4
Introduction 5
Key to Route Map Symbols 8

Llangollen and the Berwyns 9
1: World's End and Beyond 10
2: Pistyll Rhaeadr and the
Berwyns 13

Anglesey Coast 16
3: Holyhead Mountain and the
Stacks 17
4: Newborough and Llanddwyn
Island 20

The Carneddau 23
5: Conwy Mountain 24
6: Aber Falls and Foel Fras 27
7: The Cwm Eigiau Horseshoe 30
8: The Carneddau from Ogwen 33

The Glyders 36
9: Cwm Idwal and Y Garn 37
10: The Glyders from Ogwen 40
11: The Cwm Bochlwyd Horseshoe 43
12: The Glyders from the Llanberis
Pass 46

Llugwy Valley 49
13: Moel Siabod 50
14: Crimpiau and Llyn Crafnant 53
15: Short Walks from Betws y
Coed 56

Snowdon Group 59
16: Snowdon from Pen y Pass 60
17: The Snowdon Horseshoe 63
18: Snowdon from Nant Gwynant 67
19: Snowdon from Rhyd Ddu 70

Moelwyns and Eifionydd 74
20: Cnicht and the Moelwyns 75
21: Aberglaslyn and Cwm Bychan 78
22: Moel Hebog and Moel Lefn 81
23: The Nantlle Ridge 84
24: Yr Eifl and Braich y Pwll 87

Cambrian Mountains 90
25: Arenig Fawr 91
26: The Rhinog Ridge 94
27: Short Walks from Dolgellau 98
28: Aran Fawddwy 101
29: Cader Idris 104
30: Plynlimon 107

The Brecon Beacons 110
31: Bannau Sir Gaer 111
32: Waterfall Country 114
33: The Brecon Beacons from the
North 117
34: The Brecon Beacons from the
South 120
35: Waun Fach and Pen y Gadair
Fawr 123

South Coast 126
36: Garn Fawr and Strumble
Head 127
37: St David's and Ramsey Sound 130
38: Marloes Peninsula 133
39: St Govan's Head 136
40: Rhossili to Port Eynon 139

Appendix: Glossary of Welsh
Place Names 143

Preface

The preface, though read first (when at all), is written last. It is an opportunity for the author, with the benefit of hindsight, to excuse the shortcomings of the book and thus attempt to disarm a critical reader. It is also a good place to make outrageous claims for the subject before it slips away into other, perhaps less passionate hands.

Whenever I met people on the walks—I would usually go alone, midweek and out of season, so it wasn't all that often—I was always aware that I never knew what they were thinking. The only thing I could be sure of was that whatever they might say in greeting or conversation had nothing to do with the ideas and images taking shape inside their heads. Walkers are like that. They hold themselves back. Likewise the people who write about walking, albeit for other reasons. My words and pictures can't possibly convey the experiences that await. Take it for granted that inclusion of a route in the following pages means that it has the potential to lift your spirits sky high.

Until quite recently I used to hate walking, and would resort to all sorts of subterfuge to avoid it. Since my conversion it has gripped me like a hunger. Now I am prepared to admit—under the influence of the end-of-term euphoria brought on by writing the final sentence—that scrambling up a ridge on Snowdon, or walking above the cliffs of Pembroke, has brought me closer to enlightenment than anything else I have ever done.

Steve Ashton, 1990

At the summit of Pen Pumlumon Fawr. The Nant y Moch Reservoir lies below. Ar gopa Pen Pumlumon Fawr. Gwelir cronfa ddŵr Nant-y-moch islaw.

Introduction

Selection of Routes

I had no difficulty at all in finding forty classic walks in Wales. But which forty? Whatever I chose, the scramblers would want more scrambles and the ramblers more rambles. In the end I opted for a broad spread, from lowland strolls to mountain traverses. I enjoyed them all, and I don't see any reason why you shouldn't as well—whatever your professed speciality.

Route Classification

Classifying walks according to difficulty attracts controversy, though I can't understand why; it is mere shorthand for strings of adjectives. I have adopted a five-tiered system:

Class A: Short, low-level routes that may be enjoyed by everyone, including children and reluctant walkers.

Class B: Longer coastal or other low level routes, and ascents to small summits.

Class C: Hill walks to medium and high summits, and coastal routes with added complications. (Route planning becomes important).

Class D: Long hill walks, possibly including some simple scrambling or pathless terrain. (For experienced hill walkers.)

Class E: Ridge scrambles and exceptionally long hill walks. (For experienced and adventurous hill walkers.)

Distances and Times

Metric distances have been given priority for compatibility with metric maps. Imperial conversions are approximate. A simple calculation based on the length of the walk and the sum of its uphill sections gives a rough idea of its duration (1hr for every 5km walked, plus 30 mins for each 300m of ascent). To this I have added extra time to take account of delays due to difficult terrain and short rests.

Maps

Advice on choosing maps is given in the ten regional introductions. Grid references (eg GR:684 589) are used frequently in the information boxes to identify the start and important turning points on the walks. Recent OS maps explain how the system works. Note that I have omitted the national grid prefix letters

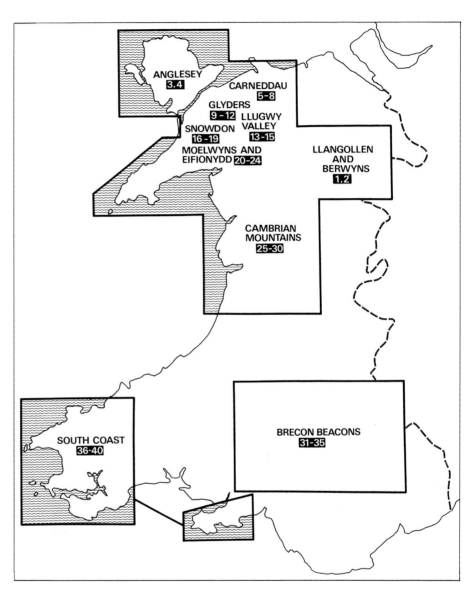

(eg. SM, SH) from the references; it will be clear from the text which map is being used (the initials GR simply stand for 'Grid Reference').

Route Descriptions

You will already have discovered that the book does not fit into your jacket pocket. You might therefore now be wondering why I have included a field-guide route description for each walk. It is there so that when planning a trip you can follow the route line on the OS

map (aided by the sketch map) and perhaps extract a few notes to take with you on the walk.

Weather and Ground Conditions

I have assumed that these walks will be attempted in 'summer' conditions. Some of the low-level and moorland walks benefit from frost (it freezes the bogs), but in almost every other case the difficulty of the route increases dramatically under snow or ice. Some of these

Huntsman's Leap. *Naid yr Heliwr.*

routes give magnificent expeditions under such conditions, but they are then no longer walks and demand the skills and equipment of the winter mountaineer.

TV and radio forecasts are adequate for building up a general weather picture before travelling, while the expensive recorded phone forecasts (eg. Weatherdial, Weathercall) are best for detailed, last-minute information. The Snowdonia National Park Authority sponsors a recorded forecast which includes a prediction of mountain-top conditions. This can be accessed at normal phone rates on Llanberis 870120. Bear in mind that the temperature falls with increased height (there may be a 10°C difference between valley and summit), while wind speed and precipitation generally intensify as well.

Equipment

Walking boots are the appropriate footwear for most of these routes, although trainers and other ultra-lightweight footwear are adequate for the coastal and low-level walks during fine weather. Another important distinction between low and high-level routes is the need for spare clothing (pullover, gloves, hat, waterproofs) and other emergency items (compass, first-aid kit, survival bag, torch, whistle). Advice on choosing an emergency rope for the two main scrambles appears in the body of the text.

Accidents

When practical it is a good idea to leave word of your probable route with someone at your accommodation, but don't forget to tell them if you change your plans and return elsewhere. If you find yourself in difficulty on the mountain, try to attract attention using the international distress signal: six successive whistle blasts or torch flashes repeated after a one-minute pause. If you have witnessed an accident and need to call out the mountain rescue, phone 999 and ask for the police.

A cloud sea pours over the Nantlle Ridge into Cwm Silyn. *Llifa môr o gymylau ar draws Esgair Nantlle i mewn i Gwm Silyn.*

A Note for Photographers

First of all, I ought to say that I make no special claims for these photographs. Enjoying the walk took priority, and if it was a choice between waiting for optimum lighting conditions and finishing the walk in daylight then I would move on. That said, I was lucky enough to be able to pick and choose my days out (no, I'm not going to apologise for the preponderance of blue skies).

All the colour pictures were taken on Kodachrome (usually ISO64 but in a few cases 25 or 200), the black & whites on Ilford XP1. I mostly used Canon SLR equipment, although on some of the more arduous routes I was forced to use Olympus XA compacts to save weight. I used a 28-55mm zoom (or fixed 35mm) for the majority of shots, supplemented by sparing use of a 17mm ultra-wide-angle and 80-210mm telephoto. Apart from UV and an occasional polarising filter, I steered well clear of accessories. A lightweight tripod accompanied me on most of my solo walks. It wasn't up to much conversationally, though with the help of a long-delay shutter release it knew how to include a figure in the composition for added interest.

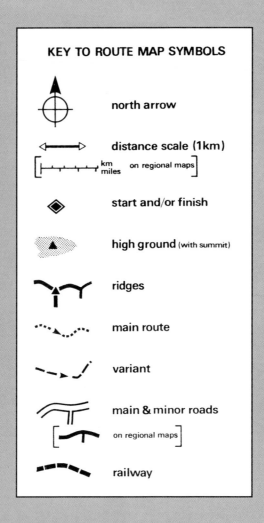

KEY TO ROUTE MAP SYMBOLS

north arrow

distance scale (1km)

km
miles   on regional maps

start and/or finish

high ground (with summit)

ridges

main route

variant

main & minor roads

on regional maps

railway

LLANGOLLEN AND THE BERWYNS

Maps: 1:50,000 scale is adequate for the walks in this section. Unfortunately the region falls on separate Landranger maps: Sheet 125 (Bala & Lake Vyrnwy) for the Berwyns, and Sheet 117 (Chester & Wrexham) for Llangollen.

Bases: No single base is ideal, although Llangollen itself, which offers a full range of accommodation, is the obvious choice for the World's End walk. It may be approached by bus from east or west via the A5 (the nearest railway station is at Chirk, 13km/8miles to the east). The Berwyns are rather isolated but can be reached by car from Llangollen over the mountain road to Llanrhaeadr ym Mochnant. Otherwise approach via Bala from a base in Snowdonia, or direct from the Midlands via Oswestry.

North-east Wales is not easily categorised. Almost every aspect of Welsh life and scenery is here, from the sprawling industry of Wrexham to the bustling tourism of Llangollen, and from the dense forests of Clocaenog to the empty moorland of the Berwyns. Only the rugged mountains are missing. That puts constraints on the selection of routes.

Leaving aside the innumerable forest tracks and lowland trails, the character of the region best emerges through two very different walks. The first of these explores the hillside above Llangollen, discovering a ruined castle, a limestone escarpment, and a navigable canal. In complete contrast the second route wanders over the lonely and sodden hilltops of the Berwyns in search—not always successful—of solitude and a bit of dry grass.

Narrowboat on the Llangollen Canal. The towpath provides a pleasant finish to the walk. Culfad ar gamlas Llangollen. Y mae'r llwybr yn ddiwedd hyfryd i'r daith.

1: LLANGOLLEN AND THE BERWYNS —
World's End and Beyond

Route summary: A walk of many colours. Visits a ruined hilltop castle, contours below a limestone escarpment, wades across a heather-clad mountain, and strolls along a canal towpath.

Difficulty: Class D.

Main summits: Dinas Brân 305m/1000ft; Eglwyseg Mountain 511m/1678ft.

Duration: 19km/12miles; 550m/1800ft of ascent; allow 6hrs.

Terrain: Mainly good paths and tracks but includes a substantial section of trackless heather bashing.

Special difficulties: Extremely difficult route finding on Eglwyseg Mountain in mist (consider one of the shorter alternatives in such conditions).

Approach: From Llangollen on the A5. Park in the town centre or opposite the school at GR:215 423 (see sketch map).

Route directions: Take a path signposted "Dinas Brân" up steps and alongside the school, continuing by the pasture's edge to a track followed across a junction of lanes to a gate. A path on the right now leads over a grass plateau and rises steeply up the unmistakable conical hill of Dinas Brân (GR:222 431).

Descend on the east side to reach the Panorama Drive and follow it left for 2km. Fork right on a gated track (obscure "Offa's Dyke" signpost) to Bryn Goleu (GR:219 454). A good path contours scree below the limestone buttresses and finally rises through the diminished crags at the northern end to a grass track above the escarpment.

After following the track around the forest edge to the head of the World's End indent, ascend south-east (vague path) to a slight saddle (GR:239 471). Turn right and ascend a shallow ridge over heather (few signs of path) to the summit of Eglwyseg Mountain (GR:231 463). Continue south, over a minor top, then descend south-west over heather to a grass path near an isolated group of pine trees (GR:226 450). Ignore all forks and junctions and follow the improving path (the 'green lane') in its gradual descent around the hillside to Panorama Drive (GR:241 429).

From a viewpoint 10m right, turn sharp left and descend to a green track followed left to a gate. Turn right and descend a steep narrow path, initially by a wall, to quarry levels. Carefully descend through the levels, trending right where practical, to arrive at a network of lanes and paths. Choose the downhill option at each junction and, hopefully, you will emerge on the main road at the Sun Trevor Inn (GR:241 423).

Follow the canal towpath back to Llangollen.

Alternatives: (1) Turn right on Panorama Drive after descending from Dinas Brân and rejoin the main route at the viewpoint. (2) Arrange return transport from World's End and quit the route after walking the Dinas Brân and Eglwyseg escarpment sections. (3) Turn right at Bryn Goleu and ascend a break in the escarpment to emerge near the start of the 'green lane' section.

Llangollen railway station, closed since the mid-sixties, has been brought back into service by enthusiasts from the Flint and Deeside Railway Preservation Society. And yet despite their efforts—or perhaps because of them—the place lacks authenticity. It is too clean, too efficient. You can sit on the benches without inspecting them first. You can see daylight through the waiting room windows. You can set your watch by the platform clock.

Every half hour or so a steam train puffs into the station returning dozens of smiling trippers from their brief ride down what was once a section of the Great Western Railway. The shrill whistle announcing the train's arrival is a cue for grown men to hurry from station buildings and immerse themselves in the steam and smoke emanating from the little saddletank engine. Their bemused and tutting wives, meanwhile, stand impatiently in the doorway of the cafeteria and cast meaningful glances at each other. My sympathies were with the wives, but in a rush of nostalgia I joined the men at the platform edge and inhaled deeply, evoking childhood memories of skin rashes from hairy seat fabric. Rejuvenated and smelly, I shouldered my pack and set off for Dinas Brân.

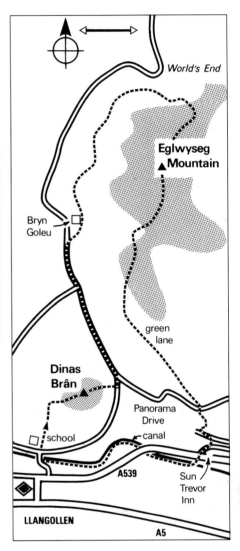

The ruins of Castell Dinas Brân stand in a position of strategic advantage on top of a conical hill overlooking Llangollen and the Dee. What we see today are the thirteenth-century remains of the most recent of a succession of defended buildings and earthworks dating back to the Iron Age. The historical record is a little fuzzy, however, so there's always a risk of conjuring up false images of the contemporary scene. Better to come here alone on a stormy day and let your imagination weave its own fantasy around the surviving archways and corner pillars. My own mental construct was

Above: Dinas Brân, a prominent landmark seen on the descent from Eglwyseg Mountain. The Panorama Drive contours the hillside below.
Dinas Brân, a welir yn glir wrth ddisgyn o Fynydd Eglwyseg. Y mae'r Ffordd Banoramig yn cylchynu'r bryn islaw.

Right: Narrow crossing below the Eglwyseg escarpment, shared with Offa's Dyke long distance path. Croesfan gul islaw sgarp Eglwyseg, sydd yn rhannu'r tir yma â llwybr Clawdd Offa.

shattered by the sudden appearance at the western entrance of an elderly lady in a sensible cardigan. She was not prepared to repel an attack with her handbag so I had to let the image go.

Over the centuries Castell Dinas Brân has inspired more than a sense of security in its occupants. Bards have sat here composing love poems at sunset, and young men have practised proposals of marriage at dawn. Not wishing to be left out I sat awhile among the stones and composed the following verse:

My love is like this rocky ruin,
Skin cracked and temper crusty,
And if I had my time again
I'd choose one young and lusty.

One of the delights of this walk is the sudden switch to new scenery and terrain at each turning point. Nowhere is this more evident than where the path leaves the lush meadows and woodland of the valley to contour the delicately poised scree plinth of the Eglwyseg escarpment. The escarpment traverse is a highlight not only of this walk but of the Offa's Dyke long distance path from the Severn estuary to the Dee. Excitingly narrow in places, this is one place where backpackers must do it one behind the other.

I have a zoological observation to make at this point. The sheep which graze below this slope are astonishingly nimble when it comes to evading stones dislodged from the path—quite different from their cousins who may stand transfixed while a car bears down on them at forty miles an hour. Perhaps they are of a different breed, an evolutionary approved sub-species. Earlier I had seen one of them eating gravel.

Quarried limestone is white, but in its natural state the rock can vary in colour from light grey to a sickly yellow with streaks of black. Limestone buttresses are never shapely, always imposing. Craig Arthur, the largest of these cliffs, is no exception. As I passed below I watched a climber working his way up a blank-looking wall, his fingers searching the rock above like the feelers of a cautious insect while his rope trailed down into the expectant hands of his partner waiting beneath.

World's End, the forested indent at the northern limit of the escarpment, lay tucked in gloomy seclusion at a bend of the moor road far below. It looked ordinary and I thought the name a trifle pretentious. A moment later a shaft of sunlight pierced the cloud and ignited a limestone crag which rose above the trees. For a few seconds the rocks burned like magnesium and then expired. World's End? Sounds fine to me.

Eglwyseg Mountain is not a mountain at all

Looking towards Llantysilio Mountain from the ruined walls of Castell Dinas Brân. Mynydd Llandysilio o furiau dadfeiliedig Castell Dinas Brân.

but a pathless mound of bracken, bilberry and heather. Especially heather. Crossing it is like wading through a cornfield with your legs tied together. You are unlikely to meet anyone else on the mountain, and never anyone who has been there twice. I had the summit to myself—the entire mountain for that matter—apart from a solitary grouse startled into flight. I fancied myself adrift in a sea of heather. If I had been here at nightfall I would have navigated by the stars.

If anything the heather on the southern slope is deeper. At the point of exasperation I came across a sheep track that appeared to lead down to deliciously short grass. But sheep have such dainty little legs that my only means of making use of the narrow trail was by skipping or hopping along, though even this was preferable to more of that aimless wallowing. I came ashore near a clump of poorly conifers at the start of the so-called 'green lane', here no more than a partially worn path at the edge of a field. Compared to the heather it was ecstasy. The lane gradually asserts itself as it rounds the southern limb of the mountain and in its descent to the Panorama Road brings new views of the river, the disused quarries, and of Dinas Brân.

After the tortuous uncertainty of the descent among trees, bracken and quarries to the Sun Trevor Inn, the return walk along the Llangollen Canal towpath was at least going to be direct—and pretty. Before that day my experience of canals had been confined to the steely grey waters of the Leeds—Liverpool, a forbidden playground where we would fish for stunted roach and ride our bikes along a perilous towpath. The Llangollen Canal, with its colourful narrowboats and large population of talkative ducks, could not be more different. Chubby fish rose for flies, rodents scurried among exposed tree roots, courting couples held hands and speculated on the future. Best of all was the hydrological certainty that the height gain during the thirty-minute walk back to Llangollen could be no more than a few centimetres. I whistled as I went.

2: LLANGOLLEN AND THE BERWYNS —
Pistyll Rhaeadr and The Berwyns

Route summary: Visits the highest waterfall in Wales, ascends to a secluded lake, and then traverses a ridge of rounded summits.
Difficulty: Class C.
Main summits: Moel Sych 827m/2713ft; Cadair Berwyn (Craig Uchaf) 830m/2723ft.
Duration: 11km/7miles; 600m/2000ft of ascent; allow 4hrs.
Terrain: Mainly grass paths but with frequent boggy sections.
Special difficulties: Marshland on the descent to Llyn Lluncaws could pose problems after very wet weather.
Approach: From Llanrhaeadr ym Mochnant on the B4580 (refer to regional map). Take the narrow lane signposted "Waterfall" to Tan y Pistyll (GR:073 295). Parking for a small fee by the café, or in lay-bys shortly before the roadhead.
Route directions: A signed path leads from the café to a footbridge and fine view of falls. Don't cross the bridge but take the path which passes back above the car park through woodland. Continue by a track on the west bank of Nant y Llyn to a confluence of streams. Cross the minor stream and ascend the spur between the two (discontinuous path) to Llyn Lluncaws (GR:072 316).

Ascend a narrow path from the south shore of the lake up the eastern spur of Moel Sych to its summit. Follow the main ridge path north, over the rocky summit of Craig Uchaf (GR:071 323, not named on current maps), to the trig point at the summit of Cadair Berwyn. Retrace the path over Craig Uchaf to a stile over the transverse fence line. The usual descent follows the fence line down to the left, precariously, on to the eastern spur of Craig Uchaf. A better route continues south on the ridge path, almost to the saddle between Craig Uchaf and Moel Sych, and then follows a diagonal ramp/path which descends back left to join the normal descent below the nasty bit. Now follow the fence to a stile at a slight col and turn right to descend marshy scrub to regain the approach path near Llyn Lluncaws.

Follow the stream, cross to its left bank,

and continue on a pleasant grass path. After fording a tributary on the left, just above waterfalls, a divine grass track brings you gently down to earth on the approach lane not far from the parking areas.
Alternatives: Detour north along the main ridge from Cadair Berwyn, adding Cadair Bronwyn to your bag of summits.

Some mountains stay forever at the bottom of your list; you always intend to climb them, but without a catalyst your curiosity remains dormant. For me the Berwyns were those mountains, and the catalyst a magazine article in which the writer claimed to have 'discovered' a summit on the Berwyn Ridge higher than any marked on the Ordnance Survey map. I'm not one for pedantry in these matters, but I was curious enough to unfold the Bala map and look for those ambiguous contour lines that might harbour 'Craig Uchaf' ('highest rocks').

By itself this was insufficient reason to prompt a visit, but by now I had begun to browse over the map—you know how it is— and had spotted the words Pistyll Rhaeadr. If I chose my route carefully, I reasoned, I could visit the highest waterfall in Wales and still have time to walk a section of the Berwyn Ridge. But I would have to be quick.

Creeping along the A5 at bicycle-pace while a wagon train of Swallows and Monzas bobbed and swayed across the Cerrig y Drudion prairie is not my idea of quick. Finally rid of the caravan convoy I stopped for a few moments at Bala Lake and soothed my temper with its calm water. Others were here too, leaning over the parapet in romantic contemplation of the blue haze while restless dogs, impatient to resume the walk, tugged at their master's leads.

Despite the late hour, infrequent traffic on the minor road between Bala and Llangynog had failed to shift ice and wildlife hazards, both equally unexpected. Pheasants dived on to the verge as I flashed past, and a grey squirrel miraculously saved itself from a two dimensional destiny with an astonishing leap from under the front bumper. Then I rounded a corner and saw a drainage streak frozen into a treacherous band across the road. This

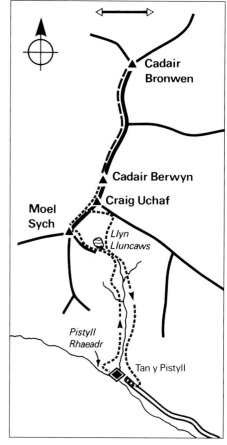

obstacle didn't budge, and had it been wider than a Ford Cortina's wheelbase I'd now be telling a different tale.

Pastureland gave way to moorland more typical of the Peak District than of Wales. It could only be the south-east Berwyns. Soon the road dipped again into an unfamiliar valley with villages reminiscent of those in Mid Wales: timeless, self-contained and wary of tourists. At this moment a car heavily laden with tourist paraphernalia appeared, and as it accelerated up the street a man leaned out of the passenger window and began to video the scene. I hadn't realised the natives were quite that hostile.

My first view of Pistyll Rhaeadr was of a white ribbon draped over a cliff barrier at the head of the valley. No sound, no movement. A pale moon hung above the falls and for a second I sensed a dual significance. What could it mean?

The residents of Tan y Pistyll have taken tasteful commercial advantage of the waterfall. Visitors can enjoy the setting while drinking coffee on the wooden verandah, but for the best view they must walk the short distance to a footbridge over the river, here to marvel at the main fall which drops almost vertically into a basin before emptying through a natural arch as foam and spray. Star billing in the tourist guides is the kiss of death for most waterfalls, but Pistyll Rhaeadr survives the treatment.

An upper path drags you away from the falls and into mature woodland—a good place to empty the thunder from your head and reset your thoughts to mountains, of which there has been barely a hint during the approach. At last, while strolling up the Nant y Llyn track, comes a tantalising glimpse of high ground at the head of the valley.

Llyn Lluncaws was partially frozen from the cold of successive clear nights, and delicate ice rods protruded from drain holes in soil banks at its shore. I sat down to plan the next move. The lake was cupped in the arms of two subsidiary spurs which extended east from the main Berwyn Ridge; I would ascend by the left-hand spur to Moel Sych, traverse the main ridge to the 'new' south summit of Cadair Berwyn, and then descend by the right-hand spur, hopefully avoiding the upper steep section by following a ramp line which appeared to cut across its left side.

I had been alone since leaving the falls but now I could see a dozen figures on the skyline, and a group of five descending the left-hand spur, hooting and laughing as they made rapid progress towards me. One of them was afflicted by a peculiar cackle which I had earlier mistaken for a grouse. Let's hope he doesn't decide to trespass on Kinder on the Glorious Twelfth. I left them taking pictures of each other at the lakeside and put my head down for the grind up Moel Sych.

Near the top the path ventures worryingly close to the headwall of the cwm. Mesmerised by the drop, I circled too far around the headwall and missed my turning for the summit of Moel Sych. I went back on discovering my mistake but I needn't have bothered; the summit is a forlorn place, consisting of a low pile of stones beyond ugly (and possible unlawful) post-and-wire fences.

The cold wind gusted unhindered across the broad back of the ridge. People passed and we smiled our greetings between thin lips and slit eyes, our balaclavas twisted on our heads. We looked like hastily dressed gnomes.

On the rock pile of Cadair Berwyn's south summit I had hoped to satisfy myself of Bernard Wright's claim. But the air was too hazy

Pistyll Rhaeadr at moonset. *Pistyll Rhaeadr yng ngolau'r lloer.*

14

Llyn Lluncaws, set in a rough sea of moor below the east flank of the Berwyn Ridge. *Llyn Lluncaws yng nghanol y gweunydd garw islaw ystlys dwyreiniol Crib Berwyn.*

to check if I could see land to north and south beyond the summits of Cadair Berwyn and Moel Sych. No matter. This craggy prominence deserves the accolade of Craig Uchaf on aesthetic grounds alone.

By now the sun had lost its warmth, but not the wind its cutting edge. I was not encouraged to linger. Ignoring the unpleasant direct descent from Craig Uchaf, I retraced my route along the main ridge towards Moel Sych and found the funnel exit of the ramp line I had seen earlier from the lake. To my delight it led effortlessly down to the gentle section of the east ridge, from where I took a direct line over heather and marsh to regain the approach path—the most unpleasant ten minutes of the day.

Determined to make a circular route of it, I crossed the Nant y Llyn, forded a tributary, and followed a broad path of yielding grass high on the valley side. Looking back I saw the last of the sun's rays grazing the crest of the Berwyn Ridge and wished I'd stayed up there an hour longer. And to think that a few days ago I couldn't be bothered with the Berwyns.

The track is reluctant to come to ground and instead of descending to Tan y Pistyll rounds a spur on to the flanks of the main valley. In doing so it provides the best view of Pistyll Rhaeadr. The sight brought me to a halt. I'd forgotten about the falls. How could such beauty result from mere geological discontinuity? What could it mean? It didn't mean anything at all, and that was the beauty of it.

ANGLESEY COAST

Maps: Landranger Sheet 114 (Anglesey) conveniently maps the entire island. Although the 1:50,000 scale is adequate for the Newborough walk, it lacks detail for following the intricacies of the paths around Holyhead Mountain. In this case a few notes from the text should avoid having to buy a separate 1:25,000 map (Pathfinder Sheet SH28/38—Holyhead). Inexpensive tide tables are sold in local newsagents.

Bases: The two walks described in this section lie at opposite ends of the island, with no single base convenient for both. It is more usual to approach them on a daily basis from Snowdonia. Holyhead can be reached by rail, and both it and Newborough lie on bus routes.

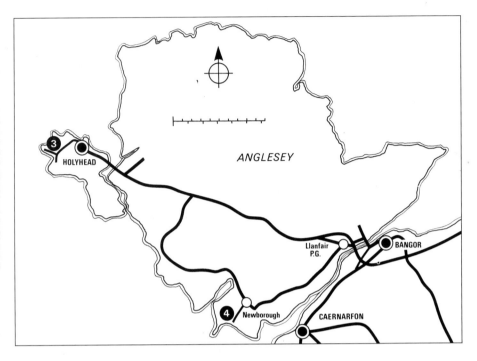

Only the narrow Menai Strait separates Anglesey from the mainland, and yet its island integrity is unchallenged. First impressions are of a land that is absolutely flat; though not strictly true, this is close enough to divert attention away from the interior and towards the coastline in search of scenery.

Both walks described in this section are coastal in nature, yet both find something of interest inland; be it the forest ecology of Newborough or the remains of an Iron Age settlement on Holy Island. With so much fascinating coastline to choose from, the selection may seem rather meagre. However, since the Anglesey coast is primarily about rock and sand, choosing two walks which between them visit the most spectacular cliffs and the finest beaches would seem to be a fair compromise.

Above the cliffs of Gogarth Bay.
South Stack in the background. Uwchben clogwyni Bae'r Gogarth gydag Ynys Lawd yn
y cefndir.

3: ANGLESEY COAST — Holyhead Mountain and The Stacks

Route summary: A short and undemanding coastal walk at the western tip of Anglesey. Includes a small summit and visits Iron Age sites. Impressive cliff scenery with opportunities to observe sea-birds in a rugged setting.

Difficulty: Class A.

Main summits: Holyhead Mountain 220m/722ft.

Duration: 8km/5miles (with detours); 250m/825ft of ascent; allow 3hrs.

Terrain: Tracks and stony paths.

Special difficulties: The descent to the Wen Zawn promontory can be unnerving and is unsuitable for children or anyone unused to mountain walking. The cliffs around South Stack drop away with unforgiving suddenness, and young children and myopic adults must be closely supervised.

Approach: Via the A5 from Bangor to Holyhead. Continue along the A5 almost to the ferry terminal, then turn left on to the harbour front. Take the second left and follow signs to South Stack. There is a car park just before the road dips to a final parking area at its end (GR:206 822).

Route directions: Take paths and tracks inland, passing to the right of the radio relay stations. Ascend steps on the west flank of Holyhead Mountain then turn right for the summit (GR:218 829). Descend east, aiming towards Holyhead harbour, and pass through a gap in the wall of the Iron Age fort to where the path swings right. Bear left here, descending to a better path which in turn leads on to a track. Follow the track leftwards to its end (possible detour to the Wen Zawn promontory — GR:215 838). Turn left and ascend a steep path (ignore a right fork leading along the cliff-top), later rejoining the approach path at the steps.

Retrace the outward route as far as the old radio relay station then turn right to follow a narrow path on to the promontory overlooking South Stack lighthouse. Descend to the roadhead, resist the ice-cream van, and detour down steps leading towards the lighthouse for views of the South Stack cliffs. Finally reclimb the steps to the car park.

To visit Ellen's Tower observatory, walk seawards from the café car park at GR:208 821. To visit the hut circles, follow the signed path opposite the large car park at GR:211 819, 1km from the roadhead.

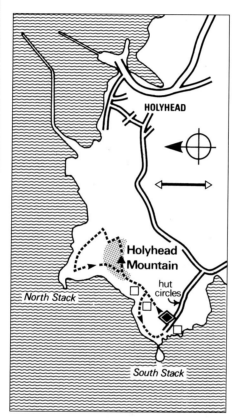

Unless you're sitting on the top deck of a bus when you cross the Britannia Bridge you won't see much of the swirling Menai Strait beneath. But even without that confirmation the transfer from mainland North Wales to island Anglesey is unmistakable; the sky seems to take up more space, and there's a whiff of seaside in the air. Crossing the causeway to Holy Island doubles the effect, finally severing what links remain with Snowdonia and its mountains.

This walk is an excuse to see something of the birdlife, cliff scenery and structures—ancient and modern—around South Stack and Gogarth Bay. The most interesting places are found within a few minutes of the car park, though to ease the sense of guilt that comes with effortless sightseeing, the day begins with an ascent of the miniature Holyhead Mountain.

Leaving the clamour of gulls and children at the ice-cream van, the route turns inland to follow paths and tracks of quartzite stone over heather scrubland towards the Mountain, a craggy lump not so very far away. At half distance the track passes a quaint radio relay station, now entering a state of pleasing dilapidation while its modern replacement, bristling with dishes, hums technologically near-by. Efficient it may be, cute it ain't.

On the track to Holyhead Mountain.
Ar y llwybr i Fynydd y Twr.

Above: On Holyhead Mountain, highest point on Anglesey, looking across the island's south coast towards the mainland and Snowdonia. Ar Fynydd Twr, y man uchaf ar Ynys Môn, yn edrych dros lannau deheuol yr ynys tuag at y tir mawr ac Eryri.

Right: At a gap in the defensive wall of the Iron Age hill fort of Caer y Twr during the descent of Holyhead Mountain. The huge breakwater protects the ferry port of Holyhead from westerly gales. Mewn bwlch ym mur amddiffynnol Caer y Twr, dinas gaerog o Oes yr Haearn, wrth ddisgyn o Fynydd y Twr. Cysgodir porthladd Caergybi oddi wrth wyntoedd cryf y gorllewin gan y morglawdd mawr.

A left fork in the track below the Mountain ushers nervous rock climbers towards the Gogarth sea cliffs. You might follow them as far as the platform where rucksacks are left, and from where you can see the profiled Main Cliff rising a hundred metres vertically from the sea. It is a sight certain to terrify climbers on their first visit, and even veterans of the crag must struggle to overcome the feeling of inadequacy it brings.

Back on the main path, a flight of steps and a final scurry among rocks will bring you to the summit. Here you will find the remains of a Roman lookout tower (which in my ignorance I mistook for a dismantled coastguard post of twentieth century origin), and also a trig point on which to lean while gasping at the tremendous panoramic view of the island and its surroundings: the sea curving west to the limits of visibility; the fertile flatlands of Anglesey stretching east towards the mainland; and the mountains of Snowdonia, reduced by haze and distance to a lumpy strip. On a clear day each mountain group can be identified, from the squat domes of the Carneddau in the north to the pimples of the Lleyn Peninsula in the south. In winter a dusting of snow elevates the whole chain in an illusion of Himalayan grandeur.

Spread below the east slope of the Mountain is the ferry port of Holyhead, and from time to time you will see a passenger boat glide serenely past the snaking breakwater which protects the moored dinghies from westerly storms. It is towards the harbour that the descent from the Mountain now makes its way. Though longer than strictly necessary, this route is worth following if only to examine the defensive wall of the Iron Age fort of Caer y Twr (which at first I took to be an ordinary pasture wall).

To the north a track rises from a disused quarry—a source of rock during construction of the breakwater—and heads over scrubland towards North Stack. The route will follow the final part of this track before veering off to return to South Stack, though adventurous walkers will first pursue its continuation—down a grass funnel between crags and on to a promontory high above the sea—for truly spectacular views into Wen Zawn. On calm days the sea licks against the base of the rock while T-shirted climbers, watched by grey seals bobbing from the water, inch across the slab above. But during storms the waves slam against the cliff with such force that the spray shoots fifty metres up the face. No frantic sounds of climbers or gulls then, only the dull thud of waves punching through the natural arch beneath the promontory, and the pitiful

South Stack lighthouse. *Goleudy Ynys Lawd.*

moan of the North Stack fog siren.

The most famous climb in Wen Zawn takes a diagonal line from right to left, beginning on the friendly grey rock of the slab and eventually threading through the sickly yellow overhangs above the arch. It is called *A Dream of White Horses*, a name which not only tells of the compulsive attraction of sea-cliffs but also betrays the pretensions of the people who climb them.

Returning from the promontory, the climbers' path continues along the cliff edge above Gogarth Bay; it visits nowhere of special interest and is really quite dangerous. Far better is to return to the main path and follow it over the west flank of the Mountain, descending steps to rejoin the approach track. Rather than simply retrace the route back to South Stack, a worthwhile variant leaves the main track between the two radio stations and detours on to the lookout promontory for retrospective views of Gogarth Bay.

West of the promontory sits South Stack lighthouse on its island base. Sadly, recent automation means that access across the suspension bridge is forbidden. Nevertheless, a descent of the concrete steps leading down towards the bridge will be rewarded by a tremendous view of Mousetrap Zawn and its 100-m cliff of convoluted metamorphic rock where, during spring, hundreds of sea-birds gather on ledges formed by preferential weathering of the soft layers. About two-thirds way down the steps, you can look down through a gap in the rocks into the zawn and hypnotise yourself with the calls of wheeling gulls and the steady beat of waves pulsing into the inaccessible boulder bay at its foot.

The South Stack cliffs continue some distance south of Mousetrap Zawn, gradually diminishing in height as they do so. Above the next main promontory, and visible from the lighthouse steps, stands the prominent Ellen's Tower. Built in the nineteenth century as a summerhouse for the wife of an Anglesey dignitary, this square tower stood empty for many years until restored by the RSPB as an information centre and observatory. From it can be seen herring gulls, razorbills, puffins, choughs, guillemots, fulmars, and occasionally an exotic off-course or stormbound migrator. The tower is most easily reached from the café a short distance along the road from the parking area.

Before leaving South Stack you must visit the remnants of the Iron Age settlement of Cytiau'r Gwyddelod. The site lies just a couple of minutes' walk from the road, where more than a dozen stone circles have been unearthed from the bramble scrubland so convincingly that they were obvious even to me. The circular structures we see today were originally topped by centrally supported conical roofs and used as living quarters (stone recesses used as hearths are still evident in some of them). The smaller, rectangular buildings were probably used as sheltered workrooms. When threatened with invasion the inhabitants of this and nearby villages would have taken refuge in the fort on Holyhead Mountain.

So despite the quarrying, the spread of housing, and the clutter of communications buildings, all traces of archaeological evidence have yet to be wiped from the flanks of Holyhead Mountain. But we mustn't judge our own time too harshly. Perhaps one day the ruins of the lighthouse, the radio relay station, Ellen's Tower, and the Holyhead breakwater, will hold a similar fascination.

4: ANGLESEY COAST — Newborough and Llanddwyn Island

Route summary: A coastal walk in three parts for frustrated beachcombers. Approaches the southern tip of Anglesey along forest tracks, explores an island nature reserve, and returns via beach and sand dunes.

Difficulty: Class B.

Duration: 13km/8miles; allow 4-5 hrs.

Terrain: Forest tracks, good grass paths, sandy beach.

Special difficulties: Llanddwyn Island may be cut off from the mainland for up to an hour at high tide.

Approach: From Llanfairpwllgwyngyll (abbreviated version) on the A5, take the A4080 via Brynsiencyn to Newborough village. Turn left in the village centre (signposted: "Beach, Llanddwyn") to a car park after about 100m (GR:423 656).

Route directions: Continue along the beach road for a few hundred metres then take a track leading right then left behind the church. Continue parallel to the road on a sometimes indistinct field path (stiles at intervals) to open ground where it merges with a grass track. Enter the forest at a gate (GR:414 652) and continue by a sand/grass track, forking right after 100m. Cross straight over a stony track and proceed directly, ignoring turns to left and right, to a terminus from where a sand gully leads out on to the beach (GR:395 636).

Walk along the beach to the right for a few hundred metres then by a good track to the southern tip of Llanddwyn Island. Return to the mainland by a series of paths along the east side after exploring the bays and buildings.

Walk eastwards along the beach for about 2km, passing the exit from the car park, to where the warren borders on to the forest at GR:410 631 (this is not obvious from the beach and you will have to climb the dunes periodically to check progress). An improving path leads inland between forest and warren until, about 200m past the forest edge, a farm track leads left, improving in stages and eventually joining the beach road near the church.

Alternatives: For a short route to Llanddd-

wyn Island, turn left in Newborough as for the normal approach and continue to the forest car park at the roadhead (GR:405 634). Exit on to the shore and turn right for a 2km beach walk to the island. Return by the same route.

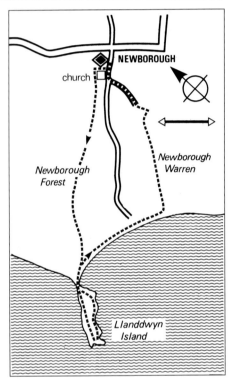

What we really wanted to do this Whit bank holiday Saturday was pack towels and swimming costumes and join the queue of a hundred thousand cars trundling across the Menai bridges towards the Anglesey beaches. But what to do about those guilt feelings? Now here was a plan: park at Newborough village, walk forest trails to the coast, explore the rocks and ruins of Llanddwyn Island, stroll along the beach, and then return through Newborough Warren. Lots of sun and sand and a good excuse to enjoy them both.

Newborough is the 'New Borough' founded in 1295 to house villagers ruthlessly evicted by Edward I during the construction of Beaumaris castle. Peasant welfare came pretty low down the list of priorities in those days and their new seaside home was a poor substitute. Tree fell

ing exposed the dunes to wind action, and during a series of severe storms the sand migrated inland, ruining fields and burying houses—some of which have only recently been excavated. Marram grass was sown in the sixteenth century to bind the dunes, and after the Second World War half the acreage was securely pinned by a plantation of Corsican pine. Once stabilised, the dunes became an unexpected source of income; first from rope and mats woven from the marram grass, and later from rabbits trapped in the warren (before myxomatosis struck in 1954 the annual yield was in the order of tens of thousands). Today Newborough Warren is one of the largest dune habitats in Britain and has been designated a nature reserve.

From Newborough there are two ways of approaching the beach: by car (on payment of a substantial fee) to a parking area within flip-flop distance of the sea, and on foot (for free) along 3km of paths and forest trails. Not only for pecuniary reasons did we choose the latter.

Although a right of way, much of the field path is indistinct, and some of it—tut, tut—has gone under the plough, so you must seek confirmation from the occasional fossilised footprint or collapsing stile. In contrast the forest trail could not be more obvious. Not that it sees any more pedestrian traffic; in the forty minutes or so it took us to walk from edge to edge we saw just two other people—and this on one of Anglesey's busiest days.

After the breezy twittering of the open scrubland only the hollow cry of a crow sounded within the forest. We expected a claustrophobic path but trod instead a broad trail set in a sun-filled strip between mature pines. The strip flourished with an ecology all its own. Colourful butterflies rose from under our feet as we walked, drifting past us like confetti on the breeze. Some were violet, others red and slate grey. We didn't know their names, but were delighted by them none the less.

From a clearing at the far side of the forest we waded through a gully deep with soft sand and out on to a beach which gently shelved into a lethargic sea. People in skimpy beachwear wandered to and fro in front of us, unconcerned, as in dreams, by our alien presence. Sara kicked off her trainers and ran

A sand-filled gully leads out from the forest on to the great curve of Newborough beach. *Rhych tywodlyd yn arwain o'r coed at draeth mawr Niwbwrch.*

into the sea, dragging us both into the fantasy.

To our left the beach curved into the hazy distance as a great arc of fine yellow sand backed by dunes tufted with marram grass, while to our right the coarser sand and shingle swung in a tighter radius on to the nearer promontory of Llanddwyn Island—our next destination. A quick survey revealed that population density on the beach dwindled in geometric proportion to the distance walked from the car park. By that reckoning the island would be practically empty.

Llanddwyn is an island only during the highest tides, when for an hour or so the sea washes over the connecting neck of sand. And yet a grass top and rocky shore set it apart from the main coastline at any time. At a cove on its west side we rested our backs against the low cliffs and stretched our feet out on the unpolluted, litter free sand, there to be entertained by a pair of oystercatchers, larger than life in their stage make-up of red eyes and beaks, repelling intruders with some furious wing flapping and verbal abuse. As predicted,

and despite the bank holiday migration of dozens of people on to the island (an untypically large number), we had the cove entirely to ourselves. Walk and ye shall find.

Most visitors are drawn to the island by its collection of ruins and artefacts, among them a modern Celtic cross with puzzling inscription, a ruined sixteenth-century church, and a modern Latin cross commemorating St Dwynwen, the fifth-century patron saint of Welsh lovers (although she herself died of a broken heart, laying doubt on her

Harbour on Llanddwyn Island, once used by pilots whose empty cottages still stand near-by. *Harbwr ar ynys Llanddwyn a ddefnyddid gynt gan beilotiaid y saif eu bythynnod gwag gerllaw.*

qualifications for the post). Other curiosities on the island are concerned with seafaring. The row of cottages housed the pilots whose boats were moored in the bay near-by, while the stone tower on the south-east point served as a navigational mark from 1800 until 1875, when it was superseded by the lighthouse built on the south-west point. You can walk around the base of the lighthouse, though since automation there is nothing much to see. Interest centres instead on a denuded offshore rock colonised by shags which, in silhouette, look like the blackened tree stumps of a land devastated by fire.

For all its historical interest, the island's greatest attractions are the rock spurs and shingle coves of its southern tip. With a bit of effort you can isolate yourself here for the remainder of the afternoon, soothed by the sound of the sea and a romantic view of the Snowdonia mountains.

Reluctantly we left the island and plodded back along the beach, past the concentration of sunbathers sprawled near the car park exit, to where we would climb the collapsing dunes to find our return path between forest and warren. But first we sat down, bared our shoulders to the sun, peeled off our socks, and wriggled our toes into the sand. After all, isn't this what we had come for?

One of a thousand butterflies travelling the sunlit strip through Newborough Forest. *Un o filoedd o ieir bach yr haf yn hedfan trwy'r heulwen yng Nghoedwig Niwbwrch.*

THE CARNEDDAU

Maps: The whole region appears on Landranger Sheet 115 (Snowdon), the 1:50,000 scale being generally adequate for this type of terrain. An unfortunate split means that at 1:25,000 scale, both Outdoor Leisure maps 16 (Snowdonia—Conwy Valley Area) and 17 (Snowdonia—Snowdon Area) are required, although Sheet SH66/76 (Bethesda) in the Pathfinder Series neatly covers the two most popular mountain walks (routes 7 and 8) at less expense.

Bases: Starting points for the four walks are spread around the perimeter of the range, so any of the towns located on the encircling roads could make a suitable base. However, hill walkers will probably feel more at home in the mountain villages of Llanrwst, Bethesda or Capel Curig, than in the coastal towns of Conwy or Bangor. All three provide hotel and bed and breakfast accommodation, whereas Capel Curig is best for camping. Conwy and Bangor are on main rail and bus routes (branch line to Llanrwst and Betws y Coed). Bethesda can also be reached by bus. In the summer months an infrequent bus service operates between Bethesda and Betws y Coed via Capel Curig.

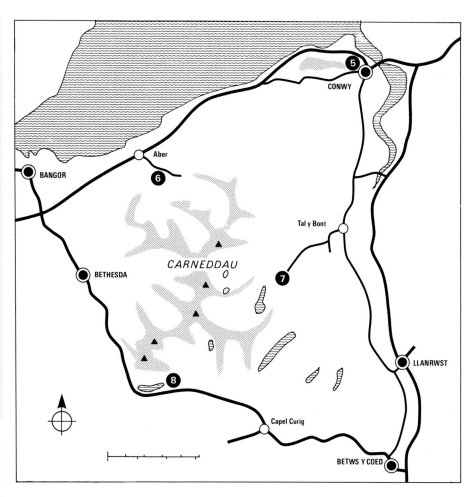

Seven of the fifteen highest peaks in Wales lie within the Carneddau, a large tract of land with no roads and few paths in the northern extremity of the national park. Rounded rather than craggy, these summits gain stature from their huge settings. Some say the region provides the finest hill walking in Snowdonia.

A chain structure of domed peaks and smooth link ridges provides the ridge traverser with ideal material. These are big undertakings even in summer, and in winter they can become very serious indeed. Three of the walks selected take sweeping horseshoe ridge circuits over the highest summits—the preserve of the committed hill walker—whereas a fourth climbs a small hill overlooking the historic town of Conwy.

On Conwy Mountain, tiny northern outpost of the great Carneddau. *Ar Fynydd Conwy, amddiffynfa ogleddol y Carneddau mawr.*

5: THE CARNEDDAU — *Conwy Mountain*

Route summary: An unusual mix of coastal and hill scenery captured in a short walk from an historic town.

Difficulty: Class A.

Main summits: Conwy Mountain 247m/809ft.

Duration: 10km/6miles; 250m/820ft of ascent; allow 3–4hrs.

Terrain: Mainly good paths and tracks plus some road walking. One muddy section (avoidable).

Special difficulties: None.

Approach: From Conwy on the old A55 road. Park at the east end of the estuary bridge (GR:786 775), or at one of several car parks elsewhere in town.

Route directions: Follow the main road until about 150m beyond the town wall arch. Turn left (signposted "Conwy Mountain") and then right once over the railway bridge. Fork left at the next junction then turn right (signposted "Mountain Road") to a T-junction. Turn left ("Mountain Road") then fork right on a track by a row of houses.

Follow a good path slanting up the south flank of the ridge (detour right at a large rock for the viewpoint) and continue by its crest to the summit. Descend by a good path and track on the west side to the broad saddle between Conwy Mountain and Allt Wen. Trend left to a track and follow it rightwards until it merges with a superior farm track leading down to the Sychnant Pass.

Turn left and follow the road for 1km— a hazardous undertaking during peak periods. Turn right to follow a track through Crow's Nest Farm. Continue first by a muddy sunken lane, then by a good track and surfaced road leading past a large hotel, to a T- junction. Turn left to regain the Sychnant Pass road and follow it to an arch under the town wall. Steps lead up on to a walkway, which can then be followed to its end a short distance from the castle.

Alternatives: Avoid the muddy lane of the Crow's Nest diversion by following the Sychnant Pass road straight back to Conwy.

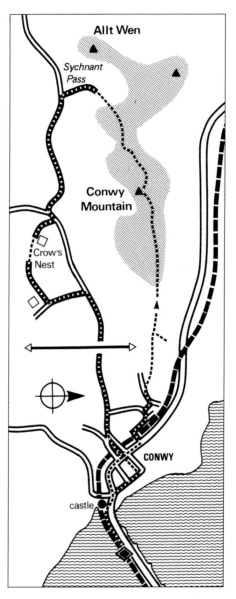

Lowland pastures and coastal squalor converge at Conwy town, amputating the northern limb of mountainous Snowdonia. Even the hilly stump that remains is almost nipped off by the deep incision of the Sychnant Pass, a tourist thoroughfare once precariously traversed by horse-drawn coaches. Thus are the mighty Carneddau reduced to a trio of diminutive summits: Penmaen Bach, Allt Wen and Conwy Mountain. Allt Wen is the highest of the three, but Conwy Mountain has the prime position overlooking the town and castle strategically built at a bridged constriction of the Conwy Estuary.

To fully appreciate Conwy Mountain you should sandwich it between two thick slices of town walking. Quietness becomes tranquillity only when it supplants the raucous din of trucks, motor cycles, horns, power drills and barking dogs, all of which are here in abundance.

An elegant suspension bridge, complete with mock turrets, spans the estuary and abuts against the castle base like an elongated drawbridge. This is the Telford Bridge, built in 1826 to replace a dangerous ferry crossing over turbulent tidal waters; it makes an appropriate starting point. Though redundant now, and dwarfed by Robert Stephenson's rail bridge of 1846 on one side and the modern road bridge of 1958 on the other, the bridge is in the care of the National Trust and remains open to pedestrians.

The castles of Conwy, Caernarfon and Harlech were commissioned by Edward I in 1283 to help consolidate his gains against the Welsh. Conwy is arguably the finest of the three, and at £15,000 (several million at today's rates) the most costly. Unassailable by direct military assault, it enabled Edward to successfully resist a long siege. For centuries the castle continued to safeguard its residents against attack, though not against their own gullibility: Richard II was betrayed here in 1399 by the Duke of Northumberland, and a few years later its defenders were tricked into opening the portcullis to Glyndwr's army. The Royalists successfully resisted an attack from Cromwell's army here in 1646, but capitulated after a three month siege. Today the castle is regularly invaded by tourists and school parties, though casualties are generally light.

Escape from the walled town lies through the north-west arch, under which lorries—if not their wing mirrors—continue to squeeze while awaiting completion of a by-pass through an estuary tunnel. Beyond lies a suburban maze partially solved by signs promising "Sychnant Pass", "Conwy Mountain" and, more ambiguously, "Mountain Road". Tolerant residents provide the final clues.

Having been assaulted by the visual, aural

and nasal discord that comes with sharing a confined space with too many people and their dogs, Sara and I arrived at the start of the mountain path eager for the soothing caress of heather, birdsong and sea breezes. We gained height steadily on the flanking path, keeping our heads down until certain we had broken free from the turmoil. At a flat rock near the ridge crest we looked back with satisfaction on the town and castle we had left behind, secure in our exalted position.

It was here that we noticed a subsidiary northern spur promising extensive views to seaward. It wouldn't take long to explore. Beyond a grassy neck the spur plunged down to a road creeping around the base of the mountain. A sign announced, accurately, that here was a "sheer drop" and advised, wisely, that we "do not proceed beyond this point". Sara watched disapprovingly as I sidled beyond it towards the edge, anxious to capture an entire view with my wide-angle lens.

Such fascinating desolation! Caravan parks, industrial scrap yards, road works, railway debris, port-a-cabin estates . . . An ebbing tide had exposed the sand banks of the estuary, completing the appearance of a half-eaten gravy dinner. Returning to the ridge we left behind industrial rot and regeneration and resumed our quest.

The long ridge teased us with several false summits. This was too much to bear for a group of three lads who had passed us earlier. Disillusioned now, they were amusing themselves by throwing pebbles provocatively down rock slabs towards us. I thought of amusing myself by throwing them playfully over the much bigger northern precipice.

Just half an hour after leaving the promontory we arrived at the Iron Age site of Castell Caer Leion at the summit. A thickening afternoon haze blocked our view inland to the peaks of the Carneddau but strengthened our sense of isolation and elevation, shared only with two figures on the near-by rounded top of Allt Wen.

From the summit we followed a path and track down to a shallow col where ponies grazed, photogenically reflected in a pool flecked with reeds. Into this perfectly composed scene trekked an airman carrying a dismantled hang-glider. We left him dragging his folded wings about the heather looking for updraughts and descended a surfaced lane towards the Sychnant Pass. Delaying the inevitable encounter with road traffic as long as possible, we lingered at the viewpoint and gazed into the dry valley reduced to shades of purple by the evening sun.

By now the wind had dropped completely

Above: Viewpoint on the ascent to Conwy Mountain. A coastal squalor of railway lines, road works and caravan parks. Gwylfan ar y ffordd i fyny Mynydd Conwy a phla o reilffyrdd, gweithfeydd ffordd a meysydd carafanau.

Below: Near Crow's Nest, exclusive residential area beyond the fringe of Conwy housing estates. Gerllaw Nyth y Frân, ardal ddewisol y tu hwnt i ffin ystadau tai Conwy.

Conway Castle at dusk from the ancient town wall walkway. *Castell Conwy fin nos o'r llwybr ar wal hynafol y dref.*

and at the roadside we saw the frustrated hang-glider pilot in the queue at the ice-cream van, shrugging off his disappointment with a Double-99 liberally topped with raspberry sauce. Brittle hopes fly on brittle wings, and the cliffs of the Sychnant would have been unforgiving.

The road over the Sychnant Pass returns directly to Conwy, but after jousting with tourist traffic through the walled defile of Death Alley we opted for a detour through Crow's Nest Farm, not least because we liked the name. At a luxury development in tasteful timber and red tiles we paused to watch the sun puncture itself on trees at the Pass while a restrained guard dog—a wolf at sunset—howled its fury at being unable to maul our bodies.

Our plan to link a series of field footpaths

back to Conwy foundered in a pile of steamy cowshit at the first gate. My guess was that we would have got stuck halfway across. A bull watching and waiting with lowered head at the dry isthmus beyond thought likewise. We took the lane back to Conwy.

It was almost dark when we arrived. A sign at the archway invited us to walk as far as the quay along the raised pathway of the town walls. How could we resist? As we strolled along in the twilight we could regard the town with equanimity, affection even. Darkness had all but stilled it, so that the only movements were those of cars in the distance, of people wandering the streets in vain search of an open chip shop, and of black cats lurking in black shadows between the dustbins. A corner of Wales was settling itself in for the night.

6: THE CARNEDDAU — Aber Falls and Foel Fras

Route summary: Traverses a series of high, remote hills after a pleasant approach beneath an impressive waterfall. The short walk to the fall is worthwhile in itself if time is short or the weather doubtful.

Difficulty: Class D (or A).

Main summits: Drosgl 758m/2487ft; Garnedd Uchaf 926m/3038ft; Foel Fras 942m/3091ft; Drum 770m/2526ft.

Duration: 19km/12miles; 950m/3125ft of ascent; allow 7hrs (2hrs for the fall only).

Terrain: Good paths and tracks to start and finish, with pathless grassy hillsides between.

Special difficulties: Extremely difficult route finding in the Drosgl area in mist.

Approach: From the village of Aber on the A55, follow a narrow lane inland (marked "Aber Falls: unsuitable for coaches") to a large parking area at Bont Newydd (GR:662 720).

Route directions: Follow the riverside path upstream, cross by a footbridge, then turn right to follow a track and path to Aber Falls (GR:668 701).

Cross boulders below the fall (if you can) and follow a grass path below Rhaeadr Bach to a third stream beyond a gate. Ascend the stream bank to a marshy saddle between Drosgl and Moel Wnion at the edge of nowhere (GR:653 690). Turn left and ascend open slopes

Above: Entering the forest on the shortened return route from Aber Falls, here seen cascading over the wooded cliff barrier behind. Wrth ddod i mewn i'r goedwig ar y ffordd fyrrach yn dychwelyd o Raeadr Aber, a welir yma'n tasgu dros y terfyn coediog.

Below: At the summit of Carnedd Uchaf. Carnedd Llewelyn and, in the distance, Carnedd Dafydd, framed between Foel Grach (left) and Yr Elen. Ar gopa Carnedd Uchaf. Carnedd Llywelyn, a Charnedd Dafydd yn y pellter, rhwng Y Foel Grach a'r Elen.

Below: On the approach to Aber Falls, where the broad track narrows to a stepped path through woodland.
Wrth ddod at Raeadr Aber lle mae'r llwybr llydan yn culhau yn llwybr grisiog trwy'r goedwig.

27

(occasional path) to Drosgl summit, a mound of stones in the middle of nowhere. Continue over the minor rocky tops of Bera Bach and Yr Aryg to the summit rock pile of Garnedd Uchaf.

Walk east to find the main ridge path and follow it to the left over Foel Fras to the summit of Drum. Descend the west slope (signs of path) to Llyn Anafon and follow the track downstream until possible to descend over grass to the roadhead at GR:676 715 within limping distance of Bont Newydd.

Alternatives: (1) Return from Aber Falls along the approach path to a kissing gate, then slant diagonally across the hillside on the right to cross a stile at the forest edge (GR:669 704). Follow a path through forest and woodland, rejoining the approach just beyond Nant cottage. (2) Fork right from the forest path of (1) after just 10m for a winding trail uphill to a viewpoint and bench. Follow the track left to a T- junction and turn left on a broad forestry track which later curves right then sharply left and leads back to Bont Newydd.

Escaping the clutches of Bera Mawr and Llwytmor, the Afon Goch giggles innocently coastwards only to plunge over forty screaming metres of Aber Falls. End of Afon Goch. But wait, from among a pile of slimy boulders beneath the fall we hear the first murmurs of a resurrected river. Under the alias Afon Rhaeadr Fawr it proceeds more cautiously down the valley, maturing with every meander and clothing itself with trees. Disguised in its green cloak it passes under Bont Newydd as the Afon Aber—a river by any other name.

Looking down from the stone arch of Bont Newydd I watched the river stretching itself over a bed of boulders smooth as bowling balls, its frothy white tongues licking the green swirls between. Small birds flickered strobe-like in the filtered sunlight from bank to bank, or perched on brittle twigs to inspect the water surface for drowning flies. And it seemed to me then that rivers stand still while time flows by. Whatever that means; it's hard to think straight when your head is filled with the sound of frothing and twittering. Before I could decide if it was a riddle or a muddle, a group of men approached asking for a rope to help rescue a dog stuck on an inaccessible ledge above the

river. I gave them a length of nylon hawser I kept in the boot as a tow rope and they went off on their mercy mission. I wasn't needed so I set off to see this waterfall I had heard so much about.

At first I followed a picturesque path along the riverbank and fancied it would be like this throughout. But in a little while the path crossed the river by a wooden footbridge and joined a track ascending the valley base, broad and open.

Natural woodland once filled the valley—the grandest survivor is a prosperous oak more than 220 years old which stands at a bend in the track—but over the centuries this has been progressively cleared for timber and to make space for crops and grazing. On the valley sides today thrives a timber crop of conifers raised in blocks within a perimeter fence, while sheep and Welsh mountain ponies graze the intervening pasture.

At the crest of a rise I got my first view of the fall, already grand though distance had robbed it of sound and motion. Then the track narrowed to a path among the exposed roots of tall trees and it was hidden from view again. Now with each step what began as a distant

Bont Newydd, starting point for the walk to Aber Falls. Bontnewydd, man cychwyn i gerdded hyd at Raeadr Aber.

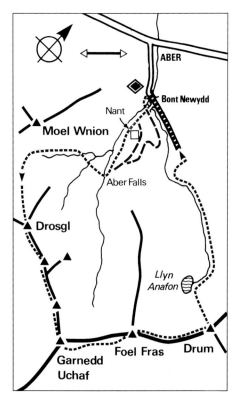

28

throb built steadily to a thunderous roar.

People stood motionless below the fall, chilled by the spray and shadow but compelled to remain by the force of spectacle. Prevented from cutting back into the mountain by a resistant barrier of rare outcropping granophyre, the stream funnels down an upper chute and sweeps over the cliff with just three slight deflections into the swirl pool carved out at its base. To right and left, mosses and liverworts favoured by the constantly damp atmosphere thrive on ledges inaccessible to sheep, hinting at a luxurious lowland growth not seen in North Wales for centuries.

Some say the fall is a disappointment, especially when dry weather reduces the gushing stream to a sputtering trickle. But I have been here three times and have been three times impressed. And I will come again, perhaps when the fall has frozen—as it has before—into an ice buttress hung with icicle chandeliers. If I had music in me I would compose it here.

Most visitors return by the same route after viewing the fall, but there are three worthy alternatives to consider. Those following either of the two forest paths first retrace the approach route until a narrow path, indistinct at first, slants diagonally across a hillside of stunted hawthorn. At a stile they will cast a final backward glance at the fall before entering the aromatic gloom of the forest. Here the two routes divide. Those following the shorter route will continue straight on along a delightful forest path carpeted with pine needles to emerge in woodland above Nant Cottage, just ten minutes from Bont Newydd. While those wishing to complete the Nature Conservancy trail will fork right soon after entering the forest and ascend to its top by a strenuous zig-zagging path, returning to Bont Newydd along a series of winding forest tracks—pleasant in dry weather but churned into ankle-deep mud when forestry vehicles are extracting felled timber.

The third alternative is much more ambitious and uses the Aber Falls walk as a mere preamble to a high-level circuit around the lonely hills of Drosgl, Foel Fras and Drum. The first task is to boulder-hop the stream below the falls. Given that the lichens growing on these rocks are permanently bloated by the incessant spray, this is a potentially embarrassing exercise at the best of times—and wholly impractical when the river is in spate. From the renewed calm of the far bank the path wanders below Rhaeadr Bach, less impressive than Rhaeadr Fawr but worth the detour to see water sluicing down rock troughs. Continuing its traverse the path comes to the

Aber Falls. *Rhaeadr Aber.*

third stream of Afon Gam, whose shattered banks it follows to the barren saddle between Moel Wnion and Drosgl where the wind blows unhindered.

Few people walk this way and not until you have crossed the pimply summits of Drosgl, Bera Bach, Yr Aryg and Garnedd Uchaf will you find a path to follow. In mist you must navigate carefully over these featureless mounds, or retreat and come back some brighter day.

Just beyond Garnedd Uchaf the route merges with the Great Ridge, one of the highways of the Carneddau, and by the time Foel Fras approaches the path could not be more obvious. With no more thinking to do you can

stride out and revel in the simplicity of it all. A squalid coastal plain infringes on the final scorpion tail of the ridge so it seems best to descend the west flank of Drum, following the Llyn Anafon track down to the surfaced lane which leads back to Bont Newydd.

Returning weary to the car park I was confronted by an excitable German Shepherd, evidently the one rescued with my tow rope earlier that day. It would be a cruel twist of fate if I was to be savaged by the very beast I had indirectly helped to save. It lunged at me with fangs bared and tongue slavering, but then after circling me once lolloped back to its owner, evidently having decided to show its gratitude by not biting off my arm. Good boy.

7: THE CARNEDDAU — The Cwm Eigiau Horseshoe

Route summary: A prolonged and serious high-level ridge walk around a remote cwm. Traverses several summits, including the highest in the Carneddau.

Difficulty: Class D.

Main summits: Pen Llithrig y Wrach 799m/2622ft; Pen yr Helgi Du 833m/2733ft; Carnedd Llewelyn 1064m/3485ft; Foel Grach 974m/3196ft.

Duration: 18km/11miles; 1000m/3300ft of ascent; allow 6–8hrs.

Terrain: Grass ridges with few paths to start and finish. Good paths in the middle section.

Special difficulties: Short scrambles to enter and exit Bwlch Eryl Farchog, although neither will tax experienced hill walkers familiar with rugged terrain. In mist the whole of the descent from Carnedd Llewelyn requires considerable navigational skill.

Approach: From Llanrwst or Conwy along the B5106 to Tal y Bont. Follow a lane rising steeply westwards out of the village (*not* the road to Llanbedr-y-cennin) and continue for about 5km to the roadhead at the entrance to Cwm Eigiau (GR:732 663). Parking is limited so take great care not to obstruct the gate.

Route directions: From the roadhead continue directly by a rough track to the Llyn Eigiau dam. Cross the outflow on to a lakeside track then fork left to Hafod y Rhiw (GR:723 646). Gain the ridge above its first steep rise and follow its broad back (intermittent path), via a final steep rise, to the summit of Pen Llithrig y Wrach.

Descend north-west then west to find a narrow path leading down to Bwlch y Tri Marchog. Continue up the far side on to Pen yr Helgi Du (the actual summit lies at the north-west end of its flat top). Scramble down the north-west ridge to Bwlch Eryl Farchog (emergency descent

into the Ogwen Valley from here; note that the opposite descent into Cwm Eigiau is complex and difficult without prior knowledge). Escape the col by an easy scramble and continue along the broad ridge, initially around the lip of the Craig yr Ysfa Amphitheatre, to the summit of Carnedd Llewelyn.

Descend north-east to a slight saddle and continue north along an obvious path to the summit of Foel Grach (stone shelter on north-east side). Retrace the path for about 300m then veer south-east to descend the shallow grass spur between Cwm Eigiau and Melynllyn (intermittent path). Go east then north-east across a marshy plateau to a rock promontory at its far side (GR:713 655). Descend the ridge north-east to a track which leads rightwards back to the start.

Alternatives: Descend the spur from Foel Grach on to the marshy plateau as for the main route, then veer south to descend by an improving path into Cwm Eigiau, arriving near ruined quarry buildings. Follow a good track down the valley to rejoin the approach at the Llyn Eigiau dam.

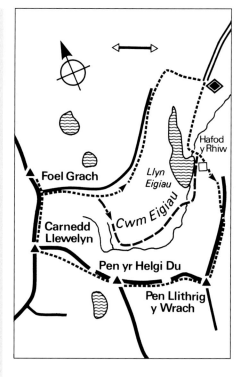

Evening on Pen yr Helgi Du, looking back towards Pen Llithrig y Wrach.
Yr hwyr ar Ben yr Helgi Du, yn edrych yn ôl tuag at Ben Llithrig y Wrach.

Above: On the shoulder above Hafod y Rhiw, looking across Cwm Eigiau to the main objectives of the horseshoe walk Pen yr Helgi Du (left) and Carnedd Llewelyn. Uwchben Hafod y Rhiw, yn edrych ar draws Cwm Eigiau tuag at ben draw llwybr y bedol Pen yr Helgi Du (chwith) a Charnedd Llywelyn.

Below: Cwm Eigiau from the link ridge between Carnedd Llewelyn and Foel Grach. The ascent ridge to Llewelyn is on the right. Cwm Eigiau o'r grib gysylltiol rhwng Carnedd Llywelyn a'r Foel Grach. Mae'r grib sy'n codi at Garnedd Llywelyn ar y dde.

North Wales regulars like to keep the Carneddau to themselves. Selfish, you see. Thomas Pennant toured the region in 1775 and found them 'very disagreeable, of dreary bottoms or moory hills', but then he was a confirmed Glyders man. Spared the deep cols and boulder strewn flanks of a typical Snowdon ridge, the sinuous Carneddau highways of fine stones and short grass gently dip and weave from summit to summit, leaving your feet to get on with the business of walking while you fill your head with wind and sky and fanciful ideas.

This circuit of Cwm Eigiau's bounding ridges delights in the pathless terrain of the remote north-east sector. Only the section between Pen yr Helgi Du and Carnedd Llewelyn—a sixth of the total—is at all well used. The walk begins near the entrance to Cwm Eigiau, on moorland bounded to the west by a breached and now redundant dam wall (which burst in 1925, killing sixteen people). Scramble on to its flat top and follow it round to the sluice gates if you want to avoid the muddy ruts of the track.

Beyond Llyn Eigiau the cwm curves to the right, hidden from view by a craggy arm of high ground on the lake's west shore. Those impatient to explore the cwm could follow the old quarry track to the disused workings below the north slope of Pen yr Helgi Du, though they might regret this decision when faced with the arduous ascent to rejoin the ridge at Bwlch Eryl Farchog. It seems best to leave the track almost at once, striking up the hillside past the restored hut of Hafod y Rhiw, and to save Cwm Eigiau for the return journey.

The highlight of the walk—the skyline ridge between Pen Llithrig y Wrach and Carnedd Llewelyn—is visible in its entirety from a shoulder above Hafod y Rhiw. But you might as well put it from your mind; the ascent to Pen Llithrig y Wrach is wickedly foreshortened, and with few signs of previous passage the heathery plod seems interminable.

For my walk around Cwm Eigiau I chose to go alone one midweek afternoon out of season. Consequently I have many vivid recollections of the day but few words to describe them. Much of the experience, like those of early childhood, is couched not in words but in sensations. One exception is the view from the summit of Pen Llithrig y Wrach. I knew as soon as I arrived that here was something I would want to tell people about when I got down, so out came the camera and the mental notepad. Isolated clouds I had seen drifting about earlier in the day were now revealed to be mere symptoms of a chronic low cloud condition afflicting most of Snowdonia. Even as I watched the blight began to spread,

spilling over the Glyders into the Ogwen Valley like a dam disaster filmed in fascinating slow motion. Not so fascinating from the inside. A gob of cloud had migrated across the valley and had stuck in Bwlch y Tri Marchog, the col between Pen Llithrig y Wrach and Pen yr Helgi Du. I pulled up my anorak hood and swam through to the next island in the sun.

The summit of Pen yr Helgi Du, flat and grassy, isn't much of a place in itself. But to the north-west the Llugwy and Eigiau cwms have scoured so deep into the mountain that only the slender divide of Bwlch Eryl Farchog remains. A ridge, rocky and occasionally exposed, leads down to it. Perched between familiar south and mysterious north, this is an inspiring place to sit alone for a while. Everything about it seems to have pivotal significance. Philosophers ought to draft their theories here, preachers their sermons.

A blocky little crag obstructs a clean exit northwards from the bwlch. Walkers coming the other way appear to be unaccountably delayed by it, but only because the best route down—a short zig-zag—is less easily located in descent. It is all perfectly obvious from this side. Above that minor obstacle the ridge rapidly eases while maintaining interest as you creep around the lip of Craig yr Ysfa's impressive rock amphitheatre, sad or glad not to be tying to the end of a rope and climbing up one of its walls. Beyond Craig yr Ysfa the path

ignores the ridge it is meant to be following and makes a beeline for Carnedd Llewelyn across the gentle south-west flank, saving five minutes but losing a little of its purpose.

Route finding on Carnedd Llewelyn can be demoralisingly uncertain in mist. Though not in this instance. All you have to do is abandon hopes of finding the actual summit (you won't be missing much) and instead follow the Cwm Eigiau rim as it swings from west to north-east towards Foel Grach. Whether or not you can subsequently find a way down into Cwm Eigiau in these conditions in another matter. The trick is not to descend too soon but to follow the well-worn path on to the broad saddle between Carnedd Llewelyn and Foel Grach before aiming south-east down the broad spur (in clear weather you might decide first to detour to the summit of Foel Grach). The map shows a path on the spur but don't hold your breath trying to find it. Path or not, you will eventually find yourself on an extensive grass plateau with a choice of two routes to follow. The first crosses the plateau north-eastwards and descends a blunt ridge to the Melynllyn track, which in turn leads back to the parking place. The second descends grass slopes southwards into Cwm Eigiau itself, arriving near ruined buildings at the end of the quarry track which leads back to the start via Llyn Eigiau and its dam. Either route offers plenty of scope for therapeutic delay.

Craig yr Ysfa from the ruined mine buildings in Cwm Eigiau. A scree cone descends from the shaded central Amphitheatre. Craig yr Ysfa o adeiladau dadfeiliedig y gwaith mwyn yng Nghwm Eigiau. Y mae llethr caregog yn disgyn o'r amchwaraefa gysgodol.

8: THE CARNEDDAU — *The Carneddau from Ogwen*

Route Summary: A tremendous high-level ridge walk over barren mountains. The classic Carneddau traverse.
Difficulty: Class D.
Main summits: Pen yr Ole Wen 979m/3211ft; Carnedd Dafydd 1044m/3423ft; Carnedd Llewelyn 1064m/3485ft, Pen yr Helgi Du 833m/2733ft.
Duration: 16km/10 miles; 1050m/3450ft of ascent; allow 6hrs.
Terrain: Mostly good paths over stony ground or grass, but with a few boggy sections near the start and finish.
Special difficulties: Short scrambles on Pen yr Ole Wen and at each side of Bwlch Eryl Farchog, none of which will deter the experienced mountain walker. Locating the descent from Carnedd Llewelyn in mist requires care.
Approach: From Capel Curig or Bethesda along the A5. Park on the roadside near the bridge at Glan Dena (GR: 668 605).
Route directions: Cross the bridge on the track to Glan Dena and continue past it towards Tal y Llyn. Turn right just before entering the farm, later crossing the wall by a ladder stile. Follow the stream into Cwm Lloer. Ascend the ridge on the left side of the cwm, initially by a short gully, to the summit of Pen yr Ole Wen.

Circle the rim of Cwr Lloer northwards on a good path to the stony top of Carnedd Dafydd. Descend east on a rocky path, then curving north above the Black Ladders cliffs. Continue north beyond a slight col, rising steadily to the summit of Carnedd Llewelyn.

Descend south-east then east, along the ridge path above Craig yr Ysfa, finally descending to Bwlch Eryl Farchog by a short scramble. Ignore a flanking short-cut on to Y Braich and scramble up the rocky ridge to the summit of Pen yr Helgi Du.

Descend the grass ridge of Y Braich southwards by a good path and pass through a gap in the transverse wall (GR: 699 609). Contour to the right, then descend diagonally to cross the leat (man-made waterway) by a footbridge left of a stone wall. Turn right and follow the leat for about 500m to the Ffynnon

Llugwy access road, which in turn leads down to the A5 about 2km from the starting point.
Alternatives: Descend to the right from Bwlch Eryl Farchog to Ffynnon Llugwy and follow its access road down to the A5, thus avoiding the ascent to Pen yr Helgi Du.

Spread a map of the Carneddau on your knees and your eyes will automatically focus on Carnedd Llewelyn. Why? Because it stands at the T-junction of the range's two primary ridges and, by implication, terminates the three big intervening cwms. Closer scrutiny also reveals—for what it is worth—that the summit rates third highest in Wales (pile another few rocks on the cairn and it becomes number two).

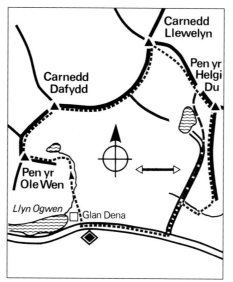

As on paper, so on the ground. Carnedd Llewelyn is the largest celestial body in the Carneddau universe and its gravitational pull draws walkers inexorably towards it—regardless of their starting point. Only after several orbits (the precise number being directly proportional to the impenetrability of the mist) does it release them to complete the second part of their journeys, which may or may not be as originally intended.

This route blasts off in the Ogwen Valley, reaches escape velocity on Pen yr Ole Wen,

cruises sub-sonically along the first stage of the near-infinite Great Ridge, orbits Carnedd Llewelyn, expires on Pen yr Helgi Du, and then falls gently back to earth along Y Braich. As a hill walk it's going to be out of this world.

Some people start the day with an unmitigated grind up the south spur of Pen yr Ole Wen. This is not a good idea. I wouldn't send my nephew up it. A much better start is that by the east ridge. This crafty flanking route begins at Glan Dena, that suburbanesque home-from-home for Midland Mountaineers, before branching uphill towards Cwm Lloer. Among other benefits it offers a terrific view of exquisitely proportioned Y Garn beyond the calm waters of Llyn Ogwen.

Calm? On most days your head will be inside your hood, hiding from a vile west wind that shaves wave tops from the lake and fetches rain up the valley by the tubful. Nothing to see then, and no reason to linger by the miniature waterfalls of the Afon Lloer. Unlike the hot afternoon when I came upon a young woman bathing in a pool here, tossing her hair back beneath the spray and . . . You think I made this up! Maybe I did. The sun plays tricks.

At the top wall a diverging path heads directly towards the east ridge, but my advice is to ignore this and instead follow the main path into Cwm Lloer, a gorgeous place in which to idle away the morning. If you have time to explore you will eventually find the engine blocks and bleached wings of a wrecked airplane, the scars of disaster long since healed by time and heather.

And now to more pressing matters: the east ridge. The crux of it is clearly going to be a rock gully, glistening with drainage, which cuts into the steepest part of the craggy shoulder. Not to worry, decades of scrabbling feet have excavated a staircase of good footholds, and after little more than five metres of concentrated scrambling you will emerge on the heathery back of the ridge. A winding path now works up the crest, switching sides to avoid difficulties and occasionally providing airy views down into Cwm Lloer, deserted but for a few sheep and perhaps a circling crow.

A detour southwards from the summit of Pen yr Ole Wen reveals the Glyders arranged in a splendid arc from Tryfan to Foel Goch,

On the ascent to Cwm Lloer. Tryfan rises from the shore of Llyn Ogwen. *Dringo i ben Cwm Lloer. Cyfyd Tryfan ar lan Llyn Ogwen.*

the near-empty cups of Cwm Bochlwyd and Cwm Idwal at their feet, and the trough of Llyn Ogwen at yours. Descend a little further and you can peer down the sinister Braich Ty Du gullies on to the vulnerable A5 far below. No wonder rocks from fist to football size, dislodged by frost or sheep, regularly tumble on to the road. Not that there's anything new in this; according to the naturalist Edward Lluyd, in 1685 there was "a great fall of rock from the crags overlooking Nant Phfrancon", out of which one large boulder finally came to rest on the opposite bank of the Afon Ogwen. The gullies periodically empty their burden of soil and scree, and over the centuries several farm houses in the valley have been buried. The

most recent landslide occurred in 1983, when flash floods swept hundreds of tons of rubble on to the road. Fortunately it happened at night when there was little traffic, and although one car was trapped between two slides, no-one was injured.

Circling the rim of Cwm Lloer loses just fifty metres of height, and it is only another hundred up to Carnedd Dafydd. At first a typical Carneddau mix of fine stones and gritty earth lies underfoot, but the stones get bigger as the summit approaches, and at the very top huge mounds of them have been heaped up to provide shelter from the gales. Stand at the summit and bare your face to the inevitable north-westerly and your eyes will be drawn

coastwards along the lizard tale of the Llafar Ridge to the Menai Strait, Anglesey and beyond. On a good day you can see the Isle of Man and the Lake District.

But there are bad days too. One grim February evening my partner and I sheltered here after climbing a gully on Black Ladders. Visibility was down to about five metres, and by some unfortunate misunderstanding neither of us had brought a map, compass or torch. During our deliberations we also discovered that neither of us had stood on Carnedd Dafydd before. In half an hour it would be dark. Crystals of hoar frost formed on our clothes and beards as we navigated by the wind down what we hoped was the Llafar Ridge.

34

At the bwlch below Carnedd Llewelyn, looking back across the Black Ladders headwall to Carnedd Dafydd. Y bwlch islaw
Carnedd Llywelyn, yn edrych yn ôl dros yr Ysgolion Du at Garnedd Dafydd.

The wind, swirling around the headwall of the cwm, proved an unreliable guide and fifteen minutes later we were dismayed to find ourselves back at the summit. With no time left for subtlety we took a beeline over the headwall and resolved to descend whatever came our way. By pure luck we chose the only feasible descent into the cwm, and two hours later we were reliving the reckless adventure in front a blazing fire.

The path to Carnedd Llewelyn circles above the grim crescent of the Black Ladders cliffs then rises up the summit dome, which may be striped with snow as early as October or as late as June. Ridge paths arrive from north, south, east and west, though not all converge on the same 'summit'. On misty days you can find yourself wandering aimlessly around the plateau, unsure of where you arrived and where you should depart. You might think to wait for someone to come along who has a better sense of direction. If so you could be there a very long time.

Carnedd Llewelyn stands at the western end of the watershed ridge between Ogwen and Conwy valleys—the next stage of the walk. At first the path slants across its broad back, but later passes above the Craig yr Ysfa Amphitheatre with its rock walled funnel of heather and scree. Beyond the cliffs the path steepens to descend the final step of the ridge; by the easiest line this rocky scramble is no more difficult than the little gully on Pen yr Ole Wen's east ridge, so try elsewhere if confronted by undue difficulties (the correct route is well marked).

The far side of Bwlch Eryl Farchog rises up in a bristling ridge to the summit of Pen yr Helgi Du. It looks longer and more difficult than it proves to be, and some are needlessly intimidated into traversing directly on to the descent ridge of Y Braich. Persevere: it can't be that bad if I once (but never again) got up it with a mountain bike slung over my shoulder. Assuming you arrive at the summit in a better state than I did then there's no reason to linger and you can trot off at once down the yielding grass of Y Braich, a panoramic view of the Glyders, backlit by a dipping sun, spread before you.

THE GLYDERS

Maps: The whole region appears on Landranger Sheet 115 (Snowdon) at 1:50,000 scale, although given the intricacy of the terrain, the lack of detail is unhelpful. Much the best choice is Outdoor Leisure 17 (Snowdonia—Snowdon Area) at 1:25,000 scale, which is especially good value in that it also includes the whole of the Snowdon Group.

Bases: Three of the four walks start from the Ogwen Valley, and so a base somewhere along the A5 between Capel Curig and Bethesda is best. Bethesda can be reached by bus from Bangor (which is served by rail), whereas the continuation to Capel Curig runs only in summer, and infrequently at that. Capel Curig is the first choice, and despite its small size offers everything from bunkhouse to hotel accommodation. There are several campsites in the village and on the road towards Ogwen.

Tightly knit and thoroughly rugged, the Glyders are the spiritual home of mountain walkers and scramblers in Wales. The summit plateaux of the two main peaks are littered with rocks, some stacked up into ramparts, others laid out into pavements. Evocative names such as Bristly Ridge, Castle of the Winds and the Devil's Kitchen convey both the atmosphere and the appeal of these intricate and fascinating mountains.

For all that the region is really quite small, essentially consisting only of a single bent backbone of a ridge, several subsidiary ribs, and a couple of satellite peaks. Other, far less famous ranges can claim as much. The difference is that here, where the thoroughfares are spiky ridges and tortuous paths, each route up each peak has a unique character.

Climax of the ascent to Y Garn. Braich Ty Du face of Pen yr Ole Wen opposite. Diwedd y dringo i ben Y Garn Mae wyneb Braich Tŷ Du o Ben yr Ole Wen gyferbyn.

36

9: THE GLYDERS — Cwm Idwal and Y Garn

Route summary: A short but unremitting ascent to a high satellite peak of the Glyders. The descent passes beneath the notorious Devil's Kitchen and wanders through a mountain cwm noted for its rock climbing, rare plants and evidence of glacial action. The short walk around the cwm is a worthwhile alternative for a less strenuous day.

Difficulty: Class C.

Main summits: Y Garn 946m/3104ft.

Duration: 8km/5 miles; 650m/2125ft of ascent; allow 4hrs.

Terrain: Some boggy ground to start, then improving paths over grass and stones. Rocky path and cobbled track to finish.

Special difficulties: The ascent ridge is broader than it appears and involves no genuine scrambling; nevertheless, it is best avoided during strong winds. Some care is required to locate the Devil's Kitchen descent. The descent itself is not difficult, although unstable rock and scree demand respect.

Approach: From Capel Curig or Bethesda. Turn off the A5 at Ogwen Cottage to a car park with toilets, phone and snack bar (GR:649 604). The car park is often full but overspill parking is available in lay-bys to the east.

Route directions: A path leads up a shale bank behind the toilet block and divides after just a few metres. Fork right through a quarried ravine, exit right from near its end, and cross a ladder stile soon after. Continue by a less obvious path, over a second stile, until overlooking Llyn Idwal. Ascend the broad north-east shoulder of Y Garn by a zig-zagging path and continue by the exposed and steepening ridge above to a junction with the main ridge path between Y Garn and Foel Goch. Turn left for the summit.

Descend south then south-east to Llyn y Cŵn (take care in mist not to stray on to the difficult knife-edge of Y Garn's east ridge). Follow a path north-east from Llyn y Cŵn and down through a stone filled runnel on to a broad ramp which slants across cliffs to the Kitchen Cleft entrance. From the entrance, descend awkwardly

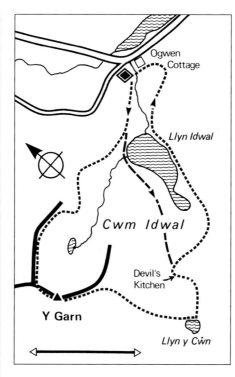

The Idwal Slabs rise beyond Llyn Idwal to the summit of Glyder Fawr. Remnants of snow in Cwm Cneifion sometimes linger into June. Creigiau Idwal yn codi, y tu hwnt i Lyn Idwal, at gopa'r Gluder Fawr. Weithiau fe erys yr eira yng Nghwm Cneifion tan fis Mehefin.

on gritty paths to a better path slanting across the hillside to the foot of the Idwal Slabs. Follow the lakeside path, through a gate near the outflow, and return to the start along a stone track.

Alternatives: Enter Cwm Idwal as for the main route then circle the lake on constructed footpaths—an entertaining short walk among magnificent cliff scenery.

The Glyders have been nipped and bent in the middle, forming two disparate limbs which defy common description. Experience of one does not mean experience of both, and an ascent of Y Garn will be quite different from an ascent of neighbouring Glyder Fawr. Let this be a warning to those of you who have 'done' the main Glyders not to neglect Y Garn.

The walk begins at Ogwen Cottage, where the A5 road squeezes past the end of Llyn Ogwen and starts its descent of the Nant Ffrancon. Before its expansion into an outdoor pursuits centre, Ogwen Cottage offered basic accommodation to travellers and mountaineers. Archer Thomson based himself here while

exploring the cliffs of the Glyders and Carnedau in the late nineteenth century. Other changes are more recent. The winding lakeside road has been straightened into a sweeping highway, and the wooden roadside tea shack replaced by a solid building adjacent to the new car park. Since then attempts have been made to retrieve lost values, such as replacing ugly roadside fencing with stone walls.

On leaving the car park the path divides almost at once: left for the main Idwal path, right for Y Garn. We turn right, over a stile and through the narrow ravine of the disused hone-stone quarry, which was a valuable local resource during construction of both the toll road and Telford road during the early nineteenth century. Today its walls are used for abseil practice by young people from the outdoor centre.

Cwm Idwal is extremely popular with stu-

Above: The Cwm Clyd headwall during the descent to Llyn y Cŵn. In the background, from left to right Tryfan, Glyder Fach, Upper Cliff of Glyder Fawr. *Ar ben Cwm Clyd wrth ddisgyn at Lyn y Cŵn. Yn y cefndir, o'r chwith i'r dde Tryfan, Y Gluder Fach, a chlogwyn uchaf Y Gluder Fawr.*

dents of the earth sciences (or rather with their teachers—on rain lashed afternoons the students have other things to say about Cwm Idwal). In particular this famous rock-walled hollow is a classic example of a glaciated cwm, and every young person who files around the lake with a clipboard in one hand and a can of Coke in the other is expected to point out the evidence. It all seems so obvious. But theorising with hindsight is like solving a jig-saw puzzle with the picture in front of you. This is what Charles Darwin wrote about his visit to Cwm Idwal in 1831 with Professor Alan Sedgwick:

"We spent many hours in Cwm Idwal, examining all the rocks with extreme care, as Sedgwick was anxious to find fossils in them; but neither of us saw a trace of the wonderful glacial phenomena all around us; we did not notice the plainly scored rocks, the perched boulders, the lateral and terminal moraines. Yet these phenomena are so conspicuous that, as I declared in a paper published many years afterwards in the *Philosophical Magazine*, a house burnt down by fire did not tell its story more plainly than did this valley."

From the grass dome overlooking Llyn Idwal a constructed path can be taken around the lake—a worthwhile walk in itself for a short day or if bad weather threatens. Otherwise to begin the ascent of Y Garn you must drag yourself away from the pebble beach and zig-zag up a broad shoulder which, in its upper part, narrows into the north-east ridge which is so distinctive when viewing the mountain from Llyn Ogwen. Despite appearances there are no scrambling difficulties, even on the steep final section. Nevertheless, there are few situations more dramatic than this when a breath-snatching north-westerly gusts across the crest. The ridge emerges quite suddenly on the gentle north shoulder of Y Garn, a few minutes short of the summit and within strolling distance of companion hills to the north—Foel Goch, Mynydd Perfedd and Elidir Fawr.

Initially the descent circles the rim of Cwm Clyd, bringing views into the cwm and across to the knife-edged East Ridge (take care in mist not to circle too far around the cwm or you'll find yourself on the promonotory of this difficult scramble). Further down, the path descends an open slope of grass and stones direct to the boggy saddle partly occupied by Llyn y Cŵn. Cloud permitting, this descent provides an interesting view of the rocky northern side of the two Glyders: the north-west face of Glyder Fawr, its grey cliffs striped with sunlit pillars; and the columnar crags of Glyder Fach, partly hidden behind the Gribin.

Locating the Devil's Kitchen descent into Cwm Idwal requires care. Some people, confused by the terminology, have mistakenly tried to descend by the Devil's Kitchen Cleft itself. If you have been inside the Cleft you will know that all such attempts are futile. But then some walkers are persistent. To be certain of finding the correct route you must follow the path north-east from Llyn y Cŵn, down through a stone filled runnel, and out on to the ramp which slants diagonally across the Devil's Kitchen cliffs. Broad at first, the ramp narrows as it descends, forcing you to pass directly beneath huge cliffs. Rare alpine plants survive here, protected by rotten rock from the destructive cleansing hand of the climber. The perpetual drainage which makes the cliffs so repulsive to climbers in summer has precisely the opposite effect in a severe winter. Then, each slimy gully freezes into an icy cascade—ideal terrain for the techniques of modern winter climbing. The most famous of these icefalls is the Devil's Appendix, a hundred metre route to the right of the Cleft. First climbed in the severe winter of 1978, it is now regarded as one of the finest ice climbs in Britain.

The ramp leads with a final short scramble down to the jumble of boulders at the entrance to the Kitchen Cleft. You might consider scrambling up the stream bed as far as the huge chockstone which blocks further unroped progress. Even here, some way short of the waterfall that spouts over the back of the Cleft, the atmosphere is tremendous. During periods of prolonged cold weather the waterfall itself freezes into a tapering column of ice, and it was by this route, in 1895, that the Cleft was first climbed. To complete their epic eight hour ascent, Archer Thomson and H. Hughes hacked out hand and footholds using a coal hatchet borrowed from Ogwen Cottage. Somewhat better equipped, I climbed the route in similar conditions during the good winter of 1983, finding it more difficult than some of the ice pitches first climbed in the sixties. But conditions vary tremendously; during the exceptional winter of 1979, so much snow drifted into the Cleft that almost the entire 25m ice pitch banked out, and for a couple of weeks the route was used by parties of winter walkers as a quick approach to Llyn y Cŵn.

From below the Cleft a scruffy descent over gritty boulders leads to a path which slants across the hillside to the base of the Idwal Slabs. On dry afternoons dozens of climbers can be seen making erratic progress up this unique sweep of rock. But why all the fuss? The Slabs, barely steeper than 45 degrees, look easy enough to walk up. That is until you try to get some purchase with your boot soles on the polished holds. True, none of the main slab routes are difficult by today's standards, though only the Ordinary Route up the wide crack near the left edge is genuinely straightforward. Being much steeper, the East Wall of the Slabs attracts comparatively few climbers, and hardly any to its upper left side, known—with some justification—as Suicide Wall.

Sometimes it feels good to turn away and leave the rock climbers to their intense little moments, knowing that your own string of moments on Y Garn is safely in the bag, and that in just twenty minutes you can be down at the Ogwen snack bar stuffing a hot pasty down your throat.

At the shore of Llyn Idwal, below the foreshortened ascent shoulder to Y Garn.
Ar lan Llyn Idwal islaw'r ddringfa fer at y Garn.

10: THE GLYDERS — The Glyders from Ogwen

Route summary: A superb mountain walk in rugged surroundings. Traverses a rock-strewn ridge over the two Glyders then descends by the Devil's Kitchen cliffs into Cwm Idwal.

Difficulty: Class D.

Main summits: Glyder Fach 994m/3262ft; Glyder Fawr 999m/3279ft.

Duration: 10km/6 miles; 775m/2550ft of ascent; allow 5hrs.

Terrain: Mainly good paths over rocky ground during the ascent (one boggy section). Eroded scree then good paths on the descent.

Special difficulties: Difficult route finding in mist between the two Glyders and on the descent to Llyn y Cŵn. Short and avoidable boulder scrambles to the summit of Glyder Fach and across Castell y Gwynt. Care required in locating the Devil's Kitchen descent (the descent itself is not difficult, though unstable rock and scree demand respect).

Approach: From Capel Curig or Bethesda. Turn off the A5 at Ogwen Cottage to a car park with toilets, phone and snack bar (GR:649 604). The car park is often full but overspill parking is available in lay-bys to the east.

Route directions: A path leads up a shale bank behind the toilet block and divides after just a few metres. Fork left, cross the wooden bridge and follow the stone track until it curves rightwards. Bear left here on a sometimes boggy path (stepping stones), then up the constructed zig-zags into Cwm Bochlwyd.

Cross the stream outflow of the lake and follow a path rising above the east shore to Bwlch Tryfan (GR:662 588). Descend slightly on the east side to find a good path contouring the head of Cwm Tryfan, later rising on to the grassy east shoulder of Glyder Fach. (GR:667 583). Ascend the shoulder, becoming rocky, to the summit plateau. Divert left to find the Cantilever then continue a little further to the summit rock pile of Glyder Fach.

Continue south-west over the boulder-strewn plateau towards the pronounced crag of Castell y Gwynt (Castle of the Winds). Either scramble through a gap just left of its summit and descend to Bwlch y Ddwy Glyder on the far side, or make a descending detour south for about 100m, returning to the bwlch after passing beyond crags. Follow a muddy rut along the southern flank of the ridge and continue over stones to the summit rock pile of Glyder Fawr.

Descend the south-west shoulder for about 200m then turn north-west to descend a badly eroded scree path (some cairns) to Llyn y Cŵn. Take the path north-east from the lake and go down through a stone-filled runnel on to the broad ramp slanting leftwards across cliffs to the Kitchen Cleft entrance. From the entrance, descend awkwardly on gritty paths to a better path slanting across the hillside to the foot of the Idwal Slabs. Follow the lakeside path through a gate near the outflow and return to the car park by a stone track.

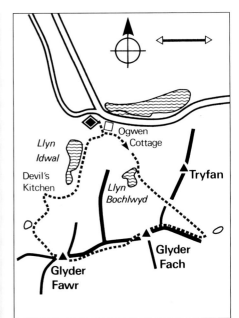

Sunset over Snowdon from Castell y Gwynt, 'Castle of the Winds'. *Y machlud dros Eryri o Gastell y Gwynt.*

The Devil's Kitchen cliffs. The descent path follows the ramp line slanting down right to the Kitchen Cleft entrance, the central dark slit. *Cegin y Diafol.*

Gwyra'r llwybr i lawr tua'r dde at y fynedfa i Hollt y Gegin, yr hollt tywyll yn y canol.

Pressed to select a representative of North Wales hill walking I would choose this roundabout route on the north side of the Glyders. The trouble is, lots of other people arrive at the same conclusion. An opportunist will come midweek in autumn and set off before sunrise.

I used this ploy to avoid the crowds one clear December morning at the end of a ten day freeze. Ogwen was still gripped by pre-dawn cold as I walked stiffly up the Idwal track by the light of a three-quarter moon lodged in the sky like a chip of ice. Weary from lack of sleep and nauseous from the draughts of cold air, it was habit, not enthusiasm, which kept me going.

Ahead lay the steepest ascent of the whole walk: the badly eroded bank of the stream which issues from Llyn Bochlwyd. This once unruly path now plods dutifully upwards on regularly spaced steps between tidy walls. Men have worked through wind and rain to unearth and lay these stones, and they can feel proud at their achievement. But was it necessary? Further up the hillside the path has worn down to bedrock and now winds up a more natural staircase. Could that same process of evolution have stabilised the lower section too? Perhaps, perhaps not; though having decided to restore the path, I think the workmen should have been dissuaded from creating a civilised path as a monument to their efforts.

Twenty minutes later I entered the hidden sanctuary of Cwm Bochlwyd. Sunlight touched the ridges of Y Garn, introducing shape and familiarity to what an hour ago had been a sinister blue-black silhouette. There was a

dusting of snow on the summit. In summer people come here to camp by the lake, to climb on the grey cliffs, or simply to sit on the boulder bridge over the outflow and listen to the whispers of an escaping stream. People speak in quiet voices here so as not to shatter the illusion of other-worldliness.

Damn the helicopter. It came thugging around the corner like a giant insect and began probing the inner recesses of the cwm. The illusion exploded. When the helicopter had gone I gathered up the bits of broken image and stuck them back together, but the glaze of perfection had gone.

North-westerlies squeeze between the gap of Bwlch Tryfan at several times their nominal speeds, but in the lee of a wall you can safely unfold a map and decide which of three routes to take. The finest rises directly from the bwlch along the crest of Bristly Ridge, but that was out of the question today, its pinnacles wrapped in treacherous hoar frost. The couloir to its left would be tolerable, but this unpleasant grind on thinning scree is more appropriate as a means of quick descent. That left me with the old Miners' Track—really little more than a good path—which contours the head of Cwm Tryfan before rising on to the gentle eastern spur of Glyder Fach. This was the route used in the nineteenth century by Bethesda men when they left home each Monday morning to work in the Snowdon copper mines.

The path up the eastern spur begins gently over marsh grass, loses itself among boulders, then reforms near the right edge with thought-

provoking views of Bristly Ridge in jagged profile (don't worry, it's not as sharp as it looks). On summer afternoons you can watch the ant-like progress of scramblers working their way up its crest. Eventually the path levels and approaches the rim of Cwm Bochlwyd, from where the Gribin and Y Garn spring suddenly into view. As I looked coastwards along the broad U of the lower Ogwen Valley I could see a bank of low cloud massing for later assault. Already a few advance clumps had worked up the back of the Carneddau, and were now creeping stealthily over Pen yr Ole Wen. Tonight it would rain. I hurried over the clumsily laid floor of the summit plateau in search of the Cantilever.

Along with the Cannon and Adam and Eve on Tryfan, this jutting plank of rock makes an ideal photo-opportunity for hill walking exhibitionists. Thomas Pennant, the eighteenth century traveller, was the first to exploit its media potential when he posed at its tip, stick in hand, while artist Moses Griffiths sketched the scene. All subsequent cavorting and picture taking on this rock are clichés. But we do it none the less. It has become a ritual. Incidentally, if you compare your own snapshot with the Griffiths sketch you will notice a discrepancy; Griffiths has blatantly tampered with the proportions in his eagerness to enhance the dramatic impact. Either that or Pennant was an uncommonly short fellow. Usually there is a queue of people waiting to stand self-consciously on the end of the rock while a companion on the ground, instructed to record the scene, pretends not to know where the shutter button is. Today I was quite alone (I checked, carefully). After ten minutes of trying without success to secure an original picture, I opted for the ordinary. What I hadn't allowed for was the short duration of the camera's self-timer and the coating of ice on the subtly tilted Cantilever. There was a certain amount of toing and froing (mostly froing, which I won't go into) before I got my picture. I may not have Pennant's poise, or Griffiths's cunning, but I know a photo-opportunity when I see one.

The near-by summit rock pile of Glyder Fach defeated me on this occasion. Under its veneer of ice the crazy pile of splinters proved insurmountable. So like a thwarted dog I circled the mound a couple of times, barking my frustration, until my spiritual master returned from his successful summit bid. I trotted dutifully behind as he strolled over the Castell y Gwynt for another dose of cosmic energy.

Castell y Gwynt—Castle of the Winds— stands at the western edge of the plateau, a fortress overlooking the notch of Bwlch y Ddwy Glyder. Macho men, who after all are only little

Coastward view down the Ogwen Valley from the Glyder Fach summit plateau, Cwm Bochlwyd below. *Golygfa i gyfeiriad glan y môr i lawr Dyffryn Ogwen o wastatir uchel copa'r Gluder Fach, a Chwm Bochlwyd islaw.*

boys trapped inside big bodies, like to sit among the crenellations, hooting and shouting and pretending to be soldiers, while their companions flank the rocks low down on the left to avoid embarrassment. There's a middle way: scramble through the gap on the left side, traverse to the far side of the tower, and then descend over a few boulders to the bwlch.

At the rim of Cwm Cneifion I met two climbers who, axes in hand and ropes, ice-screws and the other paraphernalia of winter struggle draped over their shoulders, had evidently not long emerged from Clogwyn Du Gully. "What's the ice like?" I asked. "A bit thin," one of them said, inspecting the damaged tip of his axe. Behind them Clogwyn Du appeared dispiritingly black across the desolate bowl of the cwm.

The cloud attacked on Glyder Fawr, scudding across the rock-strewn plateau in chilling waves. It must have rushed across from the Carneddau while I was looking at cliffs. The sun turned a sickly yellow, threatening to expire, and the temperature plummeted. I was amazed to discover that in an hour it would be dark.

The descent over convex slopes from Glyder Fawr to Llyn y Cŵn is extremely unpleasant. In winter it can also be very dangerous, especially if the surface is frozen but with insufficient snow cover for step-kicking or ice-axe braking. I guessed that the afternoon sun would have warmed the slope, loosening the scree and gritty soil into a more forgiving consistency. If I was wrong then I would have to go back the way I had come. My guess was correct and within an hour I had reached Llyn y Cŵn, descended the ramp across the Devil's Kitchen cliffs and arrived safely in fading light at the foot of the Idwal Slabs. It was all over bar the stumbling.

The Cantilever, the most famous of the natural rock structures found on the Glyders. *Y Cantilever, yr enwocaf o'r ffurfiadau carreg naturiol i'w gweld ar y ddwy Gluder.*

11: THE GLYDERS — *The Cwm Bochlwyd Horseshoe*

Route summary: An exhilarating ridge traverse, enjoying the best of the rugged Glyders scenery. Best tackled in fine weather by a resourceful party of competent scrambling enthusiasts.
Difficulty: Class E.
Main summits: Tryfan 917m/3010ft; Glyder Fach 994m/3262ft.
Duration: 8km/5miles; 900m/2950ft of ascent; allow 6-7hrs.
Terrain: Rough paths over rock and heather, and bare rock ridges. Some boggy ground near the finish.

Special difficulties: Even the most difficult scrambling sections should be within the capability of an experienced and agile hill walker. However, it is easy to stray on to difficult ground and carrying an emergency rope is a wise precaution (15m/50ft of 9mm climbing rope will suffice)—provided of course someone in the group knows how to tie a bowline and belay the rope. The route is best avoided in wet or windy weather.
Approach: From Capel Curig or Bethesda along the A5. Parking for several cars at

a lay-by (GR:663 603) below the Milestone Buttress, a prominent feature on the lower west side of the North Ridge.
Route directions: Ascend near a stone wall towards the Milestone Buttress then trend left to gain the first shoulder on the North Ridge. Ascend a boulder slope and break through a short barrier at its top. Continue slightly on the left side of the broad ridge to a quartz platform (the Cannon will be found over on the right). Scramble up the next high barrier near its left side and continue to another large

On the descent of Tryfan's South Ridge. Y Garn in the background. *Wrth ddod i lawr esgair ddeheuol Tryfan. Y Garn yn y cefndir.*

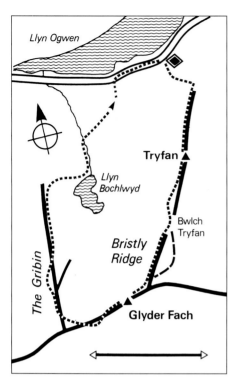

platform below a prominent nose. Scramble up the nose on polished rock to its summit and descend to a notch on the far side (or avoid by traversing its left side to the notch). Escape the notch, trending right, and ascend a gully to the North Summit. Continue easily over boulders to the twin standing stones of Adam and Eve on the Central Summit.

Traverse to the South Summit then descend the South Ridge, generally by its right side, to the broad col between South and Far South Summits. Flank the Far South Summit on the right and descend to Bwlch Tryfan (GR:662 588). If conditions deteriorate the route can be abandoned here by descending to the right into Cwm Bochlwyd.

Follow the stone wall to the base of the first crags of Bristly Ridge. Ascend a short gully 10m right, exiting left over a man-made wall to the foot of a more imposing gully (Sinister Gully) which leads, after a detour left when it steepens uncomfortably, to easier ground. Continue up a slabby shoulder to a narrowing of the ridge. Scramble over a small pinnacle on to a larger one then descend into Great Pinnacle Gap—the prominent notch of the ridge. Escape by a short wall just right of the slender Great Pinnacle then pass through a gap between a squat pinnacle on the right and the main body

of the ridge to easier ground leading up to the summit plateau. Walk south-west to join the main ridge path and follow it to the summit rock pile of Glyder Fach.

Continue south-west, scrambling around or over Castell y Gwynt, to Bwlch y Ddwy Glyder (GR:652 582). Ignore the main path to Glyder Fawr and instead circle the rim of Cwm Bochlwyd on to the promontory above Y Gribin. Descend the ridge, initially by some simple scrambling near the crest (avoid straying too far down the west flank), to a level section. Continue along the right side of the ridge until a path curves right and descends to the Llyn Bochlwyd outflow. Descend the path on the west bank of the stream then cross it for a rightward diagonal descent over boggy ground to gain the A5 at a large car park (GR:659 601) less than 500m from the start.

Alternatives: To avoid Bristly Ridge, cross the ladder stile at Bwlch Tryfan and then zig-zag up scree paths in a broad couloir on the east side of the ridge. Inferior to the main route but a useful alternative in deteriorating weather or if time is short.

Scrambling liberates the animal in us, tapping deep into dormant instincts. It restores the vitality of childhood, lost when we swung down from the trees and rubbed our hands of innocence. It turns us into rock addicts. Having once experienced the thrill of pulling clear of a gully with two handfuls of solid granite, or of balancing across a knife edge with the wind in our hair, we can't resist negotiating for another fix.

The Glyders throw down slender ridges to the north, each pair partially enclosing a glaciated cwm. Cwm Bochlwyd sits tight below the rock studded north-west face of Glyder Fach, bounded to the east by Bristly Ridge and to the west by the Gribin. Unlike the elongated Gribin, Bristly Ridge ends prematurely at Bwlch Tryfan. This col can be approached directly and the two ridges linked for a fine circuit. However, a more satisfying approach first traverses Tryfan by its North and South Ridges. This extended circuit gives the best scramble in the Glyders, and second only in Wales to the Snowdon Horseshoe.

Tryfan protrudes stubbornly from the jaws of Cwm Bochlwyd as a solitary blackened tooth. The glacier must have tugged and scraped, but the mountain, rooted deep, hasn't shifted. Now it is a landmark for travellers and a shrine for mountaineers. No other peak in Snowdonia provokes such lasting affection. The North Ridge extends a splayed foot towards the east shore of Llyn Ogwen. The lower third, broad

and featureless below a prominent heather shoulder, is usually flanked to east or west. The eastern approach begins at the farm of Gwern Gof Uchaf, passes the slabby wedge of Little Tryfan, and finally crosses the mouth of Cwm Tryfan to gain the shoulder by a scree couloir—an approach shared by the Heather Terrace, a scrambly walk which slants across the East Face from the couloir exit. The more usual western approach ascends first towards the Milestone Buttress before slanting up a bouldery rake to gain the shoulder.

Already the road looks like a grey ribbon on a playboard, its cars and trucks mere toys. The ridge teases with a dozen different lines above the shoulder. A third grind to a halt among blind alleys in outcrops on the right while another third deviate too far left and lose sight of the ridge. That still leaves four to go at, any one of which will deliver you at a glistening quartz platform.

Low down on the right here, at the base of the next barrier, the Cannon rock protrudes in unlikely equilibrium—a delightful photographic cliché. Experienced posers strut boldly to its nozzle and ask where you want them: standing, sitting, or balancing on one leg. Novices wriggle nervously *à cheval* up its back and ask you to please hurry.

The barrier itself deters direct ascents from the quartz platform but you'll find a way through on the left (not too far left, or you'll miss the fun). This is the first proper scrambling of the day and a good place for second thoughts if it seems unduly difficult. A tapering pinnacle rises from the next platform—the crucial obstacle to a direct ascent of the ridge. It can be avoided by a detour to the left, but if the rocks are dry and you are in a confident mood then you won't want to miss this highlight of the ridge. A short descent from the pinnacle summit will bring you to a boulder-choked notch between North and Far North Summits, and a reunion with companions who opted for the leftward diversion. Exit from the notch is easier than it looks, and gentle ground above leads quickly rightwards to a shallow rock gully in the final tower. The gully looks severe but soon yields to an energetic assault.

Impatient for the Central Summit, the north top passes underfoot with barely a pause. Chunks of rock lie discarded on the linking crest, the towers unbuilt. Nothing can stop you now from clambering up to the naked stones of Adam and Eve and slapping them on the back. On a fine afternoon there could be anything up to two hundred people and seagulls lunching here. One in ten will want to attempt the traditional leap between Adam and Eve (gulls excluded). Average dithering time is three minutes, so tourists glancing up from the road-side between twelve and one-thirty have a two-to-one-on chance of witnessing an apparent suicide. Don't be put off by this gladiatorial orgy—the situations and views at the rock-strewn summit of Tryfan are tremendous. The South Summit and *contre jour* lighting prevent a clear view of Bristly Ridge, although the outline of the remainder of the circuit—over Glyder Fach and down the Gribin—should be plainly visible.

Time to go. A polished neck of rock points the way towards the South Summit, from where uncomplicated scrambling on the South Ridge—gloriously sunny on a fine day after the chilling shadows of the North Ridge—leads across the west flank of the Far South Summit and down to the walled col of Bwlch Tryfan.

Bristly Ridge is an awesome sight when cloud streams through the pinnacles of its crest and pools in the cavities of its eastern flank. Frontal views are always the most intimidating, and in fact the ridge is much less steep than it appears. Provided you select the easiest line, difficulties will be no greater than those already overcome on the North Ridge. As on Tryfan, the major route-finding problems arise at the start where the ridge is broadest. One of the more obvious lines is that of Sinister Gully, which—after some exposed scrambling—exits on to a slabby shoulder below the narrower upper section of ridge. Here the prominent notch of Great Pinnacle Gap guards entry to the final bastion, and there could be a tense moment before you locate the relatively simple descent into it. Now things look much better; from a recess behind the Pinnacle a gangway leads to easy ground, above which a final raised parapet will deposit you on the familiar terrain of the Glyder Fach summit plateau.

If you've followed either of the normal routes over the Glyders (chapters 10 and 12) then you'll know all about the wonders of Glyder Fach and Castell y Gwynt. Let's just say that the traverse to the top of the Gribin will not disappoint, despite the lack of scrambling interest.

Difficulties on the Gribin are neither as severe nor as prolonged as those on Bristly Ridge. This is just as well, because scrambling down is a lot more difficult than scrambling up (ask a cat). It has something to do with feet and hands facing the wrong way, and the fact that eyes come down later when they would have been more use going down first. Not to worry, the easiest line down the Gribin—that near the crest—gives scrambling of only the most straightforward kind. In fact the interesting scrambling is confined to the upper prow, and once down on the shoulder you can relax and

Great Pinnacle Gap, climax of the Bristly Ridge scramble. *Bwlch y Copa Mawr, uchafbwynt scrambl Esgair Bristly.*

enjoy the view down the lower Ogwen Valley and across to the Carneddau.

Eventually the path veers rightwards and descends to the stream outlet of Llyn Bochlwyd. On fine evenings, columnar pillars beyond the lake glow orange in the slanting light of the setting sun, and but for the hungry bugs it would be tempting to sit by the lake and watch these candles expire one by one. As it is you will hurry down the Bochlwyd path, scratching and stumbling into the dusk. In your haste you might miss the short-cut back to the car park,

in which case you'll finish up grumbling at Ogwen Cottage, just in time to see the shutters come down on the snack bar. Don't let it get to you: tomorrow you'll wake up and believe yesterday was sublime.

12: THE GLYDERS — The Glyders from the Llanberis Pass

Route summary: The logical combination of routes on the unfashionable south side of the Glyders. Unexceptional at the start and finish, though fascinating rock scenery on the Glyders connecting ridge more than compensates.

Difficulty: Class C.

Main summits: Glyder Fawr 999m/3279ft; Glyder Fach 994m/3262ft.

Duration: 10km/6 miles; 800m/2625ft of ascent; allow 4-5hrs.

Terrain: Adequate paths over grass, heather and boulders, with boggy sections near the start and finish.

Special difficulties: Difficult route-finding in misty conditions, especially for those with no prior knowledge of the Glyders. Boulder scrambles over Castell y Gwynt and Glyder Fach summit are simple and, if necessary, avoidable.

Approach: From Llanberis or Capel Curig along the A4086 to the Pen y Gwyrd Hotel at the A4086/A498 junction (GR:661 558). Free parking opposite the hotel or in lay-bys further east.

Route directions: Walk up the A4086 to Pen y Pass (20mins) and go through a gate at the far end of the Youth Hostel buildings. Cross the wall by a ladder stile and follow the path which rises leftwards across the steep hillside. Continue north-west across a boggy area (red marker spots on boulders) then trend rightwards up a steep rise to gain the south spur of Glyder Fawr. Ascend the broad spur to the summit.

Follow the main ridge path eastwards, initially over stones then along a muddy rut, to Bwlch y Ddwy Glyder (GR:652 582). Scramble easily through a gap just right of Castell y Gwynt summit (or avoid by a long detour down to the right) to gain the Glyder Fach plateau and its summit rock pile.

Continue north-east (divert right to visit the Cantilever) to find the path leading eastwards down the broad back of the main ridge. This descends over boulders and eventually leads to the boggy saddle near Llyn y Caseg Fraith (take care not to stray on to paths leading left on to Bristly Ridge or down the scree couloir on its east

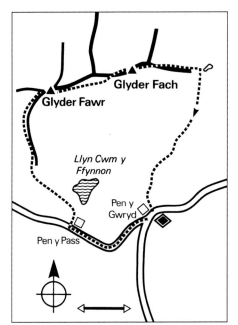

side). Turn right before reaching the lake to follow a path descending generally south over grass and stones. In the lower reaches, detour right (ladder stiles) to avoid a boggy area and cross the stream by a footbridge. Finally cross a stile to gain the main road just 100m from the start.

To me the word 'Glyders' conjures up an image of a heavily glaciated mountainside riven by gullies and buttressed by rock pillars, of evocatively named features such as the Devil's Kitchen, Castell y Gwynt and Bristly Ridge. It is an image of the northern flank of the Glyders. By comparison the south side is a wasteland strewn with boulders and choked with heather, the summits insignificant pimples on the skyline. The prospect of an ascent from this side is not an appealing one.

But we are forgetting that the south-west flank of Glyder Fawr, far from being featureless, is none other than that most imposing of

Retrospective view of Glyder Fawr from Glyder Fach. The rock tower between is Castell y Gwynt, 'Castle of the Winds'. Edrych yn ôl at Y Gluder Fawr o'r Gluder Fach. Castell y Gwynt yw'r tŵr cerrig rhyngddynt.

Evening at the summit of Glyder Fawr, the Llanberis lakes already in shadow. *Yr hwyr ar ben Y Gluder Fawr a llynnoedd Llanberis eisoes yn y cysgodion.*

hillsides which overlooks the Llanberis Pass. Not that anyone would choose to climb the mountain by this gruelling slope, but it does add scenic interest to an ascent of the more amenable shoulder at its side. And we are forgetting that any ascent of the Glyders must also incorporate a traverse of the surreal landscape of their summit plateaux, of which no-one can tire.

The walk begins at the Pen y Gwryd Hotel, the traditional home of British mountaineering. Wall cabinets display rocks from the summits of Everest and Kanchenjunga, and the hemp ropes of pioneering rock climbers. John Hunt, Eric Shipton, Tenzing, Bill Tilman and other mountaineering notables have scribbled their names on the ceiling of the Everest Room.

A twenty-minute slog up the road brings you to Pen y Pass Youth Hostel—a building which has historical associations of its own. Geoffrey Winthrop Young and his proteges from the

professions and public schools stayed here (then the Gorphwysfa Hotel) during their explorations of Snowdonia before and after the First World War.

Literate accounts of the exploits of Pen y Gwryd and Pen y Pass regulars form the basis of early climbing history in Wales, though few modern activists will trace their sporting origins to these convival gatherings of a privileged minority. C. E. Mathews, PyG regular and first president of the Climbers' Club, had this to say of mountaineering and mountaineers during his inaugural speech in 1898:

"It is a sport that from some mysterious causes appeals mainly to the cultivated intellect. 'Arry or 'Arriet would never climb a hill."

Not arf!

There's a lake above Pen y Pass almost as big as Idwal, but by the time you see Llyn Cwm y Ffynnon you're already some way past and

too eager to get going to bother with diversions. It might be more tempting on a sultry day. Red marker spots confirm the route across boggy land and up a steep rise to a grass col on the broad ascent shoulder. A backward glance from here brings a revealing view of Pen y Pass in its setting, but your attention is more likely to be held by the awesome slope of the Llanberis Pass ahead, the rotten columnar cliff of Craig Nant Peris teetering high above.

I followed signs of path up the vague, bouldery crest of the shoulder, using a scree path to avoid of a line of crags. Then the mist came down—or rather I climbed up into it. If I continued uphill then logic assured me that I would eventually arrive at the summit of Glyder Fawr. But the higher I climbed, the thicker became the mist, and the thicker the mist the greater my uncertainty. When a rocky knoll materialised from the gloom I gratefully scrambled up it, assuming it to be the summit. But it was only a bump in the shoulder which, I then realised, rose higher into the clouds. Three times more I was fooled, by which time I had stopped seeing the funny side.

I never got to the summit of Glyder Fawr. After a while I had begun to ignore the rock piles that loomed up out of the mist. Perhaps it was one of those. Instead I came upon level ground littered with plates of rock; somewhere—I guessed— between the summit and the rim of Cwm Cneifion. I couldn't be bothered going back to find the top.

I had been here so many times before that if I closed my eyes I could visualise the scene before me: the clumps of boulders, the deep indents of Cwm Cneifion and Cwm Bochlwyd, the rocks of Castell y Gwynt stacked up like spears. But when I opened by eyes again all I could see was a grey haze. I moved on and was relieved to come upon the familiar slanting trough of the path. Happier now, I followed it down to Bwlch y Ddwy Glyder and scrambled through the turrets of Castell y Gwynt on to the Glyder Fach plateau. On a previous walk, a fine December day, I waited here to photograph the sunset over Snowdon, caring little for the darkness that would soon follow. The evening was clear, a moon already rising, and I had no doubts about finding the route. On another occasion, in summer, I walked home to Ogwen this way after a family outing to Llanberis. Clouds had unexpectedly come in from the west, settling over the mountain and reducing visibility to a few metres. Near the summit I came across a middle-aged couple sitting dejected on a rock. A large bubble had formed in their compass, they told me, and they were reluctant to trust it. I suggested it wouldn't affect the reading if they were careful, but they would not be reassured and asked if I would show them the way down. They must have been getting desperate because I looked a most unlikely guide in my casual clothes and shoes. I located the exit of the couloir east of Bristly Ridge and the three of us descended its unpleasant scree in a series of skittering zig-zags. Only when we parted at the Miners' Track—they were turning left for Bochlwyd—did they ask me where I was going. "Home", I said, pointing to a little house tucked among trees below Cwm Tryfan. "No wonder you knew the way!" the lady said.

Now I wasn't so sure. The wind had got up, swirling fallen snow into an impenetrable spindrift. I could no longer see the path. Hail started falling, driven so hard by the gusts that it was painful to exposed skin. The temperature dropped ten degrees in as many minutes. A gloomy light filtering through the cloud dimmed yet further as dusk approached. In no direction could I see more than three metres. I knew I was somewhere east of Glyder Fach summit, but the terrain—disguised by snow and hoar frost—was no longer familiar. Crouching down in the lee of a boulder, I tried to study the map. Hail swirled around and stung my eyes until I couldn't see. I pulled the hood of my jacket over my face but my glasses steamed up almost at once. Kneeling on the map so the wind wouldn't snatch it from me, I took off the glasses and stuffed them in a pocket, not caring if they broke. By now my fingers were wooden from the cold and I could barely turn the compass dial. I noticed a bubble under the glass. It had been there for as long as I could remember. It had never been of much concern to me before.

When eventually I got a compass bearing it differed from my intuitive guess by ninety degrees. I repeated the calculation, thinking I must have made a technical error. But the answer was the same. Perhaps the metal of the ice-axe was influencing the needle? No: I threw the axe down on to the snow and the needle remained steady. I hesitated. A mistake would leave me stumbling among the boulders of the south-east flank as darkness fell, or on the dangerous slopes west of Bristly Ridge. Should I put my faith in the clinical instructions of a compass or trust my own intuition? I made my decision.

Fifteen minutes later I scrambled down on to an open slope of grass beneath the blanket of cloud. Though it was nearly dark I could clearly see the pool of Llyn y Caseg Fraith ahead, and the muddy rut of the Miners' Track beginning its descent towards Pen y Gwryd. I'd be home in forty minutes. A useful device, the compass.

Pen y Gwryd Hotel, once the famous haunt of pioneering mountaineers, at the start of the walk. Glyder Fach, dusted with snow, rises behind. *Gwesty Penygwryd, cyrchfan enwog mynyddwyr arloesol gynt, ar ddechrau'r daith. Y mae'r Gluder Fach, ac arni haen denau o eira, i'w gweld y tu ôl iddo.*

LLUGWY VALLEY

Maps: All three routes are adequately shown at 1:50,000 scale on Landranger Sheet 115 (Snowdon), and in greater detail at 1:25,000 scale on Outdoor Leisure 16 (Snowdonia—Conwy Valley).
Bases: Anywhere on the A5 between Capel Curig and Betws y Coed would make a good base for all three walks. Both villages offer a full range of accommodation, and there is a campsite with facilities at Dol Gam, approximately midway between the two. Betws y Coed can be approached by rail via Llandudno Junction, although the bus extension to Capel Curig runs only in summer.

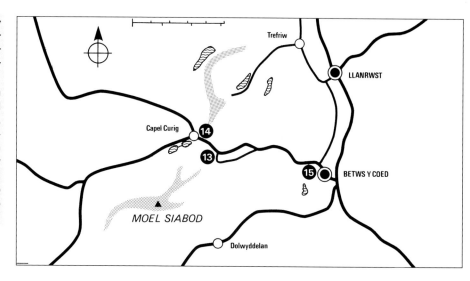

The Llugwy Valley is the forested depression through which the Afon Llugwy and the A5 road find their way from Capel Curig to Betws y Coed. In the present context the name defines not a distinct walking area but a convenient grouping of outlying routes taken from the Carneddau and Moelwyns.

The routes appear to have little in common—riverside rambling in Betws y Coed is a far cry from ridge scrambling on Moel Siabod—and yet only by following all three will you come to appreciate the diversity of Snowdonia scenery.

Looking into the arms of the Snowdon Horseshoe from the summit of Moel Siabod. From left to right Lliwedd, Snowdon, Crib y Ddysgl. Edrych ar Bedol Yr Wyddfa o gopa Moel Siabod. O'r chwith i'r dde Lliwedd, Yr Wyddfa, Crib y Ddysgl.

13: LLUGWY VALLEY — Moel Siabod

Route summary: A satisfying circular walk with a single summit as its objective. Visits a secluded lake, ascends a rocky ridge, and returns along tracks through mature forests and woodland.

Difficulty: Class C.

Main summits: Moel Siabod 872m/2861ft.

Duration: 10km/6 miles; 750m/2450ft of ascent; allow 4-5hrs.

Terrain: Narrow paths over grass (some boggy sections), a rock ridge, and forest trails.

Special difficulties: Some straightforward scrambling on the ascent of Daear Ddu. Difficult route-finding in mist on the descent.

Approach: From Capel Curig or Betws y Coed along the A5 to a car park opposite the Ty'n y Coed Hotel at GR:733 574.

Route directions: Go east and fork right on a narrow road to cross the river by Pont Cyfyng. Fork right again on reaching houses to follow a private surfaced lane to Rhos Farm (GR:732 568), and its unsurfaced continuation over the moor. Fork left at the far side of the moor, cross a stile, and follow a path passing to the right of a lake. Continue through ruined quarry buildings (GR:717 555) and by a less distinct path along the south-east flank of the mountain, over a shallow col, to Llyn y Foel. Gain the foot of the Daear Ddu ridge from the far shore and scramble directly up its rocky crest (or avoid difficulties on the left side if you must), finally trending left to reach the summit trig point.

Descend the summit ridge north-east to a slight saddle (GR:708 550) and turn left to descend over boulders to grass. Descend diagonally over grass slopes on to the spur extending towards Capel Curig (if in doubt set a course for the east end of the Llynnau Mymbyr). A vague path leads down the spur and finally over a stile on its left side. Turn right to follow a stony track among trees and over two ladder stiles to a forestry track (GR:716 573). Turn right and follow the track to its end (ignore a left turn shortly after the track merges with a lower one). Continue by a woodland path, finally descending steps to cross the river at a footbridge opposite Cobden's Hotel. Turn right to regain the start in a few hundred metres.

Alternatives: From the summit, descend the north-east ridge throughout, over rock then grass, to a junction with the approach route at the fork in the moor track.

The best thing about Moel Siabod is that it is fifty metres lower than it might have been. Only the failure to qualify for 3000ft status saves it from the punishing attentions of peak baggers. There can be no other plausible explanation for the comparative neglect of so fine a mountain. It slots uneasily into its traditional Moelwyn categorisation. No road isolates it from the main Moelwyn cluster to the south, and yet it has little in common with those distant and topographically dissimilar peaks. It is very much its own mountain.

Although Moel Siabod is a familiar reference point from Snowdon and the eastern Glyders and Carneddau, this is not its most flattering side. Moreover, the lower the viewpoint, the less interesting it seems; when viewed

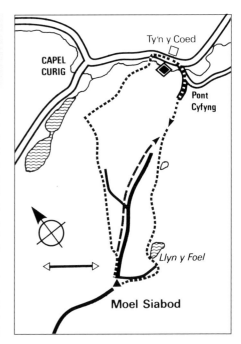

Snowdon group seen from near the summit of Moel Siabod. Peaks of the main cluster are, from left to right Lliwedd, Snowdon, Crib y Ddysgl. *Mynyddoedd Eryri, fel y'u gwelir o gopa Moel Siabod. Y prif gopâu o'r chwith i'r dde yw Lliwedd, Yr Wyddfa a Chrib y Ddysgl.*

Above: Moel Siabod from the banks of the Afon Llugwy. *Moel Siabod o lannau Afon Llugwy.*

Above right: The deceptively sharp Daear Ddu ascent ridge to Moel Siabod seen from the shore of the idyllically situated Llyn y Foel. *Esgair finiog Daear Ddu yn codi at gopa Moel Siabod, a welir o lannau prydferth Llyn y Foel.*

Right: Cobden's Bridge, picturesque crossing of the Afon Llugwy at the end of the walk. *Pont Cobden, croesfan hardd ar draws Afon Llugwy ar ben y daith.*

from Capel Curig it appears—when it appears at all—as a rather featureless mound rising above the forest. The east side, where Llyn y Foel nestles in romantic perfection within the protective arm of the Daear Ddu ridge, is far more interesting. There's a good view of this face from the A5, a few minutes out of Betws y Coed when travelling east. You will see a squat pyramid rising above the thickly forested bed of the Lledr valley, but unless the atmosphere is exceptionally clear, distance and sun glare will mask details that might reveal the nature of the walk. In fact the structure is not that of a pyramid at all, but of a long north-east to south-west ridge (foreshortened when viewed from this angle) balanced, in a visual sense, by a stubby eastern spur.

Moel Siabod can be climbed from the Lledr Valley by ascending through the forests above Dolwyddelan to Llyn y Foel. Unfortunately no satisfactory alternative path returns to this starting point—unless you have plans to traverse the high ground extending south-west to the Moelwyns and have arranged return transport from Blaenau Ffestiniog. Otherwise the finest and most convenient route begins and ends in Capel Curig, incorporating an ascent of the Daear Ddu ridge from Llyn y Foel, a descent of the north-west flank, and a pleasant return through Bryn Engan forest.

The walk begins at the Ty'n y Coed Hotel, noted for the stagecoach mounted opposite (this is now securely anchored and therefore no longer used as improvised transport by drunken revellers). The route soon branches off the A5 to cross the Afon Llugwy by Pont Cyfyng, though if the river is in spate it is worth continuing down the main road for about 100m to a viewing bay in the stone wall (for the best view

descend a worn path to a platform near the river). Although the falls are not spectacular in the usual meaning of the word, you can sense the power of the water as it thunders over a series of 3m drops, lifting spray from the shadows to create miniature rainbows in the sunlight.

Not far beyond Pont Cyfyng, where the lane passes between houses, a private road winds steeply up to Rhos farm. From here, dogs permitting, you will follow the degenerating continuation track out on to the moor with a view of Siabod's north-east ridge ahead. Although this ridge can be followed in its entirety to the summit, initially among grass runnels and later over the rocky spine of the mountain, a more interesting ascent veers left towards the flooded pits and ruined buildings of a quarry. Beyond the quarry a rising path crests out at a shoulder, and the previously hidden Llyn y Foel is revealed.

A craggy 250m face curls around the far shore of the lake and throws down a challenge in the form of a slanting rock crest—the Daear Ddu. Morning sunlight fills the basin with warmth, and pebbled bays in the picturesque lake are an excuse to linger. Doubts grow with each extra minute of delay, and the ridge looks more intimidating than ever. You have been deceived. Once established on the ridge itself you will discover that the sharp and sinister profile disguised a blunt and harmless front, with many opportunities for avoiding the difficult bits. Nevertheless, for the most satisfying ascent try to resist paths that have gone to grass on the left and instead pick a route among the wonderfully rough outcrops near the edge. Nowhere is it too difficult, and if anything it finishes too soon. The only blemish on this fine ridge is that

it doesn't quite reach the summit; you must trend left from its top to locate the trig point mounted on a pile of blocks.

The view from the summit of Moel Siabod is famous. To the north the deflated domes of the Carneddau summits can be seen spreading themselves out generously across the horizon. Space is cheap in the Carneddau. Not so in the cramped Glyders. Seen end on, their summits are all piled up together, the spiny top of Tryfan peeping out on the right. The finest view looks west into the depths of the Snowdon Horseshoe, Snowdon herself in regal mood at the head.

A grass ridge descends westwards, tempting with an enhanced version of the Horseshoe view. However, to complete the circular walk you must instead follow the summit ridge northeast and then stumble over boulders down to a delicious expanse of grass. No distinct path guides you along the correct line and if the cloud has unexpectedly come down—as it so often does on this flank the mountain—then you will need to take a compass bearing. Confirmation of route-finding accuracy comes on the north spur, where the path begins to assert itself. For a while the route is obvious, then the path dives into the murky green confusion of Bryn Engan Forest. The usual route links disjointed paths in a final descent to the footbridge over the Llynnau Mymbyr outflow near Plas y Brenin, whereas a more convenient return takes a forest track through trees to the banks of the Afon Llugwy. Where the track ends, a woodland path, complete with steps and rickety handrail, leads in fairytale fashion to a footbridge across the river with upstream views of Cobden's Falls—in spate an exciting challenge to insured canoeists.

Ty'n y Coed Hotel, at the start of the walk. *Gwesty Ty'n y Coed ar gychwyn y daith.*

14: LLUGWY VALLEY — Crimpiau and Llyn Crafnant

Route summary: A pleasant low-level walk among small hills and around a picturesque lake. On a good day the optional ascent of Crimpiau brings stunning views.

Difficulty: Class A or B.

Main summits: Crimpiau 475m/1558ft.

Duration: 13km/8 miles; 450m/1500ft of ascent; allow 4–5 hours.

Terrain: Good paths over fields and moorland but with some boggy ground (steep, narrow path on Crimpiau). Forest track and surfaced lane around Crafnant.

Special difficulties: Care required to find a problem-free route on the optional ascent of Crimpiau.

Approach: From Betws y Coed or Bethesda along the A5 to Capel Curig. Car parking near the A5/A4086 junction (GR:721 582).

Route directions: Cross the stile opposite the post office/general store and follow a path through fields, passing to the left of the prominent Pinnacles, and later through woodland. Cross the stream at a concrete bridge (GR:732 581) and fork left.

By-pass a boggy hollow on its right side and continue up the slight valley to a gap in a wall (GR:738 597) with views into the Crafnant valley. (For the optional ascent of Crimpiau, turn sharp left and ascend steeply along a narrow path, becoming vague, to the rocky summit.)

From the gap in the wall, continue down a winding path into Crafnant, passing to the right of Blaen y Nant to join a track. Follow the track towards Hendre but turn right just before reaching it and cross the stream by a footbridge. Follow a path downstream, later trending left across wet ground to join a forestry track. Follow the track around the lake shore and over its outflow on to the surfaced Crafnant road. Turn right and follow the road (cafe halfway along lake—probably shut if you are desperately hungry) to its end near Blaen y Nant. Return to Capel Curig as for the outward journey.

Alternatives: Fork left halfway between cafe and road end to follow a devious path diagonally up the hillside on the left, passing to the left of old quarry workings, to rejoin the main return path shortly after it passes through the gap in the wall. Vague in the middle section but squeezes extra variety into the walk.

A corner of heavily forested land fills the angle of high ground between the Llugwy and Conwy valleys. Strictly speaking this is the south-east tip of the Carneddau, though you wouldn't think so to judge by the scenery. No barren summit here, no desolate cwm with its grey lake. Instead the waters pool in hollows among the conifers to be gazed upon and paddled in by picnickers. For all this easy familiarity the geography of the region is indescribable. No high peak overlooks the whole, and lower viewpoints merely peep through gaps in the forests. If you get to know the place at all, you get to know it bit by bit.

The bit I like best is Llyn Crafnant and the approach to it from Capel Curig. It occupies the transitional territory between forested edge and mountainous interior, so you can have the best of both worlds.

What can I say about Capel Curig? It's my home town so I've got to be careful. It isn't a town at all, of course, nor even a village, so much as a collection of farms and houses spread out along the Llugwy valley. Nowhere will you find more than a dozen houses strung together. The school has closed, and the church is quieter than it once was, but the three hotels are thriving. At the village centre, lucratively located at a junction of main roads, you will find an enterprising post-office where

Temperature inversion over Capel Curig seen from the summit rocks of the Pinnacles. Moel Siabod (left) and the distant Snowdon group (centre) rise above the cloud. Awyr gynnes yn codi uwchben Capel Curig. Fe'i gwelir o gopâu'r Cribau. Cyfyd Moel Siabod (chwith) a mynyddoedd Eryri (yn y canol) uwchben y cymylau.

you can buy anything from low-fat yoghurt to a bottle of Pernod. This is the hub of a communications network which links each household with every other. Unsuspecting English people flutter into this web from time to time, looking for work in the hotels or outdoor centres. Those able to adapt have long since been absorbed, and those that could not have gone away. Capel Curig is like a big family: it has its unifying elders and its rebellious children, its squabblers, gossipers and feuders, but it always comes together smiling at Christmas time.

The Crafnant path begins opposite the post-office and initially flanks a sunny green hill where contented sheep graze in blissful ignorance of their fate. An attractive outcrop known as the Pinnacles crowns the hill, and if you persevere you will find an easy way on to the summit and be rewarded by a magnificent view over Capel Curig and the Llynnau Mymbyr towards Snowdon. On fine autumn mornings a temperature inversion sometimes surrounds the summit of the Pinnacles in a heaving ocean of mist, and for an hour you can pretend to be master of your own private island.

Beyond a birch wood the path ascends to open country and circles a secluded hollow which looks as though it ought to be a lake. A backward glance reveals only moorland and the distant hump of Moel Siabod. No sign of roads or habitation. The path exits the hollow by a V-shaped valley, the base of which then flattens out and tilts skyward—a take-off ramp into another world. At a gap in a stone wall is a tantalising view of a forested cwm, its lake not yet in view. This other world is Crafnant.

I urge you to postpone the walk for half an hour while you climb to the top of Crimpiau. Despite its modest height this is one of the finest viewpoints in Snowdonia. The ascent is simple enough, though steep in places, and initially follows a path circling the Crafnant rim before striking directly up a rocky spine to the top. On a clear day there is a fascinating view of the Glyders from the tiny summit cairn, the eastern spur unusually prominent while the Glyders themselves merely peep over the shapely spread of a normally unimpressive Gallt yr Ogof.

Smug Crimpiau climbers will spoil the surprise for lazy companions waiting at the wall by describing what they can expect to see while zig-zagging down towards Blaen y Nant at the head of the valley. No harm done: Crafnant isn't so much an ooh-aah as a mmm-yes sort of place. Except, that is, for the conifer blocks on the far side of the lake currently being clear-felled by hysterical chain saws. It will take years to heal the scabs of grey among the green.

Gallt yr Ogof and Tryfan (right) from the unexpected viewpoint of Crimpiau summit. *Gallt yr Ogof a Thryfan, golygfa anghyffredin o gopa'r Crimpiau.*

Llyn Crafnant. Anglers returning their boats to the lakeside cafe at the end of the day. *Llyn Crafnant. Pysgotwyr yn dod â'u cychod yn ôl at y caffe ger y llyn ar derfyn dydd.*

Harvest time comes but once a decade in the forest, and in the meantime we forget that trees are a crop, hacked and stacked when ripe for the market.

It is psychologically upsetting to walk for two hours in one direction, look at a pretty view, then turn round and walk back again. That's why this walk circles the lake (there's another reason, but we'll come to that a little later). Shortly before the track passes through the gate to Hendre, a path crosses a stream by a wooden bridge and meanders downstream for a few minutes before veering off to join the forest track on the lake's north-west shore. With yielding pine needles underfoot, and a protective arch above, this is the day's soothing interlude. Where the track exits the forest perhaps you'll see fishermen out in their boats, lazing the afternoon away with flasks and sandwiches and an occasional flick of the wrist for the sake of appearances.

The track curls around the lake end and bridges the outflow to join the surfaced lane

up from Trefriw. A few concrete channels here remind us that Llyn Crafnant is a reservoir. Things are busier now because this side of the lake is a popular beauty spot, the twisting lane a favourite with young men in customised sports cars anxious to impress their girlfriends. The walking is none the less pleasant, and those with acute hearing and lightning-fast reactions have nothing to fear.

Afternoon sunshine brings lethargy. Legs are tired, shoulders aching. Keep going, or you'll miss the cafe—it shuts at six (yes, this is the real reason for circling the lake).

Tea and scones on the lakeside lawn, watching the boats come in, ripples flopping listlessly on to the shingle. Boats with fishermen aboard, rehearsing tales of ones that got away, scrunching up on to the shelving bank. Behind their silhouettes, Crimpiau shimmers an outline, the detail of its crags and boulders lost to the haze. How long back over the top to Capel Curig—two hours? No hurry. Rest your feet a while . . .

At the V-shaped valley on the return journey there's a sense of foreboding, a warning echo from some chilling past encounter. Eyes are screwed up in the harsh light, throat dry with apprehension. Something moves high on the right-hand skyline, a glint of white. But as you turn it slips from view. A trick of the light. You go on. A dislodged stone tumbles down the slope of baked earth into your path. Another flash of white, then nothing. The air is still, rocks shimmer in the heat. Must be imagining things. Then you feel yourself rising above your body until you are higher than the valley rim itself. Now you can see: six thousand rebellious sheep in full warpaint lined up in ambush. Run! Run! But it's not you they're after; it's the farmer come to round them up for slaughter . . .

It's cooler now as the sunlight rakes low over the hillside beyond the lake. Time to go. "You know, I had this strangest dream . . ."

15: LLUGWY VALLEY — Short Walks from Betws y Coed

Route summary: A choice of short walks based on the enduringly popular village of Betws y Coed; the first through woodland along a delightful riverbank, the second through forest paths to an upland lake.

Difficulty: Class A.

Duration: River walk: 3km/2 miles (6km/4 miles with Artists' Wood extension); allow 1-2hrs. Lake walk: 5km/3 miles; 250m/800ft of ascent; allow 2hrs.

Terrain: River walk: mostly good riverside and woodland paths, but with some uneven sections among the trees and boulders. Lake walk: forest tracks and paths, some quite steep, with some muddy sections after wet weather.

Approach: From Betws y Coed on the A5. Both walks start from the car park near Pont y Pair at GR:791 568 (if this is full, try the car park near the railway station).

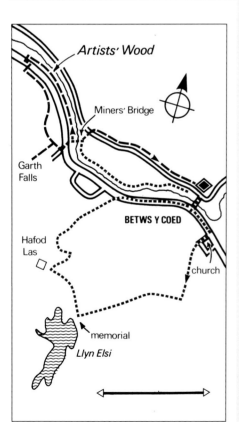

Route directions
River walk:
From Pont y Pair car park, follow the riverside path upstream for about 1.5km to the Miners' Bridge (GR:780 569). Return by the same route.

Alternatives: (1) Cross the Miners' Bridge and go up steps opposite to the A5 road. Turn left to return to Pont y Pair. (2) From the 'uphill' side of the Miners' Bridge, ascend steeply through trees to a narrow lane. Turn right and follow it back to the car park. (3) For the Artists' Wood extension, cross the Miners' Bridge, ascend steps, then turn right to follow a path through woodland (and sometimes near the river) until forced left at ruins to the A5 road. Turn towards Betws y Coed but cross after 50m on to a forestry track (GR:772 575). About 30m from the main road, take a narrow path on the left through trees. Bear left shortly after, at a junction of paths, and continue through forest and woodland (yellow markers), over several footbridges, eventually veering right to emerge from trees at a forestry track. Turn left and follow the track, passing the start of the Garth Falls walk at GR:778 568, to the A5. Cross the main road and return via the Miners' Bridge, or turn right for a direct return to Pont y Pair

Lake Walk:
From the Pont y Pair car park, cross the bridge and turn left along the A5. Turn right at the church (GR:794 565) and where the road bends left, go straight on up a forest track to a bench and 1.5m marker stone. Turn right here, crossing the stream by a footbridge, and follow a zigzagging path up through trees. Where the angle eases, pass to the left of a ruin and go straight across two forestry tracks. Continue along a break between trees to open ground and the memorial stone (GR:784 555) high above the north shore of Llyn Elsi.

Take the path leading north-west (not north) from the memorial. Ignore a left turn to the dam, and continue straight on, crossing over a forestry track, on to a narrow path. Trend left after crossing a ladder stile then turn sharp right 50m short of Hafod Las on a muddy track leading down to a barn. Here turn left on a path between stream and fence, go over a ladder stile, and pass to the right of a quarry pit. Ignore the quarry level leading left and continue down the stony track, over the stile at its end, on to a forest track leading down to the A5 a few minutes from Pont y Pair.

Betws y Coed is overwhelmed in summer by two opposing streams of pedestrians walking to the other end of town for something to do (at narrowings they spill from the pavement into the path of opposing streams of motorists). It is hard to imagine that the place has a life of its own outside the tourist season. Not that this is a recent phenomenon; in Victorian times the village attracted anglers and artists on lengthy summer vacations. Although imitators can be seen here today in their tweed suits and leather upholstered limousines, they are heavily outnumbered by day trippers in denim jeans and plastic-trim hatchbacks. Gift shops reflect this diversity, where starchy woollen goods share counter space with rows of trashy Welsh dolls. Other establishments prefer to target a specific clientele. Thus while the Royal Oak preserves an air of relaxed, if besieged, dignity, Dil's Diner dishes out the chips with frill-free efficiency.

From a hill walker's point of view, Betws y Coed lies just short of where mountainous Snowdonia properly begins, therefore to enjoy a day here some adjustment of expectation is required. The natural treasures of Betws y Coed are not mountains and moors but the valleys and woodland found along the staggered confluence of the rivers Conwy, Lledr and Llugwy; attractive rivers all three, and attaining hypnotic levels of prettiness at the Fairy Glen, Beaver Pool and Pont y Pair respectively. Where natural woodland has been cleared it has largely been replaced by pine forest, so the fenced meadows which typically border a Snowdonia village are generally missing. A network of paths surround the village. Some of them, including forest tracks and quarry inclines have—or had—a functional purpose. Others have been constructed purely for recreational enjoyment. The two described here have been chosen to represent more than a score of worthwhile short walks.

At the monument overlooking Llyn Elsi. Wrth y gofeb uwchben Llyn Elsi.

Miners' Bridge

This walk begins at Pont y Pair, the five-arched stone bridge which spans a narrowing of the Afon Llugwy near the village centre. 'Pair' means cauldron, and when the river is in spate this is no fanciful description of the pool, frothing and bubbling, below the falls. Here the salmon pause to summon strength for the mighty leap that will enable them to continue their frenetic upstream journey. Anglers casting their flies into the eddies at such a time will be certain to hook one of these marvellous fish. But nothing is certain about the outcome; the rocks on the bank are slippery, and a startled salmon running downstream through the foaming slot under the bridge stands a good chance of snapping the line, if not of drowning its pursuer. In the space of an hour one afternoon I saw an angler lose three out of four fish hooked, and twice come close to falling in. But for all that I can't help thinking the salmon have enough to worry about without fighting off some wily trophy hunter

with his glass-fibre fishing rod and barbed offer of food.

At other times the water rolls over the sill into a listless pool and the rocks are slippery not with rain but with dribbled ice cream as dozens of families spread themselves and their accoutrements about the banks. Squeeze through this sun-worshipping throng and you will find yourself on a riverside path where only the daring few will venture, tottering along in their inappropriate shoes and glancing nervously behind at the retreating security of craft shop and cafe.

The river is home to more than residential trout and migratory salmon. Scurrying things ruffle old leaves on the far bank, and flittering things ruffle new leaves above. Once I spotted a heron and followed its ponderous upstream progress from boulder to tree stump. It flew in slow motion like a jumbo jet, seeming to obey a different law of gravity from that which tried to pluck smaller birds from the sky. Eventually it grew tired of my persistent snoop-

ing with the telephoto lens and took off for a long-haul flight to some inaccessible part of the river.

The purpose of this walk—if it must have a purpose—is to cross the river by the Miners' Bridge. This is a most unusual footbridge in that it slopes at a disconcerting thirty degrees (it feels steeper but may be shallower). In fact it is an elaborate reconstruction of the rudimentary bridge once used by the men of Pentre Du to reach their work in the lead mines. In its present form it is a test of nerve for cautious toddlers and timid dogs, and I dread to think what the original crossing must have been like on a dark winter evening. The bridge can be seen from the main road, though only if you know where to look.

The bridge is not the only attraction. Beneath it the river channels through an eroded runnel of great depth, the water slurping through with the sound of a salivating carnivore while miniature whirlpools spin floating debris into spirals. From the still air above the

Start of the Afon Llugwy river walk, Betws y Coed. *Betws-y-coed, man cychwyn y daith ar hyd glannau Afon Llugwy.*

defile, dehydrated insects drop exhausted into the water, their struggling bodies radiating ripples of alarm until some unseen monster from the deep sucks them out of sight. Watch your step.

After crossing the bridge the quickest, if least satisfactory, return to the village lies along the main road. Other alternatives are to re-cross the bridge and retrace the outward walk, or re-cross the bridge and follow a scrappy path up through trees to a quiet lane which leads back to Pont y Pair at a higher level. A third alternative continues the riverside walk upstream, leaves it shortly before Swallow Falls to cross the A5, and returns through Artists' Wood to Miners' Bridge. This extension doubles the distance of the Miners' Bridge walk.

The path of this extended loop has less to do with the river than with its bordering woodland. It is all very pleasant to look at (it inspired the Victorian artists who used to stay at the Royal Oak, David Cox among them), but more often than not the din of road traffic drowns out the tinkling of waterfalls or the rustling of

dry leaves underfoot. An autumn morning is the best time to come, when the leaves have turned, a dawn mist hangs in the air, and the high-decibel motorbikes have begun their hibernation.

Near the end of the loop, and accessible by car along the forest track, a 250m pathway specially constructed for people with disabilities winds through delightful woodland to a picnic area within sight and sound of the miniature Garth Falls. Notices in braille fixed at intervals to the handrails describe the scene.

Llyn Elsi

This route is of similar length to the extended version of the previous walk, but there the similarity ends. Llyn Elsi lies some 240m above the village, and the ascent of the wooded hillside to reach it can be a tedious and strength-sapping exercise on a hot afternoon. On a cool autumn day, however, the effort will be doubly repaid.

The walk begins up a forest track behind the church and ascends steadily in the shade

of mature trees. At a footbridge it steepens even more as it branches off the main track to follow a winding path up through woodland. When the angle eases—and not before time—the path finds a way through pine plantations using muddy fire breaks and eventually emerges from thinning trees at a bench and memorial stone overlooking the lake. Lay down your rucksack, put aside your weariness, and spin around for a view of Moel Siabod, the Glyders and the Carneddau. Worth it?

Fenced pastureland and disused quarries bring confusion to the descent. Nevertheless, it is just possible to avoid the problem areas without resorting to tiresome forest tracks until the very end. It seems a pity to return to the aimless bustle of the village with so much of the day remaining. But there are compensations. The artists and anglers among us can take afternoon tea at the Royal Oak, while the rest of us get stuck into a plate of chips at Dil's.

SNOWDON GROUP

Maps: Landranger Sheet 115 (Snowdon) includes the whole Snowdon group. Its 1:50,000 scale is sufficient when following one of the popular paths (provided a few notes are taken from the route description on critical turning points), otherwise a better choice is the 1:25,000 scale Outdoor Leisure 17 (Snowdonia – Snowdon Area), which also includes the whole of the Glyders.

Bases: A base in any of the villages on the perimeter road (or even Capel Curig) would adequately serve all four of the described routes. Of these, Beddgelert is best for hotel or bed & breakfast accommodation. There are several campsites; those at Nant Peris and Nant Gwynant are best placed for the walks, whereas the Forestry Commission site between Beddgelert and Rhyd Ddu has the most facilities. Youth Hostels at Pen y Pass, Nant Gwynant and Snowdon Ranger are ideally positioned for their respective walks. Beddgelert and Nant Peris can be reached by bus from Caernarfon (nearest rail station is at Bangor), whereas extensions to Capel Curig, Nant Gwynant and Pen y Pass operate only during the summer months.

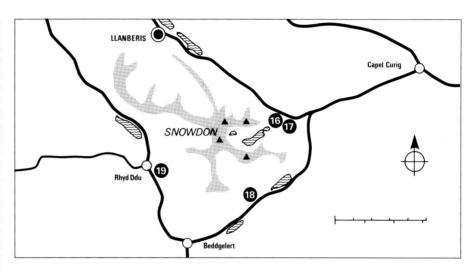

Though much maligned by those who despise the intrusion of the mountain railway and the summit cafe, Snowdon reigns supreme as the most intriguing, the most compelling mountain in the country. Each ridge and cwm has its own peculiar character and outlook – from the gentle curves of Cwm y Llan to the jagged obstacles of Crib Goch.

Hundreds of thousands of walkers annually head towards Snowdon, anxious to climb the highest mountain in Wales and encouraged to do so by improvements made to the six major paths which converge on the summit. Some of these routes are rather plodding in execution, others continuously varied and exciting. All share magnificent situations where the ridges narrow during their final approach. For a more adventurous day, the Snowdon Horseshoe provides the finest ridge scramble south of Scotland.

Sunrise near the start of the Zig-Zags. Crib Goch on the left, Moel Siabod in the distance. *Codiad yr haul lle mae'r llwybrau igam-ogam yn cychwyn. Crib Goch ar y chwith a Moel Siabod yn y pellter.*

16: SNOWDON GROUP — Snowdon from Pen y Pass

Route summary: Ascends the highest mountain in Wales by a popular track rising along the side of its impressive eastern cwm. Returns by an old miners' track winding down the lake-filled valley base.

Difficulty: Class C.

Main summits: Snowdon (Yr Wyddfa) 1085m/3559ft.

Duration: 11km/7miles; 725m/2375ft of ascent; allow 5hrs.

Terrain: Well-maintained rocky path and tracks interspersed with a few rough sections on scree and rock.

Special difficulties: In mist the precise point of departure from the Pig Track for the descent to Glaslyn is unclear. Further down this slope, try to avoid false paths leading to gritty rock slabs.

Approach: From Llanberis or Capel Curig along the A4086 to a car park (fee) at Pen y Pass (GR:647 556). When full, as is frequently the case during weekends and holiday periods, park opposite the Pen y Gwryd Hotel (GR:661 558) and walk up to Pen y Pass in 20mins.

Route directions: From the upper car park follow a well-marked path westwards, later rising steeply to the prominent col of Bwlch y Moch (GR:633 552). Continue by the main path, across the southern flank of Crib Goch, to a promontory above Glaslyn. Contour to the head of the cwm and ascend the paved Zig-Zags to emerge at a 3m high marker stone (GR:607 548). Turn left and follow the ridge or railway track to the summit of Snowdon.

Return to the 3m marker stone and descend the Zig-Zags as for the ascent route. Where the Pig Track stops losing height and begins to contour across a large scree tongue (GR:614 548), descend a steep slope of rock and scree to the shore of Glaslyn. Follow the Miners' Track via the Llyn Llydaw causeway to Pen y Pass.

Alternatives: (1) During summer months a descent could be made by one of several alternatives (refer to chapters 19 and 20), returning to Pen y Pass on the Sherpa bus. (2) For a short day the walk to Glaslyn along the Miners' Track is worthwhile in itself. Return by the same route.

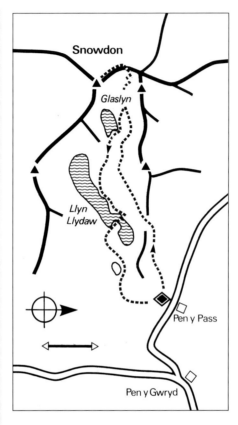

Snowdon novitiates often have a false impression of what the mountain is about: a misty, moderately boring hill, they imagine, up which trains and tourists puff and pant come summertime. Surely not the stuff of proper mountain walking. What they find on arrival is a slumbering giant, towering above its reputation with ridges sharper, trains noisier, rain heavier, summit scruffier, and views grander, than they ever thought possible. They have come to the worst and best mountain in Wales.

Two of the worst/best ways to climb Snowdon are the Pig and Miners' Tracks. Both begin inauspiciously in a 200 vehicle car park and arrive at the summit in the squalid back yard of a railway snack bar. En route the Miners' Track circles a reservoir, passes through a ruined mine building and climbs alongside a spoil heap, while the Pig Track strolls up a mountainside blasted and paved into submission. Hardly the stuff of wilderness adventure. Despite their shortcomings, these paths alone are allowed into Snowdon's magnificent inner sanctum.

The journey begins at Pen y Pass, where the Llanberis Pass road crests out after wheezing up from its rock-strewn defile. Half the accumulated throng will march off along the Miners' Track, while a quarter will come with us along the Pig Track—the superior route of ascent (the other quarter, in case you wondered, are sitting down to tea and buns in the cafe).

The Pig Track once stumbled over boulders and little outcrops but in recent years has been 'improved' to a synthetic pathway, of which more later. Admittedly in its present form it admirably fulfils its initial purpose, which is to get people quickly to the respectable altitude of 570m at Bwlch y Moch ('Pass of the Pigs' in English, hence the name of the path, though some will dispute this derivation and offer up the alternative name *PYG Track*, taken from the initials of Pen y Gwryd). Thus far the outlook has been limited to an irrelevant view down the Llanberis Pass. Now, at the bwlch, the interior of the Horseshoe is revealed for the first time. Notable landmarks are the brooding grey cliffs of Lliwedd—the hand of Snowdon's right arm—at the far side of the cwm, and far below the crumpled, shimmering oval of Llyn Llydaw, its nearest lobe nipped off by the causeway which transports walkers on the Miners' Track to the north-west shore.

Scramblers embarking on a circuit of the Snowdon Horseshoe quit the Pig Track at Bwlch y Moch and bear right to ascend the blunt ridge of a gaunt, ruddy pyramid. While they teeter along the knife-edge of Crib Goch our gentle progress along the flanks allows us to elaborate on the views of Llydaw and Lliwedd. Gradually the terrain becomes more rugged (cyclists may be forced to dismount), until at one point the path surprises itself by crossing a water-streaked slab of smooth rock. Soon after it arrives at a promontory with a spicy view of the near-alpine face of Clogwyn y Garnedd—the summit cliffs of Snowdon.

The promontory overlooks the captured lake of Glaslyn, a solitary eye tainted blue-green from copper, staring fixedly from its glaciated socket. The monstrous Afangc lives here, its reluctant home since being evicted from the Beaver Pool near Betws y Coed. Tricked from

The result of intensive reconstruction work on the Zig-Zags. *Canlyniad y gwaith adfer trwyadl ar y llwybrau igam-ogam.*

its lair by a beautiful maiden (vanity being the Achilles' heel of male monsters), it was dragged over Moel Siabod by a pair of oxen and exiled to this barren lake in the mountains. Little has been seen of it since, although it once tried to drag a fisherman into the depths. It feeds on the toes of little children who paddle out from the shingle beach against parental advice.

From the promontory the path contours the Glaslyn cwm between lake and rim, eventually merging with the Miners' Track which, finding itself too low on the mountain, has had to struggle up a slope of collapsing rubble from the lakeside to get here. Together they aim for a shallow dip in the skyline between Crib y Ddysgl and Snowdon. In the days before mountain management this section of the path had become riddled with short-cuts as people

abandoned the path and made direct assaults and descents on the slope. Now the Zig-Zags have been permanently established with the aid of paving slabs, wire cages and footpath signs. Restoration or desecration? Judge for yourself. The final leg of the Zig-Zags slants across a more solid substructure of rock and grit. No need or evidence of improvement here, so you'll need to tread more carefully—especially if the rocks are wet and slippery. During severe winters this whole slope drifts over to a great depth and reverts to its untamed origins. At such times it ceases to be a simple walk and the ascent requires ice-axe, crampons and a great deal of care. In those conditions a more suitable walk is to approach via the Miners' Track, make Glaslyn the high point, and return by the same route.

A rock finger erected at the exit of the Zig-Zags marks the transition from a gloomy confinement to a breezy freedom on the north shoulder. Here the Llanberis and Snowdon Ranger paths converge on the Pig Track to share its final ascent to Snowdon summit along the railway incline. It is customary—indeed sensible—for walkers to give way to the trains, though the doffing of caps to moneyed travellers seated within is not obligatory. A fourfold increase in walkers on the path might persuade you to forego a summit bid and instead to turn round at the rock finger and descend back into the familiar world of scree and lakes. But this walk is nothing if not a pilgrimage, and perhaps we should be more tolerant of our fellow walkers, suffering the crush of bodies at the summit in a spirit of friendship and togetherness. Oddly, the atmosphere on Snowdon summit is one of inappropriate restraint. People behave here as they do at railway stations: polite and private unless forced together by some natural phenomenon or calamity, such as a lightning strike or beer shortage. Otherwise, groups of people talk only among themselves and eye suspiciously anyone who has come up 'from the other side'. So creep away after your summit touch and return subdued to the rock finger. What should have been a moment of triumph became instead an empty gesture. The Welsh name for Snowdon summit is Yr Wyddfa—The Burial Place—but the spirits fled this place long ago.

After the clinical precision of the Zig-Zags, the descent to Glaslyn on the upper part of the Miners' Track is rather haphazard (this may change, however, if path construction continues). In mist its departure from the Pig Track is unclear, and shoddy route-finding on the lower section could have you skittering over grit covered slabs. At Glaslyn begins the track which during the latter half of the nineteenth century brought miners to their lakeside barracks. Here from Monday to Saturday they worked and slept, earning a shilling a day before walking over the Glyders or down the Gwynant to spend Sunday at home. Today the only direct evidence of their labour is the spoil spewing from the mine entrances.

The Miners' Track escapes the cwm where the lake spills over the glacier breach and sets the Afon Glaslyn on its long cascade into Llyn Llydaw. At the shore of this larger lake the track passes close to the ruins of a crushing plant then crosses by a causeway constructed in 1853 to speed the transport of ore to Pen y Pass. Llyn Llydaw is in fact the reservoir for a small hydro-electric station situated at the head of Nant Gwynant. Until 1988 two ugly black pipes channelled the outflow through Cwm Dyli and down the hillside to the generator. These were replaced during modernisation with a single pipe. In the interests of economy this too was placed above ground, losing a perfect opportunity to remove an eighty-year-old blemish. The final section of the Miners' Track returns to Pen y Pass without further complication. Time for reflection. It's been a great day. Such grandeur. But a sad day, too. Such squalor.

Early morning on the Pig Track, looking down to Llyn Glaslyn and beyond to Llyn Llydaw. *Yn gynnar y bore ar Lwybr y Moch, yn edrych i lawr ar Lyn Glaslyn a'r tu draw iddo hyd at Lyn Llydaw.*

17: SNOWDON GROUP — The Snowdon Horseshoe

Route summary: The most famous ridge scramble in Wales. Major difficulties are short but the sense of adventure is sustained throughout. Scrambling enthusiasts will be delighted by the knife-edged ridge and succession of other problems encountered on Crib Goch.

Difficulty: Class E.

Main summits: Crib Goch 921m/3022ft; Crib y Ddysgl 1065m/3495ft; Snowdon (Yr Wyddfa) 1085m/3559ft; Lliwedd 898m/2947ft.

Duration: 11km/7miles; 1000m/3275ft of ascent; allow 7hrs.

Terrain: Bare rock ridges and scree paths. Maintained paths and tracks to start and finish.

Special difficulties: Three sections require special care: the initial rock barrier and scoop on the East Ridge of Crib Goch; the traverse of the Pinnacles; and the first steep nose on Crib y Ddysgl. It is wise to carry a rope for emergencies (15m/50ft of 9mm climbing rope), assuming you know

how to tie a bowline and belay the rope. The route is best avoided during wet or windy weather. If conditions deteriorate badly while on Crib Goch then an emergency descent can be made north-west from Bwlch Coch towards Llyn Glas, or south towards Glaslyn (junction with the Pig Track before reaching the lake). In either case take care in mist to avoid outcrops and steep scree. If bad weather or darkness approaches while on Snowdon then consider descending via the Pig

Looking back down the East Ridge of Crib Goch. Llyn Llydaw is below right, Moel Siabod in the distance. The sunlit buildings of Pen y Pass, at the start of the route, can be seen far left. Edrych yn ôl ar esgair ddwyreiniol Crib Goch. Llyn Llydaw ar y dde islaw, Moel Siabod yn y pellter. Ar y chwith yn y pellter, gellir gweld adeiladau Pen-y-pass yn y haul ar ddechrau'r daith.

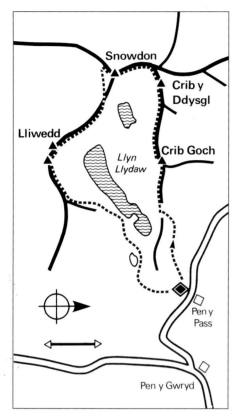

Start of the famous Crib Goch knife edge. The Horseshoe continues over Crib y Ddysgl (right) then curves left over Snowdon. Dechrau min cyllell enwog Crib Goch. Â'r Bedol ymlaen ar draws Crib y Ddysgl i'r dde gan droi i'r chwith dros Yr Wyddfa.

Track or Miners' Track rather than pressing on and being forced to abandon the route at Bwlch y Saethau with no easy descent to Pen y Pass (the Watkin Path to Nant Gwynant is the only feasible escape).

Approach: From Llanberis or Capel Curig along the A4086 to a car park (fee) at Pen y Pass (GR:647 556). When full, as is frequently the case during weekends and holiday periods, park opposite the Pen y Gwryd Hotel (GR:661 558) and walk up to Pen y Pass in 20mins.

Route directions: From the upper car park follow a well-marked path westwards to the prominent col of Bwlch y Moch. Turn right here and approach the blunt East Ridge of Crib Goch. Avoid an initial steep section on the left (refer to main text) then ascend the ridge more or less directly to the east end of Crib Goch.

Follow the ridge westwards, on or slightly below the crest, and traverse the Pinnacles with some exposed scrambling (refer to main text). An easy gully leads down to Bwlch Coch. Continue along the ridge, generally near its crest (refer to main text), rising to the summit of Crib y Ddysgl.

Circle the rim of the Glaslyn cwm, passing the 3m high marker stone at the Zig-Zags exit of the Pig Track, to the summit of Snowdon.

Do not attempt a direct descent to Bwlch y Saethau but go down the south-west ridge for about 200m to a 2m high marker stone. Leave the ridge here and descend a scree path (the upper section of the Watkin Path) diagonally across the south face to Bwlch y Saethau. Continue along the path (or ridge to its left) to a large cairn at Bwlch Cilau below the north-west ridge of Lliwedd. Scramble up the crest of the ridge to the summit.

Pass over the east summit and continue down the ridge, over the minor top of Lliwedd Bach, to where the ridge forks. Take the left fork, descending by its left flank with some scrambling to the shore of Llyn Llydaw and a junction with the Miners' Track. Follow the track back to Pen y Pass.

Alternatives: (1) After completing the Crib Goch section of the Horseshoe, return to Pen y Pass via the Miners' Track or Pig Track (as described in chapter 16). (2) During summer months a descent could be made by one of the paths described in chapters 18 and 19, returning to Pen y Pass on the Sherpa bus.

Every hill walker dreams of one day traversing the Snowdon Horseshoe. Judging by the size of queues on fine summer days, most of these dreams are coming true. Some of these people are experienced scramblers and mountaineers, for whom the Horseshoe is—at least in technical terms—an easy day. But the majority are walkers balancing on the knife-edge between reasonable risk and recklessness. Why do they do it? Because the Horseshoe combines the highest summit with finest ridge traverse south of Scotland; a ridge which, though not excessively difficult, is continuously exciting and, for much of its length, quite inescapable. Not everyone is aware of these qualities, but those who are have built a monumental reputation around the expedition. Most of the people you see lining up below the ridge are pilgrims to this reputation.

Not much is said about the second half of the Horseshoe, and in the event a majority will descend by the Pig Track or Miners' Track after completing the Crib Goch section. This is a pity, because the traverse of Lliwedd, though less dramatic, makes a perfect end to the day.

As with the Cwm Bochlwyd Horseshoe (chapter 12), with which this route compares in both quality and difficulty, the Horseshoe asks for no special skills other than an average level of agility. However, in general the rock is less reliable and must be handled with discrimination. Rope protection is not practical given the length of the undertaking, although a short length carried in the rucksack for emergencies is a wise precaution.

Good weather conditions are very important, not because of route-finding difficulties (there are none that poor visibility would amplify) but because of the exposed nature of the scrambling. Most obvious to avoid is blustery weather, remembering that average wind speed may double or treble at the ridge crests. Several people have been blown off the ridge in these conditions. Equally bad is the wet weather that makes treacherous slides of the sloping and lichenous rocks found on certain parts of the traverse. The Horseshoe provides a magnificent outing under full winter conditions. However, it is then no longer a walk or scramble but a full-blown mountaineering route, requiring ice-axe, crampons and winter climbing competence. Numerous fatalities over the years can be attributed to people underestimating the severity of the route under snow. Frost or verglas conditions are less easy to detect from the valley. At these times the rocks may appear dry and clear whereas in fact they are covered in a thin, transparent coating of ice. Wintry conditions can arise at any time between November and April.

Hundreds converge on Crib Goch on the few days when conditions are perfect and are forced to adopt an ant-like discipline. There's a lot to be said for following the less popular clockwise circuit, beginning with Lliwedd and returning along Crib Goch. The snag then is that the most difficult scrambling sections are taken in descent and at the end of the day, when you are least alert. Besides, if you arrive too soon on Crib Goch it would be like driving the wrong way down a busy one-way street. Better to get up early, beat the crowds, and follow the conventional anti-clockwise route.

A popular alternative to the complete Horseshoe is a descent via the Pig Track after completing the traverse of Crib Goch and Crib y Ddysgl. This accounts for the relative quiet of Lliwedd. I suspect the reason why most people abandon the route is Lliwedd's daunting appearance from Snowdon. In fact its height and steepness is an illusion, and it can be incorporated with relatively little extra effort. A second, more ambitious alternative is to descend from Bwlch y Saethau to Glaslyn via Y Gribin —an excellent sustained scramble of similar difficulty to the East Ridge of Crib Goch. However, it would be unwise for anyone to consider this descent unless they felt completely at ease on Crib Goch.

Feral goats high on the huge north-facing crag of Lliwedd. *Geifr y mynydd ar glogwyn mawr Lliwedd, yn wynebu tua'r gogledd.*

The Horseshoe shares its approach to Bwlch y Moch with the Pig Track, firing the imagination with glimpses of the Crib Goch pyramid rising ahead in rocky contrast to a line of green hills to the left (the true but little used start to the Horseshoe). On fine mornings Bwlch y Moch is a place to sit and stare. The austere cone of Crib Goch towers above while down below the sun glints on Llyn Llydaw and begins to disperse mists gathered in the night. From the lake's far shore rise the buttresses of Lliwedd, a grey curtain of rock drawn against the glare.

Crib Goch extends a boulder-studded arm towards Bwlch y Moch, a gentle prelude to the East Ridge proper. The first difficulties arise above a cairned shoulder. An obvious solution is to take a well-scratched, right-slanting line across fluted rock. A cunning alternative slants up left before returning to the right, above the steep part, along an exposed ledge. A good place for second thoughts if neither option appeals. 70m of sustained scrambling up a shallow depression above the barrier completes the difficult lower part of the East Ridge. Shattered rock steps characterise the upper part of the ridge. Flanking paths tempt you left or right, though it's wise to stay on the crest where the rock is firmest. East and North Ridges converge at the east end of Crib Goch (literally 'Red

Comb'). Although this is not the highest point on the ridge, nor even a prominent top, it is generally referred to as Crib Goch summit.

From this 'summit' you can see back down the East Ridge to Bwlch y Moch with green hills and the isolated clutter of Pen y Pass beyond. Looking north, the barren flank of the North Ridge sweeps down into Cwm Glas from where the Clogwyn y Person Arete, a shorter but harder scramble than this one, finds its way through the headwall on to Crib y Ddysgl.

But let the traverse commence. The first section, across a rock table, is simple enough, then the ridge narrows to a ragged knife-edge. On a calm day a competent and confident scrambler can walk along this section no-hands, while the more cautious will find footholds on the left side and use the crest like a handrail. Eventually the ridge eases and dips to the base of the first of three huge pinnacles. The first can be easily flanked on the left whereas the second looks more difficult. You might be tempted into taking avoiding action by following a trail low down on the left, but this can get you into all sorts of trouble with gullies and loose rock. Far better is to traverse the left side of the pinnacle by a ledge and short scramble, and thus gain a sinister notch between second and third pinnacles. The route is now bleakly obvious: a series of exposed ledges slanting from left to right across the right side of the pinnacle. An awesome drop beneath focuses concentration wonderfully. In fact the scrambling proves easier than it looks and leads quickly to the top of the third and final pinnacle, from where a simple gully scramble and scree path lead down to the delicious flatness of Bwlch Coch.

Bwlch Coch is a haven for travellers in peril. Here you can stretch out and relax for a few minutes while nerves de-tingle. Looking back at the Pinnacles you can now see their shadowy north faces which caused such anxiety. Your apprehension was not misplaced.

The ridge traverse resumes under the name Crib y Ddysgl; easy at first, then more testing where the rocks coalesce at the far side of an uncharacteristic plateau. Once again a path to the left suggests an easy option, but after flanking the ridge with promising ease it will abandon you in the middle of an unpleasantly loose mountainside. Instead, tackle the initial obstacle direct and the succeeding barrier by a series of zig-zags up little chimneys and over blocks on the left side (though never more than ten or fifteen metres from the crest). As on the East Ridge, the ridge reclines after this initial obstacle into a shattered crest of short problems separated by longer stretches of walking. The remainder of the crest consists of sheaves of rock piled up into outcrops, through which the path weaves with relative ease. A trig point identifies the summit of Crib y Ddysgl (strictly speaking this name refers only to the east ridge of Carnedd Ugain but is popularly used to identify the whole mountain, the original having fallen into disuse). On a clear day you can see every major hill group in North Wales from the Carneddau to Aran.

Strolling down the gentle west side of Crib y Ddysgl you might think you've earned a bit of peace and quiet. Not a chance. In the time it takes to hum the first verse of *Climb Every Mountain* your path has converged with the Llanberis Path, the Snowdon Ranger Path, the combined Pig and Miners' Track and, for good measure, the Snowdon Mountain Railway. So many paths, so many people. Isolationists will follow the rim of the cwm—averting their eyes from the hordes trudging up the railway trail just a few metres away—and pass over Snowdon summit without a pause.

Forcing a direct descent from Snowdon summit to Bwlch y Saethau is not a good idea. Far better to descend by the Watkin Path. If you're worried about losing the Horseshoe 'feel' then leave the Watkin at the Bwlch and follow the ups and downs of the true ridge to Bwlch Cilau. During this traverse you will see the rocky crest of Y Gribin—the alternative route for a shortened Horseshoe—leading down to the left to the east shore of Glaslyn; and opposite, the bulbous side of Crib Coch, scored by the contouring line of the Pig Track now dotted with walkers returning to Pen y Pass.

Until now the ascent of Lliwedd threatened to be a tiring and difficult scramble, but having got to grips with it, the route unfolds without complication. Stay near the left edge for greatest interest, and for tremendous views across the huge north-east face. This face—the highest in Wales—used to be the haunt of pioneer rock climbers of the early nineteen hundreds, but now languishes in almost total neglect. Today you're more likely to see feral goats than climbers on its heather ledges. The ridge path circles over the two summits and a final minor top before breaking away from the true Horseshoe. A final scramble and some scruffy work down ledges and scree brings you to the shore of Lyn Llydaw and a junction with the Miners' Track. You now have twenty minutes before reaching Pen y Pass in which to purge your head of the inevitable anti-climax that accompanies an ambition realised. Look at it this way: the first time may be the most memorable, but its rarely the best. You'll be back.

Looking across Llyn Glaslyn to Crib Goch from the elongated col between Snowdon and Lliwedd. *Golygfa ar draws Llyn Glaslyn at Grib Goch.*

18: SNOWDON GROUP — Snowdon from Nant Gwynant

Route summary: A rewarding mountain walk to the highest summit in Wales. Follows a track near waterfalls into a hidden cwm then ascends a long ridge, at one point traversing an exposed crest. After an unpleasant initial descent, returns more sedately down a scenic valley.
Difficulty: Class D.
Main summits: Snowdon (Yr Wyddfa) 1085m/3559ft; (Yr Aran 747m/2451ft).
Duration: 13km/8miles; 1025m/3350ft of ascent; allow 6-7hrs.
Terrain: Mainly good tracks and paths with one section over unpleasant scree.
Special difficulties: Exposed to strong winds at Bwlch Main on the narrow upper section of the South Ridge. The initial part of the descent crosses a slope of shattered rock; with care this presents no real difficulties, though even a frost or sprinkling of snow will render this slope extremely insecure.

Approach: From Beddgelert or Pen y Gwryd along the A498 to a car park at Bethania (GR:628 507).
Route directions: Cross the road from the car park and take the marked lane along the west bank of the river. Fork left after about 400m and follow a track, rising steadily, to an easement at the entrance

At the summit of Snowdon. Llyn Llydaw lies below the shadowed north face of Lliwedd. Ar gopa'r Wyddfa. Gorwedd Llyn Llydaw islaw wyneb gogleddol Lliwedd.

of Cwm y Llan (GR:621 520). Do not cross the stream but bear left up a steep diagonal path on to the dismantled tramway. Follow the tramway for a few hundred metres to the right then bear left on a path rising diagonally across a grassy hillside to gain the South Ridge just above Bwlch Cwm Llan. Ascend the ridge by a good path near its crest—narrow and exposed at Bwlch Main—to the summit of Snowdon.

Descend back along the south-west ridge for about 200m to a 2m high marker stone. Leave the ridge here and descend a poor path diagonally over scree and rock to Bwlch y Saethau. Continue to a large cairn at Bwlch Cilau, below the north-west ridge of Lliwedd. Here the main path swings right; follow it down the valley side to slate tips in Cwm y Llan. Veer left and continue down the valley, passing close to the Gladstone Rock, to rejoin the ascent route beyond a footbridge.

Alternatives: An approach over Yr Aran adds interest. Ascend to the tramway as for the main route, then continue uphill on a vague path, passing to the right of mining spoil, to gain the level section of the east ridge. Turn right and follow the ridge crest. Where the wall veers right, cross it by a ladder stile and continue up the ridge by a stony path to the summit of Yr Aran.

Return initially to the ladder stile then turn left and descend a stony path near a wall to a grass col. Divert left then right to continue on the right side of the stone wall to a cairn at Bwlch Cwm Llan and a junction with the main route. (2) During summer months a descent could be made by one of the paths described in chapters 16, 17 and 19, returning to Bethania on the Sherpa bus.

Five ridges converge on Snowdon, each bearing a well-worn path (and one of them a railway also, but we needn't worry about that). It would help our mental grasp of the topography if the ridges radiated from the summit like the arms of a starfish, but this is not so. The regional sketch map at the beginning of this section reveals the true complexity.

Many keen walkers first get to know Snowdon from its impressive east side, often by ascending the Pig Track, and having done so are likely to be dismissive about its gentler aspects to south and west. This is a mistake. Excepting the Horseshoe, the combination of South Ridge and Watkin Path is as fine as any on the mountain. The scenery is different—being greener, softer and sunnier—but in no way inferior. Nor is the ascent any less arduous. Quite the opposite: the walk begins in Nant Gwynant, three hundred metres lower down the mountain than Pen y Pass, starting point of the Pig Track. Though tiring, this additional climb up from the valley deepens the sense of remoteness felt on arrival in the mountain's southern cwm.

The Gwynant is the prettiest of Snowdonia's main valleys. With its winding road, sheltered lake, and clumps of natural woodland, it might belong in the Lake District. High valley sides cut off all but the merest glimpse of Snowdon's summit pyramid, and instead it is the satellite peak of Yr Aran which attracts admiring glances. It makes a fine climb by itself for a short day, or as a prelude to an ascent of the South Ridge.

Sir Edward Watkin oversaw construction of his path to Snowdon in the late nineteenth century, a trifling matter for a railway engineer prepared to tunnel the English Channel. In Cwm y Llan the path veers around a small outcrop now known as the Gladstone Rock. It was on this rock in 1892 that the then Prime Minister, 83 years old, stood to address the people of Eryri on justice to Wales. After which, the plaque records, the assembled multitude sang Land of My Fathers. Thus was the Watkin Path officially opened.

The first stage of the ascent follows a surfaced lane and rough track by the side of a wood. At open country the track winds up a steepening hillside with occasional views of the Afon Cwm Llan and its waterfalls. In time both river and track are confined between craggy slopes, birdsong and sunny calm overwhelmed by the sound of thrashing water and chill of

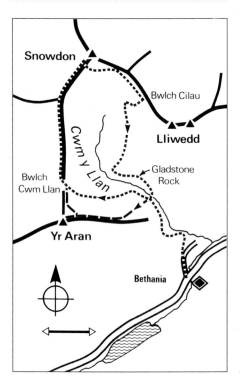

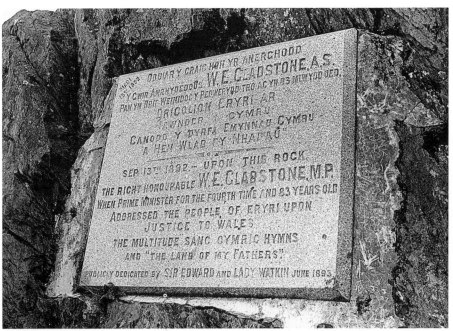

Plaque mounted on the Gladstone Rock in Cwm y Llan. *Llechen ar Graig Gladstone yng Nghwm y Llan.*

Looking back down the South Ridge ascent route towards Yr Aran. *Y ffordd i fyny'r Esgair Ddeheuol yn edrych tua'r Aran.*

mountain air. Soon the track enters the hanging valley of Cwm y Llan, where the river trickles not roars, and tranquillity returns. The Watkin Path crosses the river by a footbridge and continues along the flat base of the cwm, whereas the approach to the South Ridge bears off to the left to gain the course of a tramway, now dismantled, which once transported slate from Hafod y Llan quarry to the incline so obvious from the early part of the walk. There's a decision to be made here. Those eager to get to grips with Snowdon will use the tramway, and a grassy diagonal beyond, to gain Bwlch Cwm Llan at the foot of the South Ridge without further delay. Others will continue above the tramway to snatch an ascent of the fine miniature peak of Yr Aran, adding about an hour and a half to the total duration of the walk.

The lower third of the South Ridge is broad-backed and the path which plods along its crest, uneventful. Excitement mounts slowly. The middle third introduces no new complications, but now the right side of the ridge plunges sharply down into Cwm Tregalan over the rotten cliffs of Clogwyn Du. The upper third traverses the crenellations at Bwlch Main, especially dramatic when clouds are scudding through the gap. For a little while it feels like a section of Crib Goch, then the ridge broadens again and the path wanders harmlessly up through boulders in a final ascent to the summit.

Snowdon summit. What an ignominious end to such a fine route: up concrete steps to the back of the station cafe, alienated from your mountain by the dross of civilisation and the manic hooting of engines. Is the Snowdon Mountain Railway a fine example of Victorian engineering or an unforgivable intrusion? Stand up and be counted. In my opinion the track should be ripped up, the snack bar and souvenir shop demolished.

The shortest descent from Snowdon summit to Bwlch y Saethau, first objective of the Watkin Path, takes a direct line down the blunt ridge. This poor choice of route is rocky, steep and unstable (cup your ear and listen carefully and you may hear the pathetic squawks of walkers who thought they knew better). A rock finger a couple of hundred metres back down the South Ridge identifies the actual point of departure of the Watkin Path for its slanting, skittering descent of the south flank to Bwlch y Saethau. Even this correct line is awkward. The path of unstable scree and gritty rock slabs gives poor support at the best of times, and becomes treacherous when frozen or dusted with snow.

Bwlch y Saethau—the Pass of the Arrows—features prominently in Arthurian legend. It was here, after marching from Dinas Emrys near Beddgelert to deal with his treacherous nephew Modred, that Arthur was fatally wounded by an arrow. His victorious followers buried him and marked the grave by a huge cairn, now dispersed. Local legend maintains that his warriors are hiding in a cave on Lliwedd, awaiting the sound of the bell at its entrance that will announce the second coming of Arthur.

A long, level ridge links Bwlch y Saethau with Bwlch Ciliau, the col below the northwest ridge of Lliwedd. Unfortunately the Watkin Path shirks the few ups and downs of the ridge crest by creeping along its south flank. At Bwlch Ciliau the path veers away from the ridge and begins its slanting descent across the Cwm Tregalan hillside towards Cwm y Llan and the abandoned South Snowdon Slate Quarry, which operated on a commercial knife-edge in the mid nineteenth century. Before starting this final descent, walk up to the edge and peer over the other side into the great eastern cwm. On the far skyline you may see scramblers working cautiously along the crest of Crib Goch, and down below, carefree walkers strolling along the Pig Track. It's another world, another adventure, over there.

19: SNOWDON GROUP — *Snowdon from Rhyd Ddu*

Route summary: A popular if rather plodding ascent of the highest mountain in Wales. Interest develops in the upper reaches where the route circles the rim of a remote cwm and finishes up an exposed rock ridge.
Difficulty: Class C.
Main summits: Snowdon (Yr Wyddfa) 1085m/3559ft. (Moel Cynghorion 672m/2207ft).
Duration: 16km/10miles; 900m/2950ft of ascent; allow 6-7hrs.
Terrain: Track then stony paths. Some boggy sections in the lower reaches.
Special difficulties: The narrow upper part, in the region of Bwlch Main, is exposed to strong winds. Take care when descending in mist to locate the point of departure of the Snowdon Ranger path from the railway.
Approach: From Caernarfon or Beddgelert along the A4085 to a large car park on main road a few hundred metres south of

Rhyd Ddu village (GR:571 526).
Route directions: Go along a track from the north end of the car park for about 100m. Turn right at a gate and follow a stony track for about 1.5km. Soon after crossing a ladder stile at a gate, turn left through a swing gate (GR:583 525) and continue by a narrower path over rough ground, later rising steeply up to a broad shoulder overlooking Cwm Clogwyn (GR:597 538). Circle the rim of the cwm and zig-zag up fenced paths. Continue by the rocky left side of the ridge and across the narrows of Bwlch Main to the final ridge leading to Snowdon summit.

Walk down the railway, ignoring the first marker stone over on the right (departure point for the Zig-Zags of the Pig Track), to a second marker stone (GR:607 551). Bear left here, gradually veering away from the railway. Continue down the stony path (divert right for views down Clogwyn Du'r Arddu), zig-zagging in the

lower stages, to Bwlch Cwm Brwynog (GR:592 557). Continue less steeply across the south flank of Moel Cynghorion, finally zig-zagging down to the Snowdon Ranger Youth Hostel. Turn left and follow the main road through Rhyd Ddu back to the start.
Alternatives: (1) To incorporate an ascent of Moel Cynghorion, veer right from the Snowdon Ranger path to Bwlch Cwm Brwynog and ascend the steep and pathless south-east ridge to the broad summit area. Descend a grass ridge south-west then west to Bwlch Maes-gwm—the Telegraph Col (GR:573 559). Turn left and follow the path down grass slopes to rejoin the Snowdon Ranger path just above the zig-zags. (2) During summer months a descent could be made by one of the paths described in chapters 17, 18 and 19, returning to Rhyd Ddu on the Sherpa bus.

Looking west from Snowdon to Moel Cynghorion (right) and Moel Eilio. Yn edrych tua'r gorllewin o Foel Cynghorion (ar y dde) a Moel Eilio.

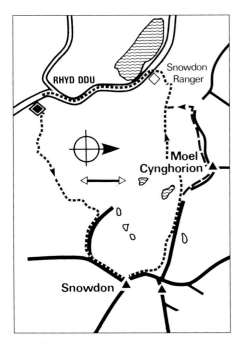

If you were to see Snowdon for the first time from the west you might wonder what all the fuss was about. Can this uninspiring mound be the Queen of Eryri, 'throned high on mighty desolation, crowned with mist of stars'? What contemptible drivel! Not much 'treach'rous splendour' here, only a slope of bracken and boulders meekly rising at an average 1 in 4 gradient to a distant and unremarkable summit where the 'silv'ry glint' is not a lingering patch of snow but the windows of a snack bar, and where the 'silken pall' is not a curl of mountain mist but smoke from the train now waiting at platform one.

I should take advice before cynicism gets the better of me:

"It is easy to say 'yonder is Snowdon', but not so easy to ascend it." (Welsh proverb)

Well, yes, I'd have to agree with that. And having learned that lesson I can now see that it is easy to write the words, 'yonder is a boring looking walk', but not so easy to eat them. The incentive to climb Snowdon from the west comes not from what you can see but what you can't: the 'gaunt red crag' of Llechog, the parapets of Bwlch Main, the imaginative chill of Clogwyn Du'r Arddu. Go to it.

You won't be alone. The Rhyd Ddu Path, one of the eight main ascent routes on Snowdon, takes its fair share of the hundred thousand pilgrims. Of course the popularity of Snowdon is not a new phenomenon. George Borrow— traveller, writer, walker—made this observation while climbing Snowdon with his daughter Henrietta and a guide: "We were far from being the only visitors to the hill this day;

On the final part of the ascent to Snowdon Summit in full winter conditions, looking back towards Bwlch Main and the crags of Llechog. *Nesáu at gopa'r Wyddfa berfedd gaeaf, yn edrych yn ôl at Fwlch Main a chreigiau Llechog.*

Summit 'hotel' on Snowdon, prior to superficial attempts at camouflage with slate cladding. *Y 'gwesty' ar gopa'r Wyddfa cyn yr ymgais arwynebol i'w guddio dan lechi.*

groups of people, or single individuals, might be seen going up or descending the path as far as the eye could reach." And that was in 1854.

In its initial stages the route follows a gently rising track and the time passes pleasantly enough. Soon it takes to a narrow path across terrain alternately bouldery and boggy and a long way short of anything splendid. I have to say that I don't hold with this nonsense about hill walking being unmitigated joy. When it is good it is very very good, but when it is bad it is horrid. Let's face it, plodding up some dismal slope in the lashing rain can be a mind-numbing chore. Sometimes we do it because it's so awful we know it can only get better, and it does (except for the times when it gets worse). When you think about it, much of hill walking is like much of life in general: thrilling in prospect, fulfilling in retrospect, tiresome in execution.

For me the pay-off came when I crested out on the Llechog ridge and peered down over the tottering cliffs to the red screes of Cwm Clogwyn below. For the first time that day I felt as though I was truly among mountains.

The cloud base was not far above; the specks of people toiling up the ridge towards it looked like soldiers marching blindly into a bank of poisonous gas. From time to time the cloud would shiver, dislodging feathers of mist which floated down into the hollow where they would mass together and escape over the ridge in a silent rush, leaving the cwm clear once more.

Above some ugly zig-zags between erosion control fences the path narrows to cross the inner flank of the cwm. Previously I had been a spectator to the unfolding drama, but now I was part of it, steadying myself in the buffeting wind as I crossed the exposed edge of Bwlch Main. Here the path merged with the South Ridge route, at a stroke doubling the cast of players. Inevitably we got in each other's way, but instead of becoming irritable we smiled grimly at each other, aware that we were all caught up in the same theatrical climax.

The lights came up for the interval and I found myself in the foyer of the Snowdon Summit Hotel. The dazzling normality of it all made a fiction out of what I had just been through. Attempts to civilise Snowdon summit

are not new. Borrow mentions "a rude cabin, in which refreshments are sold, and in which a person resides through the year", and some sort of building had been there since 1820. I wonder if Borrow was the original summit bore? Let's listen in while he pontificates into Henrietta's earhole:

"You are now on the top crag of Snowdon, generally termed Y Wyddfa, which means a conspicuous place or tumulus, and which is generally in winter covered with snow; about which snow there are in the Welsh language two curious englynion, or stanzas, consisting entirely of vowels with the exception of one consonant, namely the letter R."

He goes on to recite the stanzas in Welsh and English. Henrietta stifles a yawn. I am stood among a small group of English people, grinning with scorn. The recital over, a Welsh-man comes forward, shakes Borrow by the hand and asks if he is a Llydauan. Borrow says: "I wish I was, or anything but what I am, one of a nation amongst whom any knowledge save what relates to money-making and over-reaching is looked upon as a disgrace. I am ashamed to say that I am an Englishman."

Thus did George Borrow oil the wheels of his passage through Wild Wales.

At first the descent follows the tracks of the Snowdon Mountain Railway, the means by which civilised people get to see a cloud at close quarters. It was opened in 1896, the first and only rack-and-pinion railway in Britain. Despite an impressive safety record, the steep gradients on the railway (which in places exceed 1 in 6), and its proximity to the edge of some formidable drops, maintain a high state of nervous excitement among the passengers. This is not entirely misplaced: during the official opening a passenger leapt from a carriage after a train crashed into the back of some stationary carriages high on the mountain. He later died of his injuries. More recently, in 1987, a passenger was injured after jumping from a runaway carriage shortly before the back-up braking systems brought it to a halt.

The Snowdon Ranger Path soon leaves the railway for a stony path on the north-west shoulder of the mountain. This section of the route is unremarkable, except for the views ahead of a chain of velvety hills culminating in Moel Eilio. However, if you divert slightly to the right you will find yourself at the top of Clogwyn Du'r Arddu, the finest cliff in Wales. This is a complex face and you can never be sure which bit lies beneath. Most obvious from above is the East Gully Wall, which cuts in at right angles to the rest of the cliff and can be seen in all its awesome detail. The Abraham brothers peered down this wall in 1905 after failing to ascend the main cliff (not climbed until 1927) and predicted that climbers possessed of great strength and skill would one day cling to these holds. Fifty years later Joe Brown climbed the first route on the wall.

The path continues down the shoulder towards the bwlch above Llyn Ffynnon y Gwas, zig-zagging to ease the strain, then slants more gently across the southern flank of Moel Cynghorion, the first of those velvety hills. Now here's a challenge: quit the path at the bwlch, climb the south-east ridge of Cynghorion to its summit (tremendous retrospective views of Clogwyn Du'r Arddu and Snowdon), romp down the west ridge to Bwlch Maes-gwm, and finally descend the track leftwards to rejoin the Ranger Path just above its final switchback descent to the Youth Hostel. The hostel is just half an hour along the road from the Rhyd Ddu car park. Stick out your thumb, you never know your luck.

On the Snowdon Ranger path near Bwlch Cwm Brwynog. Moel Hebog and its satellite peaks in the distance. *Ar lwybr y Snowdon Ranger ger Bwlch Cwm Brwynog. Moel Hebog a'i gopâu is yn y pellter. Y ddau Foelwyn ac Eifionydd.*

MOELWYNS AND EIFIONYDD

Maps: Several maps may be required depending on the particular route and amount of detail required. At 1:50,000 scale (adequate in conjunction with notes extracted from the route descriptions), both Landranger Sheet 115 (Snowdon) and Sheet 124 (Dolgellau) are required for the Moelwyns, whereas Moel Hebog, the Nantlle Ridge, and the walk from Beddgelert are all shown on Sheet 115. The region is split differently on 1:25,000 scale maps. The Moelwyns appear in their entirety on Outdoor Leisure 18 (Snowdonia—Harlech & Bala), and the Nantlle Ridge on Outdoor Leisure 17 (Snowdonia—Snowdon Area), whereas the Moel Hebog and Beddgelert walks are split between the two. The two Lleyn Peninsula walks described in chapter 24 are both shown at 1:50,000 scale on Landranger Sheet 123 (Lleyn Peninsula). The scale is coarse though adequate when supplemented with notes taken from the route description.

Bases: Beddgelert is convenient for all walks apart from the Lleyn Peninsula, which in any case would normally be approached from a central base. Hotel and bed & breakfast accommodation can be found in the village, while there is a campsite with good facilities 1.5km/1mile out on the road towards Rhyd Ddu. Beddgelert lies on the Bangor-Caernarfon-Porthmadog bus route (rail stations at Porthmadog and Bangor). However, Beddgelert can be reached direct by bus from Llanberis or Capel Curig only during the summer months.

Lower than the Carneddau, less rugged than the Glyders, the straggling hills south of Snowdon remain undeservedly neglected. Even the famous Nantlle Ridge—as fine a ridge traverse as any in Wales—is rarely crowded. Naturally this adds to the attraction and the region has its own band of enthusiasts who gladly sacrifice a few hundred metres of altitude for the sake of exclusivity.

The region stretches the full width of the national park and beyond. It includes three distinct mountain groups, each separated by main roads—the Moelwyns, Moel Hebog/Nantlle, and the Lleyn Peninsula. Despite this geographical spread they share an atmosphere of threatened beauty: in the case of the Moelwyns the threat came from slate mines and is retreating; on Yr Eifl it comes from quarries and is advancing.

At the summit of Cnicht. Moelwyn Mawr, the next objective, rises above Cwm Croesor. Spoil heaps from the old slate mines at Bwlch Cwm Orthin are visible on the far left. Ar ben Y Cnicht. Cyfyd Moelwyn Mawr, y nod nesaf uwchben Cwm Croesor. Gwelir tomenydd llechi yr hen chwareli ym Mwlch Cwm Orthin ar y chwith.

20: MOELWYNS AND EIFIONYDD — Cnicht and The Moelwyns

Route summary: Combines the three main peaks of the southern Moelwyns in a mountain walk of contrasting scenery and terrain.

Difficulty: Class D.

Main summits: Cnicht 690m/2265ft; Moelwyn Mawr 770m/2527ft; Moelwyn Bach 711m/2334ft.

Duration: 16km/10 miles; 1000m/3275ft of ascent; allow 7hrs.

Terrain: Mainly narrow paths over grass. Some trackless moor walking and a few boggy sections. A short road walk to finish.

Special difficulties: The final ascent to Cnicht involves 25m of simple rock scrambling, and there is a short scramble on the descent of Craig Ysgafn. Neither will detain a mountain walker accustomed to the rugged terrain of the Glyders or Carneddau. Route-finding between Cnicht and Moelwyn Mawr is fraught with difficulty in misty conditions.

Approach: From Beddgelert or Penrhyn-deudraeth along the A4085. Take the narrow Croesor road from a junction 500m north of Garreg/Llanfrothen village. Turn left at crossroads towards the village. Large car park on the right (GR:632 447).

Route directions: Turn right at the car park exit and take the uphill road from the village to a gate and stile at its end. Continue by a woodland track until the angle eases (GR:628 451). Fork right to follow a track along the left side of the lower

On the ascent to Cnicht. Cwm Croesor is below, the Glaslyn Estuary in the distance. Wrth ddringo'r Cnicht. Gwelir Cwm Croesor islaw ac Aber Glaslyn yn y pellter.

south-west ridge of Cnicht. Shortly after the track turns to grass, turn right and cross a ladder stile on the skyline to gain the ridge. Ascend the ridge and later cross a stile on the right to a path leading over rocks to below the steep upper section. Continue up the ridge to a grass plateau below the final rock step, taken on the right by a slanting trough with good holds. Scruffier though easier scrambling above leads to the summit of Cnicht.

Descend the north-east ridge, crossing or by-passing subsidiary summits (and avoiding a false ridge on the right), to a cairn at the saddle just south of Llyn yr Adar (GR:656 477). Turn right and follow a generally contouring path (vague in places), passing the west shore of Llyn Cwm Corsiog, to ruined quarry buildings at Bwlch Cwm Orthin. Ascend a dog-leg incline just left of the largest spoil heap and continue beyond the upper level on to the open moor. Trend right—vague path—to gain the north spur of Moelwyn Mawr and follow it, curving right and steepening, to the summit trig point. Walk about 100m east from the summit before turning right to descend the blunt south ridge. Cross over the rocky subsidiary summit of Craig Ysgafn to the deep col of Bwlch Stwlan. Ascend a shale path diagonally left (*not* the contouring track at a lower level) to reach the grassy east spur of Moelwyn Bach. Turn right and ascend to the summit.

Descend the grassy west ridge and then, heading for the left side of the fore- stry plantation, continue over boggy lower pastures (stiles or open gates at fence junctions). Turn right at the surfaced lane to return to Croesor in about 1.5km.

Alternatives: (1) Turn right at ruined quarry buildings at Bwlch Cwm Orthin and descend a path diagonally across the south side of Cwm Croesor to a road in the valley bottom. Turn right at crossroads to return to the start. (2) Descend the ridge westwards from summit of Moelwyn Mawr to the surfaced lane. Turn right and return to start in less than 500m. (3) Turn right at Bwlch Stwlan and follow a path below the north flank of Moelwyn Bach's west ridge, rejoining the normal descent route at the base of the ridge.

A night of thunder has left us down-hearted. Cnicht and the Moelwyns in a rain storm? I'd been there before, snatching glimpses of hills from under the rim of a cagoule hood and knowing more about the map than the mountain under my feet. But we decided to go anyway, as if the act of making up a flask and sandwiches would somehow push back the clouds. It did. At Capel Curig the rain had stopped, at Pen y Gwryd the mist had lifted, at Beddgelert the roads were steaming, and by the time we reached Llanfrothen, Cnicht was pointing optimistically towards a mottled sky.

A narrow dead-end road protects the tiny village of Croesor from the insincere attentions of tourists. The mines have long since closed, but the village survives in defiant isolation. As we strolled up the lane from the village, the ten-tenths cloud cover fragmented into a grey mosaic set on a blue background. A hawk circled overhead, rising on an invisible spiral escalator with a few twitches of its wing tips. A track took us around the foot of Cnicht's west ridge, and a less obvious path on to its back. The Glaslyn estuary stretched out behind us but we were more interested in peering down a slope of rock and heather into Cwm Croesor, already an unreal distance below.

Beyond a rocky knoll the ridge rears up apparently unbroken to the summit, but it has a secret. I teased Sara about it, promising a lunch stop somewhere special. "Is this it?" she would ask every two minutes. "You'll know when we get there," I would say. We arrived at the hidden shoulder, where the ridge falls back and takes a breath before jutting up over a rock step towards the summit, with the last of our patience consumed by an aching hunger. Others were already here, wandering bewildered over the sheep-mown grass, or gazing out from the parapets towards Snowdon before settling down to lunch among the sun-trapping boulders. Asked to name a dozen favourite places in the Welsh mountains I might well begin with this one.

Over lunch we watched dispassionately while a group of three heavily burdened backpackers mistakenly descended the difficult northern flank of the rock step. Seen from below the best route is clearly the trough of spiky rock which slants across the south side. Even so it looked as though it might give us a tough scramble. A couple lunching near-by seemed to be going through a similar crisis of commitment. One of them strolled over to examine the problem and returned delighted with news of solid rock and huge holds. They would go on, and we with them, revelling in the push and pull of an easy but energetic scramble and encouraged by the nearness of the summit.

Cnicht has another surprise in store. The mountain proves not to be the classically pointed peak suggested by the tag 'Welsh Matterhorn', but a main summit and several minor ones strung out over a rocky spine. This is not a disappointment, because the path which twists along the summit ridge is one of the highlights of the walk.

Cnicht's eastern ridge quickly turns to grass and loses itself among a lakeland interior to which any one of four Moelwyn peaks might legitimately lay claim. This long detour out to the cairned saddle above Llyn yr Adar before turning towards Bwlch Cwm Orthin seems wasteful, but is the only way to avoid the deep intervention of Cwm Croesor. Between saddle and bwlch the contouring path wanders among bogs, outcrops, tiny lakes, and later the ruins and inclines of old slate mines. This exploratory interlude between ascents of Cnicht and Moelwyn Mawr is both the reason and the reward for linking two such disparate summits. By now the clouds had drifted away and the cold wind that had sent us scurrying over the summit of Cnicht had moderated to a listless breeze. No-one from Cnicht had followed us into this precious upland and we delayed our crossing with little excuses to sit down and bathe in its emptiness.

During the gradual descent to Bwlch Cwm Orthin we envied a group of people setting up a secluded camp by a waterfall, then hurried on to regain a schedule that might yet return us to Croesor before nightfall. At the bwlch we walked out across a floor paved with slabs of discarded slate and wandered among silent ruins, feeding our curiosity on bits of rusting machinery, poking them with our boots in search of explanations. Others were here too, preserving or burying the past with sketch pads or cameras. At the foot of the incline which would take us towards Moelwyn Mawr we

Llyn yr Adar

Llyn Cwm Corsiog

Cnicht

Bwlch Cwm Orthin

ruins

Cwm Croesor

Moelwyn Mawr

CROESOR

Bwlch Stwlan

Moelwyn Bach

Looking through the gap of Bwlch Stwlan to Moel yr Hydd during the descent of Moelwyn Bach (right). The rock spine of Craig Ysgafn, traversed on the route from Moelwyn Mawr, is on the left. Golygfa trwy Fwlch Stwlan i gyfeiriad Moel yr Hydd wrth ddisgyn o Foelwyn Bach (ar y dde). Mae Craig Ysgafn, a groeswyd wrth ddod o Foelwyn Mawr, ar y chwith.

came across the dripping entrance tunnel of a slate mine. It sucked us in with the daylight but then, after swallowing the liquid light, spat us out like pips.

As we toiled up the incline an elderly man rode carefully down in masterly control of the twitching front wheel of his mountain bike. I guessed he had ridden up the Stwlan dam road and had then followed the moorland track to get here. If so he could look forward to an exhilarating ride down the Cwm Orthin track into Tan y Grisiau. We stopped to watch his progress, expecting him to dismount for the rocky steps at the bottom of the incline. After a slight pause to inspect the problem he rode down the stairway with exquisite precision and clattered out on to the slate floor of the bwlch.

We had been dreading the ascent of Moelwyn Mawr, and now the unbroken grass of its tedious northern spur lay before us. And yet even here the Moelwyns found games and puzzles to distract us from the effort. The sun had dipped precisely to the angle of the slope so

that our shadows stretched out behind us like spindly giants a hundred metres tall. With their sharp legs and fuzzy heads they took giant strides and yet advanced only a tiny amount with each footfall—none bigger than our own small steps. Later, when we came to the moon-crater edge of the northern hollow, we saw something that hinted at secret and sinister goings-on of which I had heard rumours. From the scree slope above the bowl curled a wisp of smoke, evidence of venting from within the mountain. There may be an innocent explanation, but I know of one underground explorer who was sworn to secrecy after stumbling across suspicious activity in a neighbouring mine.

By now our day was breaking up into a series of dislocated incidents separated by periods of hazy urgency. Near the summit of Moelwyn Mawr we passed a woman rubbing her face in the last remaining patch of snow while her little dog sat patiently to one side, its head tilted with incredulity. At the summit

we took turns to stand wind-buffeted on the cemented cairn of the trig point and gaze at the silver sea. We said nothing; perhaps we would talk about it later, perhaps not. We no longer needed to share our feelings with words.

We crept cautiously down the southern slope, suspicious of hidden crags, and scrambled over the strange, knobbly rock of Craig Ysgafn to the deep col of Bwlch Stwlan. Above the summit crag of Moelwyn Bach taunted us, but I knew from previous explorations that it offered no feasible direct ascent. Instead we followed a shale path rising across the east side and outflanked the crag altogether.

There's no finer end to a mountain day than the west ridge of Moelwyn Bach. Surfaced with deep-pile grass, it dips gently towards the lowlands at the perfect angle for tired feet. After a final backward glance at the stone head of Moelwyn Bach, staring across Bwlch Stwlan at its faceless superior, we turned and gave ourselves up to normality.

21: MOELWYNS AND EIFIONYDD — Aberglaslyn and Cwm Bychan

Route summary: A delightful low-level walk based on the village of Beddgelert. Explores a river gorge and disused railway tunnels before ascending through a copper mining valley to heather uplands.

Difficulty: Class A

Duration: 11km/7miles; 275m/900ft of ascent; allow 4hrs.

Terrain: Mainly good paths and tracks. Several muddy sections after wet weather.

Special difficulties: Children need to be closely supervised on the gorge section, especially when the river is high. This sec-tion can be avoided by taking a short-cut through the long tunnel (torch useful but not essential).

Approach: From Capel Curig, Caernarfon or Porthmadog to Beddgelert at the junction of the A4085 and A498. Large car park (fee in summer) off the A498 on the south side of the village (GR:588 482)

Route directions: Go down a narrow lane from the village centre (signposted "Gelert's Grave"), cross the footbridge, and turn right along a riverside path, later merging with the dismantled railway. Follow the track through two short tunnels until about 50m short of a long tunnel. Now descend rock steps to the river and follow it downstream, over boulders and a footbridge, to the Aberglaslyn road bridge.

Instead of descending to the bridge, turn left up steps and follow a woodland path to an open area. Turn left here (signposted "Cwm Bychan") and follow a good path up the valley, passing mine workings in its upper reaches. Ignore left forks and go straight ahead over a small col (GR:607 481), descending a shallow valley on the far side. Later the path veers left and

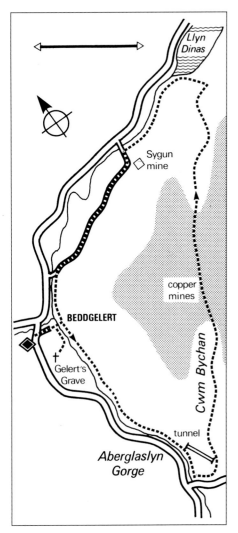

The track of the dismantled Welsh Highland Railway cuts across the steep valley side where the river begins to tumble through the Aberglaslyn Gorge.

Lein hen Reilffordd Ucheldir Cymru sy'n torri ar draws ochr serth y cwm lle mae'r afon yn dechrau byrlymu trwy Fwlch Aberglaslyn.

descends steeply to the south shore of Llyn Dinas.

Turn left to follow the riverside path (later a track), curving left to the entrance of the Sygun copper mine buildings. Ignore the path signposted "Cwm Bychan" and curve right on the main track, improving to a surfaced lane, until it bends right to bridge the river. Go over a stile to continue along the riverbank, now by a stony path, back to Beddgelert. Cross the footbridge used on the approach and turn left to visit Gelert's Grave before returning to the car park.

Alternatives: Continue through the long tunnel, emerging on the woodland path shortly before turning left to begin the ascent into Cwm Bychan.

Sometimes the prospect of struggling up a cloud-wrapped mountain is simply too much to contemplate. Yet it can be easier to conform than to confess. There's a middle way, which is to devise a respectably long but gratifyingly low-level walk. Things are made easier if you are accompanied by children. It wouldn't do to push them too hard, would it?

I doubt there's a better low-level walk in all Snowdonia than this 10km tour of the countryside around Beddgelert. It begins and ends as a riverside ramble, and in between explores a railway tunnel, a river gorge, and a copper mining valley. Kids love it (except perhaps for the uphill bit), which is some indication of the interest and variety. None of this is secret knowledge and the walk appears, in one form or another, in several local guidebooks. For some reason most describe a clockwise circuit from Beddgelert. I think they are mistaken. On the anti-clockwise circuit you come to the gorge first, when you have the vitality to enjoy it, and take the gentler slopes in ascent.

You might think that bustling Beddgelert outside the tourist season is Beddgelert without the bustle. It isn't. The shell remains—the hotels, craft shops, cute stone cottages—but the life form that inhabited it is elsewhere, or in hiding. In summer it is bloated with visitors and second-home dwellers; in winter it is undernourished. You can't help liking the place, though, with its narrow roads and frothing rivers and stone houses all cluttered together in the barely adequate gaps between the mountains.

The walk begins along the lane signposted to Gelert's Grave (of which more later), down past the gift shops and over a steel footbridge on to the far bank of the Afon Glaslyn. Here is peace, if not quiet, shared on sunny Sunday afternoons with the camera-and-ice-cream

A short tunnel on the dismantled Welsh Highland Railway. *Twnel byr ar Reilffordd Ucheldir Cymru, nas defnyddir bellach.*

wielding occupants of several motor coaches. The Second Law of Tourist Dynamics states that crowds thin in proportion to the distance walked from the car park and public conveniences (the First Law states the former will be full and the latter closed for repairs), so that by the time you reach the level track of the dismantled Welsh Highland Railway their numbers should have diminished sufficiently for you to begin nodding at people without causing alarm. Nevertheless, this empty track today carries more people per annum than in the days when it was laid with railway lines. The original narrow-gauge railway transported sightseers of the late nineteenth century from the main line near Caernarfon to Rhyd Ddu at the foot of Snowdon, from where the more energetic among them would begin their ascent. But from 1896 tourists switched to the newly completed Snowdon Mountain Railway, which would take them direct to the summit. And who could blame them. The spurned railway struggled on with its depleted custom for another twenty years before closing. In the early twenties the original line was resurrected and extended through Beddgelert and the Aberglaslyn Pass to Porthmadog. Had it remained open it would now be a major tourist attraction, but it had inherited the jinx and closed during the thirties. A small section of track near Porthmadog has since been re-opened, though all attempts to extend the line to Beddgelert have failed.

As the Aberglaslyn gorge approaches, the track clings ever more precariously to its side. In a couple of places there simply isn't room for both a river and a railway, and since the river got there first—by about 10,000 years— the railway has to tunnel through a couple of projecting buttresses. Then the gorge gets really serious, and so the railway gives up trying to be as spectacular as nature and instead tunnels straight through the cliff for three hundred spooky metres (if ever the railway restoration project succeeds then we can expect this section of the walk to become even more exciting). Due to a slight curvature, there is at first no light at the end of the tunnel. Those of you carrying fertile imaginations but no torch will find this disconcerting. I had both, and though I can reveal that no concealed shaft or ankle-breaking boulder lies in wait, I can't guarantee that there won't be something nasty lurking in the shadows. If you're lucky there will be other parties walking through, also talking in loud voices and laughing hysterically in an attempt to ward off evil spirits.

The tunnel emerges near the entrance to Cwm Bychan—the next stage of the walk— but in our haste to scare ourselves we've missed the best part of the gorge. I recommend back-tracking through the tunnel so as to resume the walk along the riverside path. You won't be disappointed. The river turns white with rage and rushes down a boulder-choked incline, a famous canoeing challenge (you might see a pale face peering over the road-side wall on the far bank as some intrepid paddler inspects the course). Negotiating the gorge on foot is much less exciting but incomparably safer. Most of the party can expect to emerge alive at the far end.

Shortly before the river passes under Pont Aberglaslyn the path rises up the bank and enters an area of mature woodland, the noise and glare of white water replaced by the soft calm of a moss-covered glade. Rounding the hill into the entrance of Cwm Bychan completes the character transformation. Now the path works up the side of a picturesque valley painted with trees and tumbling streams against a background of Moelwyn hills. As the uphill climb progresses, the valley narrows, the trees thin, and the stream becomes a trickle. Cwm Bychan is running out of ideas. Then above a slight rise appears what looks like a warren for giant rabbits—a hillside riddled with tunnel entrances and heaped with spoil. A curious place, but not a place to indulge your curiosity; these are the old copper mines, and the disused tunnels and shafts are dangerous. The mines had been worked for centuries, although the overhead ropeway which carried buckets of ore down the valley to the crushing plant, and from which a few of the pylons remain

The steep descent to Llyn Dinas. *Y ffordd serth i lawr at Lyn Dinas.*

standing, is of course much more recent. Unlike the near-by Croesor and Ffestiniog slate mines the workings here are lilliputian in scale and relatively inoffensive to the eye.

The path given prominence on OS maps veers left near the head of Cwm Bychan and tries very hard to get you lost, whereas the best route ascends the narrowing cwm to the col and continues down a heather-filled valley on the far side, zig-zagging in its lower stages to the shore of Llyn Dinas. At the lake the path returns to its previous character and becomes a riverside ramble again. On a craggy hill rising from trees on the far bank can be seen Dinas Emrys, a strategic defence site from Iron Age to Middle Ages. The site is also associated with Merlin the Magician, Vortigern the vile, two dragons and one human sacrifice (mix ingredients incredibly together and cook for fifteen hundred years for a tasty legend; season with a pinch of salt before serving).

The path becomes a track near the entrance to the disused Sygun Copper Mine, now a tourist attraction, and for a while loses touch with the river. Eventually the path returns to the bank and follows it over boulders and stepping stones while the river—shallow, chill and white like glacier meltwater—tumbles alongside. Beyond the footbridge is the lane leading back into the village, but before returning there you might spare ten minutes for a paved stroll down the riverbank and across a meadow to see Gelert's Grave, from which the village supposedly gets its name. The tale varies of how a dog called Gelert got to be honoured by a fenced grave and a slate pathway, a treatment normally reserved for dead poets, but the general drift is this:

One day Prince Llewelyn went off hunting, leaving his baby son in the safekeeping of his faithful hound Gelert. Llewelyn returned to find the cot overturned amid blood-stained blankets. Where was his son, where was Gelert? Gelert was skulking in the corner licking his lips. Llewelyn put two and two together and plunged his sword into its side. Exit Gelert. At this moment Llewelyn's whimpering child crawled unscathed from beneath the blankets—which had also concealed the body of a wolf bravely fought and killed by Gelert. 'Whoops,' said Llewelyn, or words to that effect. Aching with remorse, he buried Gelert in yonder field and erected a cairn so the brave dog would not be forgotten.

Some malicious spoil-sports have suggested it was all a wheeze dreamed up by an eighteenth century publican to generate tourist trade for the village. Unthinkable. Rest assured that while you shed a tear for Gelert the traders of Beddgelert are crying all the way to the bank.

22: MOELWYNS AND EIFIONYDD — Moel Hebog and Moel Lefn

Route summary: A strenuous ascent to an isolated mountain followed by pleasant ridge walking and a devious return through forests.

Difficulty: Class C.

Main summits: Moel Hebog 782m/2566ft; Moel yr Ogof 655m/2149ft; Moel Lefn 638m/2094ft.

Duration: 13km/8miles; 950m/3125ft of ascent; allow 5-6hrs.

Terrain: Grass, boulders, forest tracks and trails. Several boggy sections.

Special difficulties: Care required to find the best line on the boulder slope near the summit of Moel Hebog. Complex route-finding in the forest (a 1:25,000 scale map is a useful aid).

Approach: From Capel Curig, Caernarfon, or Porthmadog, to the junction of the A4085 and A498 at Beddgelert. Large car park (fee in summer) off the A498 on the south side of the village (GR:588 482).

Route directions: From the village centre, follow the Caernarfon road for about 500m then turn left on a track, bridging the river, to buildings at Cwm Cloch about 1km from the main road (GR:581 478). Cross a ladder stile on the right near a barn and follow a path over wet ground, later rising to gain the north-east ridge of Moel Hebog. Ascend a stony path up the broad ridge to a final rocky slope. Wind up through boulders and scree to emerge at prominent twin cairns. Turn left and ascend the ridge over a rock step to the summit trig point of Moel Hebog.

Descend north-west down steep grass, right of a stone wall, to a deep col (GR:560 475). Ascend through the cleft in the outcrop and pass to the left of pools. Avoid a crag on its right side and scramble over boulders to the summit of Moel yr Ogof. Descend north-west, stepping over a fence at its junction with a stone wall, to grass and the rocky summit of Moel Lefn. Continue northwards, avoiding cliffs by descending a steep path right then left. Trend slightly right over the broad foot of the ridge to a quarry pit. Descend steeply on the left side of a stone wall to the col of Bwlch Cwm Trwsgl (GR:553 496).

This is where the trouble starts. Turn

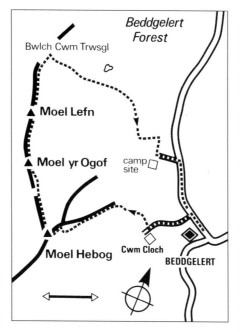

right, pass through a break in the wall, and cross the fence by a stile to enter the forest. Descend a muddy break and turn left on a track. Leave it after about 100m and follow a narrow path on the right, over a footbridge and through trees, to emerge at a stile with open ground ahead (GR:558 496). Cross the open ground by a vague path and re-enter the forest at another stile (GR:563 497). Continue through trees to a track; turn left and follow it around a right bend but leave it at the next left bend, descending through trees to emerge at yet another track. Go 5m right then turn left on a narrow path, crossing over the next two tracks, to a wide stream. Do not ford the stream but turn left, descend a rough track to a superior forest track, and follow it to the right into the forest camp site. Finally turn left to reach the main road (GR:579 491) about 1.5km from Beddgelert.

Alternatives: An ascent of Moel Hebog is rewarding by itself. Return by the same route (having previously noted the twin cairns which identify the start of the boulder slope descent).

Beddgelert and the Gwynant valley seen from high on Moel Hebog. Moel Siabod, truncated by cloud, rises in the distance. *Beddgelert a Chwm Gwynant, fel y'u gwelir o Foel Hebog. Cyfyd Moel Siabod, a'i hanner yn y cymylau, yn y pellter.*

I have to admit I was never greatly impressed by Moel Hebog. I knew it merely as a foothill enriching the coastal view from Snowdon's South Ridge, or as a distant protuberance on a limb of the Nantlle Ridge. But to climb it—why bother? Then one day it winked at me as I drove by on some mundane errand. You know how it is.

Previously I had thought of Moel Hebog as a straight-up-and-down mountain of the Grand Old Duke of York type, but having opened the map I discovered a promising complexity. Here was an opportunity to climb Moel Hebog, traverse the lesser summits of Moel yr Ogof and Moel Lefn, and return to Beddgelert along forest trails.

As we drove into Beddgelert Sara wanted to know where Moel Hebog was. I pointed up to a bank of grey cloud. "Behind that." The cloud base was at a hundred metres. "It'll lift, honest".

Beddgelert is a pretty little village, but a Saturday afternoon in high summer is not the best time to see it. We didn't linger and took a short-cut over the river from the car park on to the Caernarfon road. Not until we'd turned off on to the Cwm Cloch track and bridged the Afon Colwyn, steamy under its canopy of ivy strangled trees, could we start to relax. Is hill walking a pursuit or an escape?

The Hebog path from Cwm Cloch squelches across a boggy meadow before gaining the bracken covered north-east shoulder of the mountain. The air was sultry beneath its cloud blanket as we toiled up the blunt ridge, soaked in sweat and dizzy with effort. Synchronised to our lethargic pace, the cloud lifted and thinned, hinting at a blue future. As we rested at an easing of the shoulder it occurred to me why I had never felt comfortable with the usual justification of climbing mountains for the 'view'. The word has no

meaning. It robs memory of its emotional impact. It is an inadequate word used by inadequate people.

"Nice view" I said to Sara, looking out beyond Beddgelert nestling in its confluence of wooded valleys to Llyn Gwynant and the swelling of a distant Moel Siabod, truncated by cloud. She smiled politely but said nothing.

Bracken had given way to grass, and now grass gave way to boulders. Twenty minutes ago we had seen a cliff barrier through a break in the clouds; the path had responded by trending leftwards but now it had gained a breach and we were expected to make a bid for the summit. A family group came clattering down towards us, preceded by a shower of stones. They had timed their ascent too soon and had spent most of the day wrapped in

cloud. They didn't look happy.

"I'm not happy," the mother confided as she passed, her boot soles skittering over the gravel covered boulders. I know how she felt; it was like walking on ball-bearings. We took our time and picked the best line through the unstable terrain, duly emerging at two large cairns—important markers for anyone descending this way in mist. The cold wind that had shifted the clouds now blasted in our faces as we turned to survey the wider panorama recently revealed; of the Cwellyn valley, clinically divided into slabs of grazing and forestry, and of the southern flank of Snowdon, blandly lit but creatively hung with fluffy remnants of cloud.

It was almost five-thirty at the summit trig point so we postponed celebrations and set off

On the ascent to Moel Hebog. The village of Beddgelert lies in the confluence of valleys below. *Dringo Moel Hebog. Mae pentref Beddgelert yn gorwedd yn aber y cymoedd islaw.*

Retrospective view at sunset from the rocky top of Moel Lefn, across Moel yr Ogof, to Moel Hebog. *Golygfa adeg y machlud o ben creigiog Moel Cefn, i gyfeiriad Moel yr Ogof a hyd at Foel Hebog.*

at once on the uncomfortably steep grass descent to the north-west col. Relatively few people come this way, and only where the route channels between rock outcrops is the path distinctive. We ascended the Moel yr Ogof side of the col by a curious slot cut ten metres deep in a guarding outcrop and came upon enchanted pools, hopelessly pretty in the evening calm. We squandered precious minutes of remaining daylight in exploration and picture taking.

It was eight o'clock by the time we'd traversed Moel yr Ogof and raced over the grass link to the rocky summit spine of Moel Lefn. The sun, already within a few degrees of the horizon, was reflected in the coastal waters of the Lleyn Peninsula. Land silhouetted against a silver sea introduced a biting con-

trast to distant views; through a dip in the Nantlle Ridge we could see the distinctive shape of Holy Island at the western tip of Anglesey.

Sara trusts my weather forecasting but not my sense of timing. I'd promised we'd be down by seven o'clock. The last time I had made such a prediction we had navigated safely off the Nantlle Ridge in thick mist only to be caught by nightfall deep in the forest. A sickly yellow moon had risen to light our way through the clear-felled devastation. Bats fluttered overhead and huge birds cawed from perches high in the few shattered trees that had remained standing. Bewitched, we had lost the path and waded through a marsh before arriving at the roadside sometime after eleven o'clock. And this looked like being a repeat

performance. Sara was stoical.

Before light faded we zig-zagged carefully down the north ridge of Moel Lefn, passed a dripping quarry pit—its walls cloaked in lurid green ferns—and followed the drainage stream down to the col of Bwlch Cwm Trwsgl. We congratulated ourselves on completing in daylight what we assumed to have been the tricky section. Then we stepped over the stile into the gloom of the forest, laughing prematurely.

23: MOELWYNS AND EIFIONYDD —
The Nantlle Ridge

Route summary: An entertaining, scrambly ridge traverse over a string of small summits. A double traverse or circular alternative avoids transport problems.

Difficulty: Class D

Main summits: Y Garn 634m/2080ft; Mynydd Drws y Coed 695m/2280ft; Trum y Ddysgl 710m/2329ft; Mynydd Tal y Mignedd 655m/2148ft; Craig Cwm Silyn 734m/2408ft; Garnedd Goch 701m/2301ft.

Duration: 11km/7miles; 875m/2900ft of ascent; allow 5hrs (7-8hrs for the alternatives).

Terrain: Generally fast going over grass with some rocky sections.

Special difficulties: The ascents to Mynydd Drws y Coed and Craig Cwm Silyn involve scrambling. The first is simple, the second avoidable. The narrow sections of ridge are exposed to strong winds. Care required in mist when crossing featureless ground between Craig Cwm Silyn and Garnedd Goch. Also note the false lines immediately before and after the ascent of Trum y Ddysgl.

Approach: From Caernarfon or Beddgelert along the A4085 to a large car park 500m south of Rhyd Ddu (GR:571 526). Park a second vehicle in the field adjacent to the start of the Cwm Silyn track (GR:496 511). For alternative (1), park just before the gated bridge over the Afon Dwyfor in Cwm Pennant (GR:532 476).

Route directions: Take the slate path opposite the car park, later bridging the stream. White markers beyond a ladder stile indicate the negotiated route to a junction with the B4418 (no parking here).

Turn sharp left (footpath sign) and follow the path on to the grassy flank of Y Garn. Soon after crossing a ladder stile, leave the main path (at a rock marked "ridge") and ascend steeply to the summit of Y Garn.

Follow the ridge southwards, narrowing and becoming rocky, to the summit of Mynydd Drws y Coed.

Continue along the ridge, descending to a slender col. Ignore a contouring path on the left and ascend through shattered rock to resume the ridge traverse to the summit of Trum y Ddysgl.

Follow the ridge south-west, taking care to follow the right-hand branch at a fork, and scramble down to a notch. Cross a narrow neck of ridge and continue to the summit obelisk of Mynydd Tal y Mignedd.

Take the broad ridge south and descend steeply to the double col of Bwlch Dros Bern. At its far side, ascend the crag easily from right to left, starting about 100m right of the stone wall (or scramble directly up the crag with difficulty). Continue steeply by a rocky path, finishing over boulders to the summit of Craig Cwm Silyn.

Continue along the broad and featureless ridge, over a stile at a junction of walls, to the rocky summit of Garnedd Goch.

Descend northwards by a grass shoulder and follow the Cwm Silyn track to the parking area.

Alternatives: (1) Circuit from Cwm Pennant. From the parking place (refer to *Approaches*), follow the road to its end, cross the ladder stile and ascend a grass spur, later trending right past a ruin. Cross a ladder stile, pass through ruined mine buildings, then veer left to ascend an overgrown incline. Continue by a level tramway then ascend a second incline, diverting right at the third level to follow a track and path to the stile at Bwlch y Ddwy Elor (GR:553 505). Do not cross the stile, but turn left to ascend a grass hill and steepening ridge beyond to the summit of Trum y Ddysgl. Continue by the main traverse to Garnedd Goch.

Descend towards the col south of Garnedd Goch then veer left to enter the heather-filled Cwm Ciprwth. Descend near the stream to a waterwheel in the lower valley then cross to the left bank and follow it, bending right, to a sheep bridge. Turn left to follow sheep tracks through gaps in walls and down through woodland, trending right. Turn left at open ground and follow a vague path (occasional marker posts) back to the start. (2) The double traverse. The outward traverse can be re-traced throughout. Alternatively, descend the ascent ridge of (1) to Bwlch y Ddwy Elor, turn left over the stile, and follow a good path, forestry tracks, and finally a boggy path below the east slope of Mynydd Drws y Coed, to a junction with the approach path below Y Garn.

There was a time when the Nantlle Ridge was the worst-kept secret in Snowdonia. Now it isn't even that. And were it not for two protective obstacles, this superb traverse over six neighbouring hills might receive the trampling suffered daily by the classic ridge walks of the Glyders. The first is that the ridge is tucked away in that unfashionable corner of the national park west of Snowdon, where the hills are small and villages dowdy. The second is that the ridge does not curl round in a tidy semi-circle like the Snowdon Horseshoe but

Moel Hebog (far left) from the summit of Trum y Ddysgl. An alternative approach to the Nantlle Ridge from Cwm Pennant ascends the sunlit spur centre left. *Moel Hebog (ar y chwith eithaf) o gopa Trum y Ddysgl. Y mae'r ffordd arall at Esgair Nantlle o Gwm Pennant yn dringo'r clogwyn heulog (canol / chwith).*

strings itself out with linear inconvenience.

The first obstacle isn't really one at all. You approach with an open mind, that's all. Removing the second requires a little more ingenuity, because there is no practical means of returning by public transport to the start at Rhyd Ddu. Three possibilities suggest themselves. The first and most obvious is to park a second car at Cwm Silyn beforehand (or arrange to swap keys with a party walking the ridge in the opposite direction—hard luck if you happen to pass each other in the mist). The second is to ignore convention and not begin at Rhyd Ddu or Cwm Silyn at all, but in Cwm Pennant on the south side of the ridge. Unfortunately this route misses an interesting scramble at the start, and faces a heathery struggle at the end. It compensates with circular convenience and the charm of Cwm Pennant. The third is simply to turn

around at Garnedd Goch and walk back along the full length of the ridge. Double the traverse: double the pleasure. Naturally this presupposes you enjoyed it the first time around.

Stories of gun-toting farmers and man-eating dogs have passed into folklore since the national park authority negotiated a ceasefire in the long-running access war between farmers and walkers in the Nantlle area. Now a waymarked path crosses the once bloody battlefield where sticks were shaken and ankles bitten and young men gave up their trouser bottoms so that future generations would be free to walk up Y Garn without threat or hindrance. Halfway up that demoralising grind up the east slope of Y Garn you might begin to wish they hadn't bothered.

Y Garn summit might be a good place to sit down and admire the craggy south side of

Mynydd Mawr opposite, or study the west flank of Snowdon behind, except that it comes too soon. A quick slug of mountain air for medicinal purposes and it's time to go, scrambling up the ridge towards Mynydd Drws y Coed, teetering around gendarmes and gasping at the consequences of tripping over your boot laces. A less consequential route creeps up the gentler left side of the ridge, but there's little point choosing an intoxicating route like the Nantlle Ridge only to dilute the thrill with watery variations.

A retrospective view from Trum y Ddysgl, the third summit, reveals the west face of Mynydd Drws y Coed in all its fascinating ugliness. You wouldn't believe grass could cling to a cliff face set at so severe an angle. Sheep would need abseil ropes to graze it. At Trum y Ddysgl the ridge undergoes one of its many abrupt changes of character, becoming a strip

Y Garn, first summit on the Nantlle Ridge, from Rhyd Ddu. The path ascends the grass shoulder on the left. *Y Garn, copa cyntaf Esgair Nantlle, o'r Rhyd-ddu. Mae'r llwybr yn dringo'r trum glaswelltog ar y chwith.*

of grass so smooth and level that you could run a motor mower over it. When low cloud isolates it from the rest of the world it looks like the popular vision of Heaven. In normal conditions the neck of ridge which follows barely warrants scrambling status, but on a gusty day you'll see people clinging to each other like sailors in a stormy sea.

On Mynydd Tal y Mignedd the ridge reverts to the character of a gentle hill walk. Here is a great carpet of grass and a stone wall guiding the way to the summit obelisk, a five metre stone tower built by quarrymen to celebrate Queen Victoria's jubilee. Ignoring the advice of your companions, you may attempt to climb the obelisk. There's not much to choose between the four faces, though it's worth remembering that the higher you climb, the less is the overburden pressing down on the stones. In other words, at the bottom you would need a jemmy to prise out the blocks,

whereas near the top you can pull them out and slide them back like drawers in a dressing table.

A fence leads the way to Bwlch Dros Bern, the deepest col of the traverse. Here the ridge narrows and steepens until even the fence is unable to keep its feet and tumbles over in a tangle of rotting wood and rusting wire. If we weren't so preoccupied with staying upright ourselves this disgraceful mess might be something to get really angry about.

Gentle valleys to left and right of Bwlch Dros Bern invite with uncomplicated solutions to the problem of the crag at the far side of the col. But that would be cheating. Scrambling enthusiasts will pounce eagerly on the direct line and spend a happy half hour getting stuck and foisting loose blocks on to each other's heads. Everyone else will take a cunning zig-zag to the right, for which they hardly need bother taking their hands out of their

pockets.

Rocks litter the summit area of Craig Cwm Silyn; not rocks fallen innocently from cliffs, but rocks sprouting maliciously from the ground. They make for slow going. By now all pretences at ridge walking have been dropped, and the final summit of Garnedd Goch lies some distance away at the far side of an extensive plateau. Interest is confined to the right edge, where promontories hint at concealed precipices beneath (cross the saddle between the two summits then creep to the edge above Cwm Silyn to discover the huge rock prow of Craig yr Ogof). And with that it is time to come down; over the bouncy grass of Garnedd Goch's north shoulder into Cwm Silyn, or through the interminable heather of Cwm Ciprwth into Cwm Pennant, or, best of all, back along the twists and turns of the ridge to Rhyd Ddu.

24: MOELWYNS AND EIFIONYDD — Yr Eifl and Braich y Pwll

Route summary: Rough upland walking over minor coastal summits, visiting the site of an ancient hill settlement. An optional short second walk explores the rugged coast at the tip of the Lleyn Peninsula.

Difficulty: Class B

Main summits: Tre'r Ceiri 485m/1590ft; Yr Eifl 564m/1850ft.

Duration: 8km/5miles; 500m/1650ft of ascent; allow 3hrs. (3km/2miles and 1-2hrs for Braich y Pwll).

Terrain: Paths through grass and heather with one trackless marshy area. Road walking to start and finish. (Narrow clifftop path at Braich y Pwll).

Special difficulties: The traversing path and gully on the lower part of the descent from Yr Eifl demand caution and are unsuitable for young children, as is part of the cliff-top path at Braich y Pwll (this can be avoided, however).

Approach: Yr Eifl: Approach along the A499 from Caernarfon or Pwllheli. Turn off on the B4417 to Llanaelhaearn. Roadside parking on the south side of the village (GR:386 448). Braich y Pwll: Approach through Aberdaron (refer to Eifionydd map) and along narrow lanes to the car park at the summit of Mynydd Mawr (GR:140 258).

Route directions

Yr Eifl:

Follow the B4417 rising out of the village for about 1km. Take the path on the right (marked "Public Footpath") and follow it uphill to the left of a wall. Trend left beyond a gate, cross a fence by a stile, and continue along the path through heather and bracken. Fork right and ascend more steeply up a stony path to the summit of Tre'r Ceiri.

Descend north to the stone wall and follow it leftwards to a break. Descend to the marshy saddle between Tre'r Ceiri and Yr Eifl (GR:370 447). Continue along a vague path, rising leftwards, to an eventual junction with a better path just below the summit of Yr Eifl.

Descend initially north-east from the summit then turn north-west down a featureless slope to the track at Bwlch yr

On the descent from Yr Eifl, looking north to Gurn Ddu. *Wrth ddod i lawr o'r Eifl; golygfa i gyfeiriad y gogledd a'r Gurn Ddu.*

Eifl (GR:361 453). Turn right and follow the track until about 50m beyond the gated track leading left into the quarries. Fork right here, following a narrow path to a wall/fence line. Turn right along a contouring path above very steep slopes until a gully leads down through the cliff barrier. Contour rightwards across the hillside and go through a gate at a junction of fences. Follow the path to a forestry plantation, diverting around it through fields on the left to reach a surfaced lane. Turn right and follow the lane back to Llanaelhaearn.

Braich y Pwll:
Explore at will, (refer to main text for a suggested walk around the headland).

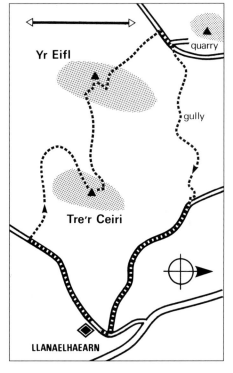

A lobster boat passes through Bard-sey Sound and rounds the rock promontory of Braich y Pwll. *Cwch cimychod yn hwylio o gwmpas pentir caregog Braich y Pwll.*

a headland or scrunch pebbles on a beach. Hence the fragmentary nature of this chapter.

Some hills are more beautiful to look at than to climb. The three peaks of Yr Eifl, otherwise known as The Rivals, belong to this category. Viewed at a distance from Nantlle or Anglesey, and therefore against the sun, they appear like the misty mountains of an enchanted land. Romantics leave the main road to view them across Caernarfon Bay from the beach at Dinas Dinlle. Hints of the Black Cuillin of Skye. Imagine Neptune's trident thrust up from the far headland and draped with a green blanket: the right-hand prong, brutally quarried, overlooks the sea; the central and highest prong is Yr Eifl summit; and that on the left, the site of the ancient settlement of Tre'r Ceiri.

A close approach textures the pure shape of Yr Eifl with bracken and boulders, and blemishes the fanciful image with fenced pastures, quarry buildings and power lines. Disenchantment. These hills are, after all, not so much low highlands as high lowlands. Precious little escapes domestication. This is not a modern trend. The collapsed walls of Tre'r Ceiri, Town of the Giants, litter the eastern summit of Yr Eifl. Pre-Roman in origin, the purpose of this hill settlement is something of a mystery. Being a conical hill, with unob-

structed views to all sides, it was an obvious choice from a defensive point of view, though there are few clues as to how the large number of residents (there is evidence of more than a hundred circular huts) sustained themselves through the winter—if indeed they did. I spent some time alone here one blustery day, trying to capture something of the way of life two thousand years ago. But my feeble knowledge of history failed to make the connections through time. I saw no ghosts. Then I felt the cold wind on my face and the hard stone under my feet and the intervening centuries contracted into nothing. Never mind the changes wrought by time, think of the common thread.

A little-used direct route to Yr Eifl's main peak finds a gap in the defensive wall, sloshes through bogs at the saddle, and finally plods upwards through heather tussocks. Nothing a pair of boots can't handle. The view from the elongated summit equals that from Tre'r Ceiri, provided you take the trouble to wander around its perimeter. Neighbouring Gurn Ddu, mottled with heather and stones, sweeps down to villages clustered on the narrow coastal plain around the curve of Caernarfon Bay. Inland the hills of Eifionydd appear over the shoulder of Tre'r Ceiri, part of a chain briefly interrupted by the Porthmadog lowlands before it re-establishes itself in the Rhinogs and Cader Idris. The most compelling view is that to the south-west, along the tail of the peninsula and into the glare of the afternoon sun. Misty enchantment again.

There are no clean ascent routes to the summit of the third peak from Bwlch yr Eifl. Eaten away by quarries, and messy with fences and buildings, it is much less attractive than it seemed. I turned away with little regret and began the return to Llanaelhaearn by the cliff path.

Watch how you go. The path skirts the top of an extremely steep slope and then descends a heather gully through the cliff barrier. Some of it is little wider than a sheep track; safe enough if you take your time, but not a place for exuberance. It was just before descending the gully that I surprised a herd of feral goats sunning themselves on the rocks. They looked at me disdainfully for a few seconds and then took off down the gully. I followed at a more sedate pace and by the time I emerged from its confines they were already back on the cliff, grazing some apparently inaccessible patch of grass.

Something happens on the drive to Braich y Pwll. The invisible twine that binds us to Snowdonia, already stretched to its limit on Yr Eifl, finally snaps. Instead of straining to see

Unequal measures of earth, sea and sky make Wales what it is. True, the earth is often folded, rarely flat; the sea angry, rarely calm; the sky tortured, rarely settled. But the stirring is incomplete. In Llangollen and Brecon the mainland mix of land and sky predominates; whereas in Anglesey and Pembroke it is the island mix of sea and sky with a thin strip of earth underfoot. Only on the Lleyn Peninsula, a forked tongue of land flattened and scalloped at the edges, do the three components evenly blend.

The best way to see the Lleyn is to drive (or cycle) anti-clockwise around its coastline, parking up at intervals to climb a hill, explore

upwards from the side window to summits and sky, we gaze out and down to beaches, head lands and the sea.

Braich y Pwll lies at the extreme western tip of the Lleyn Peninsula, opposite Bardsey Island. A narrow road winds up to a car park near the coastguard lookout post at the top of Mynydd Mawr, a hill perched defiantly at the peninsula tip. From here a concrete path leads down steps and past the site of an old signalling station on to the promontory of Braich y Pwll itself. From here you can see across the treacherous sound to Bardsey Island, once a place of pilgrimage and reputed resting place of 20,000 saints. To get the true feel of the sea you need to continue down the promontory until grass gives way to rock. Except in rough weather, or when storm rollers are breaking over the headland, you can descend the gently angled rocks to within a few metres of the waves. On returning to grass, a contouring path can be followed to the right around headlands and indents, alternating pleasant seaside strolling with nervous shuffling above sinister convex slopes.

The path degenerates on the fourth promontory and a short, breathless ascent brought me to a minor summit and a final opportunity to gaze out at Bardsey Island before nightfall. A small fishing boat struggled bravely against the tide through the sound, while above it a cormorant, black and determined, flew unswervingly into wind with some dark purpose in mind.

Looking down the north coast of the Lleyn Peninsula from the summit of Yr Eifl. *Golygfa i gyfeiriad glannau gogleddol Penrhyn Llŷn o gopa'r Eifl rhwng Ynys Enlli a'r tir mawr.*

CAMBRIAN MOUNTAINS

Maps: At 1:50,000 scale, five of the walks conveniently appear on Landranger Sheet 124 (Dolgellau), while the Plynlimon route appears on Sheet 135 (Aberystwyth). For good measure, Arenig and Aran are also included on Sheet 125 (Bala & Lake Vyrnwy), which is required for the Berwyns walk (chapter 2). This scale is adequate for all the walks when supplemented by notes extracted from the route descriptions. At 1:25,000 scale the situation is slightly more complicated. Arenig and most of the Rhinog Ridge (the devious bit) are shown on Outdoor Leisure 18 (Snowdonia— Harlech & Bala), whereas the southern tip of the Rhinog Ridge, Cader Idris, the Dolgellau walks, and the Arans, appear on Outdoor Leisure 23 (Cader Idris area). Both maps are double-sided and therefore good value.

Bases: The walks are spread throughout a large area. By far the best base for those with private transport is Dolgellau, which stands at a junction of several main roads and offers all types of accommodation, including camping. It can be reached by bus from all directions (rail stations at Machynlleth and Barmouth), though relying on the sketchy services to reach the walks will be limiting.

'Cambrian Mountains' is a catch-all heading for the five distinct mountain groups scattered about the southern limb (and beyond) of the Snowdonia National Park: Arenigs, Rhinogs, Arans, Cader Idris and Plynlimon. If they have anything in common it is their facility to surprise and delight walkers who think they have seen and done it all before.

Every type of walk is here, from the ambles around Dolgellau to the exhausting traverse of the Rhinog Ridge—the most arduous route in the book. Certain parts of the Arenigs and Arans are like the Moelwyns; parts of Cader Idris like Snowdon; and parts of Plynlimon like the Berwyns. Then again, other parts are like nothing else at all.

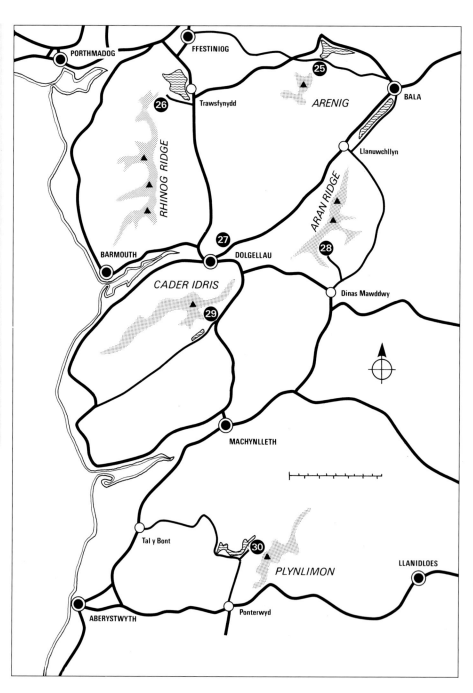

25: CAMBRIAN MOUNTAINS — *Arenig Fawr*

Route summary: Visits a mountain lake then ascends an isolated peak by rough paths. The summit brings panoramic views of all major mountain groups in Snowdonia.

Difficulty: Class C.

Main summits: Arenig Fawr 854m/2801ft.

Duration: 13km/8miles; 550m/1800ft of ascent; allow 4-5hrs.

Terrain: Stony track then narrow paths over grass and rock. Marshy ground on the descent. Track and road to finish.

Special difficulties: Difficult route-finding in mist in the region of the boggy plateau.

Approach: From Bala or Trawsfynydd along the A4212. When almost opposite the B4391 junction to Ffestiniog, turn south along a minor road and follow it eastwards for about 3km. There is parking space for about four cars at GR:846 396, opposite the track leading up to Llyn Arenig Fawr.

Route directions: Follow the stony track (gate and stile at the start) to the dam at Llyn Arenig Fawr. Cross the dam and ascend the ridge beyond the lake by a narrow path to a level area with boulders. Step over a fence (blocks in place) and continue to a boggy plateau (GR:835 378). Take the narrow path which leads leftwards across the south-east flank of the summit ridge. Quit the path when it begins to lose height and ascend steeply up to the ridge. Turn left and follow the stony crest up to the summit of Arenig Fawr.

Retrace the ascent route down the ridge then continue north-east to a junction of fences at a minor top (GR:829 373). Step over the fence (blocks) and turn left to descend the north-west ridge. Cross a marsh at its base to gain a transverse track (GR:815 379). Turn right and follow the track to its junction with the minor approach road. Turn right and follow the road for about 2km back to the start.

Alternatives: Return from the summit by the line of ascent if the marsh and road walk of the circular route do not appeal.

View south from the summit of Arenig Fawr. The Aran Ridge is on the far left. Golygfa i gyfeiriad y de o gopa Arennig Fawr. Y mae Esgair Yr Aran ar y chwith.

Is there life beyond Ffestiniog? As we drove past the 'highest petrol station in Wales' on the unfenced back road to Bala we saw no movement except for a 'closed' sign, rocking and creaking in the wind. Sheep prowled the verges and swaggered on to the tarmac with the self-confidence of wild animals in a Safari park, mildly curious at our vehicle and in no hurry to allow it through.

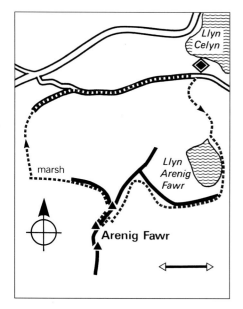

I'd forgotten about Arenig Fawr. We rounded a bend and suddenly it was there before us; a wave in the sea of moor, its crest breaking darkly. We stopped at the roadside to sniff the air and get a feel for the mountain before approaching too closely. Despite multiple summits and prominent ridges there was nothing distinctive about its shape. A patch of forestry creeps towards its western flank and a disused quarry bites into its northern shoulder, though neither impinges severely on the view. Pity about the pylons stomping across the foreground.

What brought us to Arenig Fawr on this day? It is not an impressive mountain, and it is too isolated to be incorporated into a ridge traverse. Naturally it is popular with visitors staying near Bala, who have little enough choice, but otherwise it comes low down on the hit-list of summits. It must be said that most come here when possibilities in other mountain areas have been exhausted.

Our first human encounter was with a picnicking family on the Llyn Arenig Fawr track. The father clearly felt uncomfortable at being seen with lolloping dog, sandwich boxes and deck chairs. As we passed he assured us that we would enjoy magnificent views from the summit—a pleasantry designed to assure us of his hill walking credentials.

We got no pleasure from walking over the imported rubble of the dam access track. A cloud of sticky flies added to our disgust. We flicked them off our clothing and they fell to the ground, unable to support their floppy black bodies on undersized wings. Our clumsy boots squashed those unable to crawl into the heather. There were so many. Bugs apart, we saw little of interest until we came across a large cracked boulder by the track. It must have stood untouched for thousands of years until some unknown force (a JCB bucket?) tipped it over and split it in two, revealing a pale interior yet to be colonised by lichen. We explored the boulder as if it were a fallen dinosaur.

At the lake we wandered up and down the low dam wall, dazzled by water suddenly ignited by a full afternoon sun, only now revealed by the parting strips of cloud. There was cirrus about and tomorrow it would rain, but for now we could screw up our eyes and tingle in the blaze. We forded the outflow and hid from the spray behind the dam wall to eat a conspiratorial lunch.

Eager for new sights, we took the initial rise of the ridge too fast and suffered for it. Where it steepened we put our heads down and laboured slowly upwards, hand on thigh, until the dam was far below and we felt sick with effort. A large party we had seen earlier as specks on the skyline had defected to swim in

Llyn Arenig Fawr.

On the summit ridge of Arenig Fawr, Aran Ridge in the background. *Ar y trum ar ben Arennig Fawr. Gwelir Esgair Yr Aran yn y cefndir.*

the lake. We watched their frolicking in the few minutes before the crags threw a chilling shadow over the water and sent them scurrying down the track.

Our first view of the summit was not an encouraging one. The sun was behind it, robbing the shape of detail and therefore upsetting our sense of scale. It looked a long way off. We assumed this was an illusion and plodded on regardless over the shoulder. Beyond a boggy plateau we could have made straight for the summit ridge but instead sought shelter from the wind on a path contouring the inner flank. First the Berwyns came into view, then a segment of Bala lake, and then the Aran ridge and Rhobell Fawr. Impatient for the top, we did not pause to study them. Where the path narrowed to a sheep track we struck a direct line up to the ridge, emerging into the windstream and facing a panorama of western hills. Within minutes we stood at the summit.

Now we could see every major hill group in North Wales: Cader Idris, the Rhinogs, Eifionydd, Snowdon, Moelwyns, Glyders, Carneddau. But these were mere silhouettes on the horizon, significant and recognisable only through familiarity. Instead it was the near-by smaller peaks of Arenig Fach, Moel Llyfnant, and Arenig Fawr's lower summit, that contributed most to the shape and texture of the landscape.

Erected at the summit circle shelter is a memorial to the crew of a Flying Fortress which crashed into the mountain in 1943. Now I felt guilty that earlier in the day I had cursed the screaming jet planes on training exercise. As one who lives beneath a regular flight path I am torn between admiration and fury. Sometimes we complain to the local RAF base. "The sound of a low-flying aircraft", they tell us, "is the sound of freedom".

An electric fence, piles of discarded poles

and redundant coils of rusting wire accompanied our descent. Merely the latest in a series of intrusions which began with the pylons, pine forests, quarries, tracks, dams and planes. What fools we are to think of these as *our* mountains!

Like the sun we too had lost our vitality and were being overtaken by cloud and rain. The first specks fell as we sloshed through the marsh to reach the old track that would return us to the north side of the mountain. It didn't matter any more. Darkness came on the road back to Ffestiniog. We drove along the white line to avoid sheep that had settled down on the warm tarmac at the road edge. The wind had dropped and not even the garage sign swung on its hinges. Ours was the only movement in a land stilled by night.

Route summary: A long and arduous ridge traverse, initially among wild and rugged terrain with few obvious paths. The most challenging of the walks selected for this book.

Difficulty: Class E.

Main summits: Moel Ysgyfarnogod 623m/2044ft; Rhinog Fawr 720m/2362ft; Rhinog Fach 711m/2333ft; Y Llethr 754m/2475ft; Diffwys 750m/2462ft.

Duration: 37km/23miles; 1900m/6250ft of ascent; allow 10-14hrs.

Terrain: First along intermittent paths through heather and marshland, then by poor paths over steep slopes of grass, heather and boulders, and finally on superb grass paths over rounded ridges.

Special difficulties: Complex route-finding (extremely so in mist) on the northern section. Numerous short scrambles of minor difficulty. Otherwise the main problems are cumulative, due to the unusual length of the traverse. Although there is no right of way, the National Park Authority have—with the permission of the landowners—erected stiles along the ridge. Access is withheld for one day each year (Feb. 5th).

Approach: From Dolgellau or Ffestiniog along the A470 (or from Bala along the A4212) to Trawsfynydd. Park a few hundred metres down the single-track road which leaves the A470 at GR:711 346 (or in a lay-by on the main road a short distance north).

Route directions: Map reading skills are assumed, so these directions merely outline the walk:

Leave the lane at GR:684 358 on a signed footpath leading up left. It briefly levels beyond a fourth gate (GR:678 358). Here bear left up grass and heather among rocks, carefully crossing a stone wall, to the cairned top of the first peak—Moel y Gyrafolen (GR:672 353). Continue west then south-west along the ridge over Diffwys (several craggy descents) to the Moel Ysgyfarnogod trig point.

Descend south from between the two summits and continue in roughly the same direction (more notches), passing to the left of Llyn Corn-ystwc (GR:657 335),

The Rhinog Ridge from the east. Y Llethr is in the centre, Rhinog Fach to its right, and Rhinog Fawr isolated on the far right. Esgair Rhinog o'r dwyrain gyda'r Llethr yn y canol, Rhinog Fach i'r dde, a Rhinog Fawr ar ei phen ei hun yn y canol.

Below: On the descent from Y Llethr to the walled crest of Crib y Rhiw. Diffwys is on the right, Cader Idris in the background. *Wrth ddisgyn o'r Llethr at grib furiog Crib y Rhiw, gyda Diffwys ar y dde a Chadair Idris yn y cefndir.*

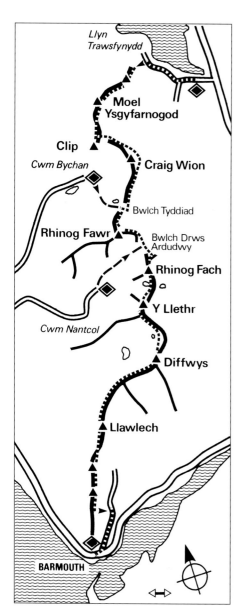

Right: Looking back to Rhinog Fach during the ascent to Y Llethr. Golygfa i gyfeiriad Rhinog Fach wrth ddringo'r Llethr.

to the saddle north-east of Clip (GR:656 330). Descend steeply south-east (path) to Bwlch Gwylim and ascend in the same direction to Craig Wion, or, more pleasantly, flank it to the left via two small lakes (path). Regain the ridge, here broad and marshy, and follow it south then south-west, now on a better path twisting through outcrops and rifts, to Bwlch Tyddiad.

Descend the Roman Steps west for a few hundred metres to a gap in a wall (GR:657 301). Turn left and ascend by the wall, following it throughout until it levels at a shoulder (GR:652 292). Turn left and follow a rising path and tongue of bouldery scree to the summit of Rhinog Fawr.

Descend east, past a cairn, on to a promontory. Fork left and descend east then south to Bwlch Drws Ardudwy. Ascend steeply up the far side and follow the easing path left then right to the summit ridge of Rhinog Fach.

Avoid crags by descending east then south, by the wall, to the bwlch above Llyn Hywel. Ascend the far side by a steep path to the right of rocks, emerging on a grass ridge. Turn right and follow its crest to the summit of Y Llethr.

From here the ridge path over Crib y Rhiw and beyond is obvious (but remember to turn right at the junction of walls just south of Diffwys for the dog-leg to Llawllech). Mostly the path follows the right side of the wall, but cross to the left by a gate at GR:635 218 to avoid climbing walls later (re-cross by a stile at about GR:622 183).

Quit the ridge at a gate and stile at Bwlch y Llan (GR:622 176) and descend left, past the transmitting station, to a surfaced lane at GR:628 176. Turn right and follow the lane into Barmouth.

Alternatives:

(1) A shortened ridge traverse avoids the tortuous northern section by starting from the car park at the head of Cwm Bychan and ascending the Roman Steps to join the main route at Bwlch Tyddiad.

(2) An even shorter version avoids Rhinog Fawr as well (and therefore almost all of the nasty bits) by starting from the head of Cwm Nantcol, joining the main route at Bwlch Drws Ardudwy.

Every book of this sort ought to include at least one route which is so daunting in prospect, so gruelling in execution, that thousands aspire but only dozens succeed. This is that route.

A terrible reputation for difficult terrain discourages many aspirants. "Up to your waist in

Llyn Pryfed on the east side of Craig Wion, one of several small lakes encountered on the rough northern section of the Rhinog Ridge. Llyn Pryfed ar ochr ddwyreiniol Craig Wion, un o amryw o lynnoedd bach a geir yn y rhan ogleddol arw o Esgair Rhinog.

heather and boulders," they say, "weaving and twisting like a roller-coaster." But that's a grain of truth buried under a mountain of exaggeration: it describes only seventeen of the thirty seven kilometres, and the final stint is as gentle as a Berwyn hillock.

The Rhinog Ridge is more than a mountain walk; it is a journey through Wild Wales from Trawsfynydd to Barmouth—thirty kilometres without touching a road. For all that the notion of 'wilderness' and the commitment to it are illusions: east or west, a road is never far away. Nevertheless, the route's adherence to the ridge ensures a strong sense of purpose. A lowland walk as arduous as this would never be completed. What began as a walk and became a journey becomes, ultimately, a challenge. So don't expect to stroll into Barmouth whistling a merry tune at the end of the day. Be content to have got there at all.

Without grit, nothing. And yet grit by itself is insufficient for the task. You have to be clever too: clever with timing and transport, clever with provisions and morale. Look at the facts. An averagely fit walker will take twelve hours or so to complete the route. That cuts out the period October to March, unless you are prepared to use headtorches on the final section (a pre-dawn traverse of the complex initial ridge section is unthinkable). In June or July you could have a lie-in and start as late as 8am, but otherwise you will need to set off at first light.

Good weather is the next pre-requisite for success. Although the ridge is feasible in almost any conditions, rain would bring misery, and

mist, confusion. The best day is a bright and breezy one. Most opt for a north-south traverse. Although that means facing the sun for much of the day, it is imperative to tackle the most difficult terrain first, saving the easy stuff for later (when nothing else will do). Ideally, park a second car at the Barmouth end. Otherwise trust to luck and hitch a lift, or catch one of the infrequent buses (four or five per day, and fewer than that out of season).

By choosing to go in summer and in good weather you can cut back on clothing and emergency equipment (hint: keep the torch) and take extra food. You can't eat a spare pair of gloves! (Then again, you can't warm your hands inside a blackcurrant and apple fruit pie). Water is not a problem. Only the section beyond Y Llethr is dry, by which time the end is in sight.

Having arranged for lots of daylight, good weather and food, all you need is lots of morale. Being 'walking fit' is good for morale, so is sharing the walk with a capable and enthusiastic companion. This is no place to introduce novices to hill walking: before the day is out you would have grown to hate them and they you. Above all, wait until the desire is strongest; set off in a negative mood and you won't finish.

I apologise if all this sounds a bit too much like planning a military campaign. I'm merely trying to emphasise the need to remove obstacles to success because, uniquely among the routes in this book, succeeding is primarily what the Rhinog Ridge is about. It is a big day.

It was a big day for me too. Though I'd walked sections of the ridge before, I'd never

The mouth of the Mawddach Estuary, crossed by the Cambrian Coast Railway, at the end of the Rhinog Ridge. *Aber Mawddach a groesir gan Reilffordd y Cambrian, ar ben eithaf Esgair Rhinog.*

strung them all together. Then my partner phoned at six o'clock that morning to cancel. What to do? The weather was perfect; I would go alone. The kids waved goodbye from their bedroom windows as I drove away into the sunrise. It was like going off to war.

I first saw the ridge from Ffestiniog, dwarfed behind the sinister twin towers of Trawsfynydd nuclear power station. The apparent domination was a trick of perspective; the plant could blow itself to bits and leave the ridge, the remnants of a several-hundred-million-year-old grit sandwich, largely untouched. A mist from yesterday's rain had already lifted from the heather, and as I walked up a sunken path between trees the patches of blue got bigger and bigger. By the time I reached open pastures it was 8.30am and hot enough for shorts and sunglasses—an ominous development so early in the day. Fortunately a breeze had got up with the sun and so a struggle up pathless bilberry slopes on Moel y Gyrafolen—the first objective —was fractionally less unpleasant than it might have been.

The first section is a ridge only in the broadest sense of the term. It is more of a longitudinal Lost World raised up on embankments, isolated in its own peculiar ecosystem of heather and bilberry and marsh. The stratified sedimentary rock which outcrops at every opportunity is unlike anything else in North Wales. A coarse-textured grit, it lies in huge, near-horizontal slabs. Subsequent weathering has produced stepped terraces on the flanks and pavements on the crest (in one place I saw a family of feral goats sunbathing on their patio). At several points the ridge is cut by unexpected lateral chasms guarded by outcrops five or ten metres high. In mist there is endless scope for misadventure.

Rhinog Fawr was not the monster I had feared. It was hard going to start and finish, but there was a pleasant interlude above beautiful Llyn Du. I found myself alone at the summit, and this on a fine summer afternoon. Perhaps this is not so surprising: this is an uncompromising and rather ugly hill to climb by itself. In the context of the ridge it is merely the toughest of several tough obstacles. The reward comes later.

A direct descent to Bwlch Drws Ardudwy is out of the question. From the map it is quite clear that you must first descend on to the eastern promontory. But here lies a trap. The path splits, and the impatient ridge traverser will be tempted by the less worn but more direct right fork. Be warned: it leads down a steep gully and over nasty boulders, losing precious time.

Bwlch Drws Ardudwy is a forlorn place of heather and boulders, and a watershed in more ways than one. Recent efforts on Rhinog Fawr have erased the mental image of the preceding part of the ridge so that you have to get psyched-up all over again. This is a severe test of will-power, because ahead lies the most dispiriting ascent of the whole traverse—a scramble up a rut of mud and boulders to escape the bwlch and get established on Rhinog Fach.

The character shift from first to second stage is complete at the summit of Rhinog Fach. A view south to where Y Llethr rises above the improbably situated Llyn Hywel brings depth and dimension to the scene. Among proper mountains at last. At the bwlch, where rock slabs sweep down into Llyn Hywel, and where the sun is trapped by a sturdy wall, I lay down with a pile of sandwiches and cakes, and for half an hour pretended not to notice the looming presence of Y Llethr.

Y Llethr is the highest summit on the ridge —a fact of great psychological significance. Of more practical importance, the peak also introduces the third character type. Gone are the heather and boulders, the chasms and the twisting paths, and in their place the short grass of rolling hills with nothing more troublesome than a few stones to interrupt the flow. There's no kinder walking terrain than this.

Heaping riches upon the already rich, the views from Y Llethr were outstanding: of craggy Rhinog Fach poised above Llyn Hywel; of Cader Idris, a rock wave breaking at its tip into wisps of cloud; of Bardsey and the Lleyn, dark shapes in a shimmering sea; and of the walled crest of Crib y Rhiw, the Rhinog equivalent of the Great Wall of China. It was all so wonderful, except that on Diffwys my knees started to wobble, on Llawlech the soles of my feet began to sting, and at Bwlch y Rhiwgyr the last sparks of enjoyment flickered and died inside my brain. From now on the walk would be a test of endurance, an exploration of will-power. I'm not saying the remainder of the ridge was interminable, merely that it went on forever.

It was entirely typical that I should arrive in Barmouth twenty minutes after the last bus had departed. The harbour looked idyllic in evening light. Brightly coloured boats lay at anchor—the rail bridge in dark geometric contrast overhead —against a backdrop of Cader Idris pulling a cloud blanket over itself for the night. Pretty it may have been, but it wasn't home. There was nothing for it but to get a steak and kidney pie and two pints of shandy down my neck while I worked out what to do next.

It is every (male) hitch-hiker's fantasy to be offered a lift by a woman driving an open-top sports car. After thirty minutes of monitoring the traffic flow (dribble) out of Barmouth that night, I had modified my dream to include spotty-faced youths on mopeds and axe murders in Reliant three-wheelers. Then a young woman drove by in an open-top MG, studiously avoiding my stare and quivering thumb. Two minutes later I heard the familiar growl of the exhaust. She had come back for me. "You've made my day," I said, with no need for exaggeration. Then with the wind in our hair we drove along the winding road into the night, our heads full of summer and thoughts of the things we do.

27: CAMBRIAN MOUNTAINS — Short Walks from Dolgellau

Route summary: Two short walks sampling the hill and woodland scenery around Dolgellau. The Torrent Walk follows the tumbling progress of a river; the Precipice Walk circles a small hill for superb views.

Difficulty: Class A.

Duration: Torrent Walk: 3km/2miles; allow 1hr. Precipice Walk: 6km/4miles; allow 2hrs.

Terrain: Generally good paths (boots or wellingtons useful after prolonged wet weather).

Special difficulties: One section of the Precipice Walk is narrow and exposed, though with normal care—and close supervision of young children—it will present no difficulty.

Approach: Torrent Walk: From Dolgellau take the A470 Machynlleth road then turn left on a minor road after about 2km. Limited roadside parking after about 1km (GR:752 187), shortly before bridging the river. Precipice Walk: Leave the by-pass to

enter Dolgellau town and take the A494 Bala road. Turn left on a minor road and follow signs for Llanfachreth. There is a large car park at the left turn for Ganllwyd after about 4km (GR:745 212).

Route directions

Torrent Walk:

From the road bridge, follow the obvious upstream path on the right side of the river for a little over 1km to a footbridge. Return by the same route.

Precipice Walk:

From the car park, walk down the Ganllwyd road (sign: "Llwybr Cynwch, Precipice Walk") for about 100m. Turn left and follow a track and path, via two stiles, to the north shore of Llyn Cynwch. Fork right and follow the obvious path which circles the hill of Foel Cynwch in an anticlockwise direction, eventually returning to the south shore of the lake. Follow the lakeside track along the west shore to rejoin the approach path.

Built from attractive grey-green stone, the sturdy houses of Dolgellau—focus of rural prosperity in southern Snowdonia—sit shoulder to shoulder in cramped streets, exuding an atmosphere of proud permanence. Though the Mawddach estuary is near-by, the dominant influence on the town is not that of open sea and sandy shore but rugged mountain and fertile lowland. Situated within a wooded valley and overlooked by Cader Idris, its National Park credentials are beyond question.

OS maps identify both the Torrent Walk and the Precipice Walk as tourist attractions, ensuring their continuing popularity. The Precipice Walk circles a small but prominent hill and in doing so provides superb panoramic views of Cader Idris and the Mawddach estuary. In complete contrast the Torrent Walk cloaks itself in greenery as it follows the tumbling progress of a river through a tree-filled valley. The two walks complement each other and are easily combined in a single afternoon.

An inbuilt deficiency of the Torrent Walk as its non-circular nature. You start at one road

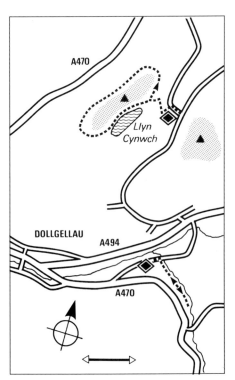

Above: The highlight of the Precipice Walk, where the narrow but secure path overlooks the river valley. Ar Rodfa'r Dibyn, Lle mae'r llwybr cul, ond diogel, yn edrych dros yr afon.

Facing page: Bird's eye view of the Afon Mawddach from the Precipice Walk. Golwg oddi uchod ar aber Afon Mawddach o Rodfa'r Dibyn.

Right: Hidden Llyn Cynwch, paradise for anglers and coots. Llyn Cynwch, paradwys gudd y pysgotwyr ac ieir y gors.

Not yet out of the woods on the Torrent Walk. *Yn y coed o hyd ar Rodfa'r Cenllif.*

bridge, walk up or down stream to the other, and then turn around and walk back again. The usual start from the Brithdir road has convenient parking but detracts with an uphill return. Besides, on my visit the footbridge near the start was in a dangerous condition and closed off (there is no alternative access from this end). Consequently I began from the lower road bridge and walked upstream. A much better arrangement, I think, provided the limited parking places are not all occupied.

Those coming to the Torrent Walk expecting spectacular waterfalls will be disappointed. In fact the path follows the river closely only at the lower and upper ends of the defile. For much of the time the river is out of sight altogether. Instead, the rushing water provides a backing soundtrack to a woodland stroll along a constructed path complete with steps and guard rails. You come here not for action but reflection, and depart with recollections not of rushing torrents but of a mossy boulder, a wild flower, a tree trunk thick with lichen (or midge bites, screaming kids, yapping dogs—it's all a matter of timing).

The Precipice Walk is entirely different in scope. It begins unpromisingly along a track which by-passes the grounds of Nannau House in its approach to the miniature reservoir of Llyn Cynwch set below a small hill. The purpose of the walk is not to climb the hill but to encircle it for kaleidoscopic views of forest, valley, estuary and mountain. Initially there is no hint of a precipice. Instead the sheep-grazed

pastures slope gently down into the valley and up the hillside opposite to where the tiny village of Llanfachreth perches (the first of several, rather patronising, information boards confirms this identification).

The outlook changes as the path curves round on to the northern flank of the hill. Sharp-eyed show-offs will identify the Snowdon group far to the north, although the dominant features of the scene are the extensive block plantations of conifers. Patches of mixed woodland are evidence of recent thinking in the Forestry Commission, but old mistakes take a long time to grow out in this business.

I once walked this path with Dafydd Elis Thomas, MP and president of Plaid Cymru (the Party of Wales). The weather had been perfect, the scenery magnificent. How lucky we were to live in such a fine country! But the mood had not been one of complacency. As we walked he pointed out the hideous rock scars of the 'improved' trunk road, the menacing bulk of Trawsfynydd nuclear power station, and the scattered cottages recently bought up as second homes. Seemingly idyllic, the scene was in fact one of contradiction and simmering conflict: narrow roads preserve character but suffocate commercial enterprise; nuclear power stations provide energy and employment but haunt with memories of Chernobyl; holiday homes attract tourists but hasten depopulation. These are the supposedly intractable problems of rural Wales, and yet the conver-

sation had been full of optimism for the 'workable' compromises that lay beyond dogmatism: sensitive road improvements, clean energy sources, alternative employment, housing quotas and quality tourism.

As the path progresses along the western slope of the hill it begins to earn its 'precipice' tag. Though level and secure, it is little more than a half-metre wide as it cuts across a 45° slope of scree and heather. It reaches a climax where the path bends sharply to cross a couloir of rocks and heather. Far below, the river meanders along the fertile base of the glaciated valley with the unreal perfection of a geography book diagram.

Beyond the 'precipice' the hillside lies back and turns to grass. Startled sheep sprint away from your approach, while the hawks hovering above the untrodden hill-top, their attention fixed to some small movement in the heather, pay no heed. With less cause for vigilance, the views broaden to include the sandy basin of the Mawddach estuary and the shadowy northern slope of Cader Idris. Its circumnavigation complete, the path comes once more to Llyn Cynwch, an irresistible attraction for anglers, coots and weary walkers.

28: CAMBRIAN MOUNTAINS — *Aran Fawddwy*

Route summary: A varied mountain walk to Aran's highest summit, approached by secluded valleys and a broad, marshy ridge. An optional route traverses the entire Aran Ridge.

Difficulty: Class C.

Main summits: Aran Fawddwy 906m/2971ft; (Aran Benllyn 884m/2901ft).

Duration: 13km/8miles; 775m/2550ft of ascent; allow 5-6hrs.

Terrain: Narrow path over grass and rock to start; boggy ground on the ridge; good paths and tracks to finish.

Special difficulties: Care required when descending in mist between Drws Bach and Hengwm.

Approach: From Machynlleth or Dolgellau along the A470 to Dinas Mawddwy. Turn off on the minor road to pass through the village. Turn left after about 1km (signposted "Cwm Cywarch") on to a single track road. After crossing a cattle grid the road enters a meadow; park considerately at its far side, where a track bears off to the left (GR:854 185).

Route directions: Walk to the end of the road, detour rightwards around a farm (waymarked), and then trend rightwards to cross a ladder stile. Turn left at once and follow a path up the hillside left of a stream. Cross the stream by a footbridge (GR:850 197) and ascend its right bank to a marshy saddle (GR:842 200). Turn right and follow the path to the right of the fence along the steepening ridge. Cross a stile over the transverse fence (GR:858 218) and continue uphill, passing a subsidiary top, to the summit of Aran Fawddwy.

Return to the junction of fences and re-cross the stile. Turn left and follow a rough path near the fence, down Drws Bach and out on to a prominent grass ridge. After crossing a transverse fence by a stile, descend slightly right on a vague path to a marshy saddle, identified on maps by a spot height at GR:875 205 (in misty conditions it may be better to ignore the path after crossing the stile and instead to follow the fence on the left until it turns sharp left at the saddle). From the saddle, follow the path (later a track) which slants down the side of Hengwm. After passing through a hawthorn tunnel, bridge the stream and turn left to follow the lane back to the parking area.

Alternatives:

(1) Continue along the ridge from Aran Fawddwy to the summit of Aran Benllyn. Return along the ridge to Aran Fawddwy and descend as for the main route.

(2) The full traverse of the Aran Ridge provides an equally rewarding and slightly longer walk (15km/9miles), though it does involve leaving a second car in Cwm Cywarch. Approach from Bala or Dolgellau along the A494 and turn off on the B4403 to Llanuwchllyn. Park at a lay-by on a sharp left bend (GR:880 297), about 1km from the junction. Cross a stile at the lay-by and follow the waymarked route on to the ridge. Ascend the ridge by a narrow path, mostly on its right side, to the summit of Aran Benllyn. Continue along the ridge crest to Aran Fawddwy and descend as for the main route.

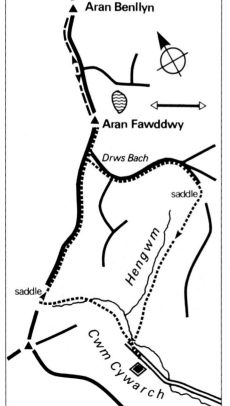

View north towards the Berwyns from the summit of Aran Fawddwy. Golygfa i gyfeiriad y gogledd a Mynyddoedd y Berwyn o gopa Aran Fawddwy.

Yesterday was summer: today is autumn. I knew it the moment I opened the front door and sniffed the air. High pressure had built overnight, pushing the rain clouds eastwards and erecting a refrigerating dome of frosty stars over the mountains. I would migrate south to Aran.

In the valleys a mist shifted upwards through foliage already turned yellow, while on intervening high ground the morning sun evaporated remnants of yesterday's showers into steamy spirals. The day was calm and bright, the clouds high and patchy. It was midweek and off-season and I would have Aran to myself.

Well, almost. In Cwm Cywarch I parked next to a car in which a woman and dog waited patiently. The woman smiled, the dog snarled. I think it wanted to cock its leg over my rucksack. Soon a man returned, binoculars bouncing on his chest and a bleached ram's skull in his hand, having narrowly outrun "the most unfriendly farm dogs you've every come across". He'd seen a buzzard—perhaps I would see it later—and a peregrine falcon yesterday. Yes, but would the skull be allowed in the car by his disgusted wife? The dog, misunderstanding, licked its lips. In the end the man got his way: it was for their son's Sunday School teacher. "Look what my Dad found!" the lad would say, thrusting it on to her lap. He would be told to put it on the nature table and then to go and wash his hands, thoroughly. Meanwhile the other children would gather round and poke pencils into its eye sockets.

Others were at work in the valley. A shepherd, buckled from age, drove his sheep to pasture. An old woman carried a zinc bucket into the field for some cow's milk for the house. Until fifteen years ago Aran was the forgotten corner of Snowdonia. Now half the homes in the valley advertise bed and breakfast or holiday cottages. The change has come too suddenly for some, leading to furious arguments over access. Precarious negotiations have secured temporary use of a small number of courtesy paths: across the saddle from Cwm Cywarch to Rhydymain; along the length of the main Aran ridge from Llanuwchllyn in the north to the Cywarch-Rhydymain saddle; from Aran Fawddwy down western slopes to Esgair Gawr (near Rhydymain); and from Aran Fawddwy to Cwm Cywarch via Drws Bach and Hengwm. From the walker's point of view this arrangement is adequate if not ideal. Discussions continue but in the meantime there is little scope for improvising routes away from the agreed paths.

Cwm Cywarch is everything a U-shaped valley should be: long, lush, and . . . well . . .

The footbridge below Craig Cywarch. *Y bont droed islaw Craig Cywarch.*

U-shaped. At each side its marshy floor curves up to high, parallel ridges where tree-lined pastures give way to bracken and open grazing. It is the sort of place you could choose to live out your life and then do so, slowly. The valley terminates abruptly below the vegetated buttresses of Craig Cywarch. From here a V-shaped valley rises steeply to a saddle on the Aran Ridge—the first objective. On the right the gently inclined valley of Hengwm bites deep into the hinterland east of the main ridge. This will be the return route from Aran Fawddwy. Between the two valleys projects a blunt spur, at the base of which nestles the climbers' hut of Bryn Hafod.

It was towards Bryn Hafod that I now walked, having failed to strike up a conversation with a grumpy fly-fisherman (the stream was barely deep enough to drown a cat, let alone hook a worthwhile fish, though I didn't venture this opinion). With no more excuse for delay I branched left up my tributary and

ascended the slope below Craig Cywarch. As I passed below its sunless and water-streaked North Buttress, a large bird soared over the top of the crag and began circling effortlessly on the updraught. It was a buzzard. Even I knew that.

After a concentrated bout of hill-bashing up the stream bank I emerged at a tranquil basin of streamlets and unidentified birdsong. Minutes later I stood at a pool on the saddle, where a signpost reminded me that I could return the way I had come to Cwm Cywarch, continue straight ahead over the saddle to Rhydymain, or turn right to "Y ddwy Aran"—the two Arans (although one would do nicely). I turned right.

Far away along the broad-backed ridge I could see the stony hump of Aran Fawddwy. Such a long way off. To stave off impatience I erased the sight from my memory and plodded off across the bogs with an empty head. Here and there I came across grotesquely

The summit of Aran Fawddwy seen from the upper part of Drws Bach. *Copa Aran Fawddwy o'r rhan uchaf o Ddrws Bach.*

slutchy hollows over which the thoughtful path-finders had laid wooden planks. Otherwise I have nothing to say about this part of the walk, except to agree with a solitary walker I met somewhere along its length that it was a "slog".

Even a slog can be satisfying when, as here, it imperceptibly draws you to within fifteen minutes of your summit. Nice surprise. Not so nice was the discovery, made only after eating a packet of salt and vinegar crisps and half of a Swiss roll, that I had left my flask in the car. I stashed the rucksack at the transverse fence and wandered sullenly up to the summit.

I recognised the pile of stones and trig point at the top, but not the unearthly stillness. The last time I stood here it had been a steely April day with old snow underfoot and a numbing easterly about my ears. The solitary walker was here, sitting on a rock slab with his feet dangling over the eastern precipice. Propped next to him was a flask from which he sipped contentedly. One little push and it would be mine.

I asked about his route to take my mind off homicide.

There was no point hanging around making small talk now that I'd decided to spare the man's life, so I scurried back down to my rucksack at the top of Drws Bach, that remarkable neck of grass which extends eastwards above Hengwm.

Above the awesome Hengwm flank stands a memorial cairn to Mike Aspain, a member of the RAF St Athan Mountain Rescue Team who was killed by lightning near here on the 5th June 1960 while on duty with the team. A donations box tucked under the cairn also contains a visitors book. In this you can record your name and moan about the weather or your companions. A quick count revealed that about four hundred entries had been made during the previous six months, confirming the increasing popularity of Aran. It had come too late for Kilroy, however.

The path into Hengwm follows a diagonal rake of geometric regularity. Though much maligned as a route of ascent, this path has the perfect inclination for a rapid descent. I suggest you slow to a jog where the path traverses the sides of stream indents, otherwise you can let rip as far as the sunken lane and hawthorn tunnel (where I suggest you duck). It was here that I saw two hyenas squabbling over the remains of what I assume was a lone walker who had overshot the path. Could these vicious wild animals be the "unfriendly farm dogs" from which the birdwatcher had escaped? They didn't see me as I hurried down the hawthorn avenue to the river, but as I turned to run the last few hundred metres to the car I could hear their hideous Baskervillean howls growing nearer. In two minutes it would all be over, one way or the other.

Route summary: A fine walk among the most impressive mountain scenery south of Snowdon. Begins strenuously through trees then circles the rim of a hidden cwm to incorporate three summits.

Difficulty: Class C.

Main summits: Mynydd Pencoed 791m/2595ft; Pen y Gadair 893m/2928ft; Mynydd Moel 863m/2832ft.

Duration: 11km/7miles; 975m/3200ft of ascent; allow 5-6hrs.

Terrain: Mainly good paths over grass, stones and rock on the ascent (some boggy sections); vague path down steep grass on the descent.

Special difficulties: In misty weather it would be better to descend by the ascent route than risk losing the way on the vague descent of Mynydd Moel.

Approach: From Dolgellau or Machynlleth along the A487. Large car park at Minffordd (GR:733 115), near the junction of the B4405 to Abergynolwyn.

Route directions: Walk down the Abergynolwyn road for a few hundred metres to the Idris Gates on the right. Go through the gates and follow a track over a footbridge to enter woodland. Zig-zag steeply up through trees on the bank of the stream to open ground where the angle eases. Continue along the path, curving into Cwm Cau, to a large cairn. Trend left up to the ridge crest and follow it to the summit of Mynydd Pencoed.

Continue circling the cwm, first down to a col then rising towards Pen y Gadair. Either continue direct to the trig point at the summit of Pen y Gadair, or divert left to the Tourist Track near Cyfrwy and follow that to the summit.

Descend north-east over boulders and follow the broad ridge, over a minor top, to the summit of Mynydd Moel. Cross a stile to the east, then descend the broad southern spur by a vague path near the fence line. Lower down the path trends right to regain the ascent route above the forestry plantation.

Snowdon summiteers gaze south on fine afternoons and point to a grey strip of land rising above an ocean of haze. "That's Cader Idris," they say, the more imaginative among them likening its shape to a submarine or some such elongated nautical object. "And if you screw up

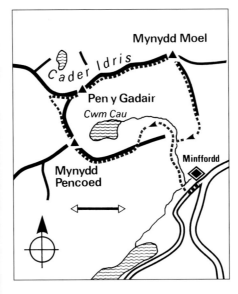

your eyes," their prosaic companions might add, "it could even be a long mountain in the distance".

But it isn't that. Get close and you will see a ruggedness and complexity in Cader Idris that is more typical of the Glyders, or Snowdon itself, than the soft simplicity of its grassy neighbours. You won't fully appreciate this until you've driven the dog-leg around the mountain from Dolgellau to Minffordd. This is the usual approach anyway, so you don't need to make a special effort. Just keep your eyes open.

First you will see the northern flank of the mountain (the broadside, if you like); the face is buttressed with cliffs for much of its length, the most dramatic of them appearing to the right of Pen y Gadair (the actual summit) in the area known as Cyfrwy. So far the mountain has been glimpsed between trees. Out of town the road rises clear of the valley and swings around the eastern end of the range. Soon after taking the Cross Foxes junction, a clear view opens up of Gau Graig and Mynydd Moel, the latter peak almost as high as Pen y Gadair itself and often mistaken for it (a traverse of the entire range could begin here). The road continues rising to a bleak pass then dips determinedly towards Tal y Llyn, clinging to the precipitous valley side as it does so. The road is narrow and bits of it crumble away from time to time, though this is less likely since completion of elaborate repairs. If you can spare your eyes from the road for a second you will see on the opposite side of the valley a for-

bidding hillside topped by crags. Only where the road levels out at Minffordd in the valley base, and from where a tree-filled breach appears to lead up towards a hidden cwm, is there any prospect of a reasonable ascent.

This is the start of the Minffordd Path, the finest way up the mountain. Follow it and you will climb up through the trees to enter Cwm Cau, circle its bounding ridge on to the main bulk of Cader Idris, view the cliffs of Cyfrwy during your ascent to Pen y Gadair, and then return over Mynydd Moel to complete a circular walk as good as any among the high cwms of Snowdon or the Glyders.

At Minffordd a set of iron gates bars entry to a secret garden. Grab the bars and shake them furiously to rouse the hunchback gatekeeper from his hovel, or slip unnoticed through the side gate and leave him to his slumbers. Inside is an unkempt avenue of trees, its once grand symmetry destroyed by a violent storm in the early eighties. Through a garden gate lies the enchanted wood, and twenty minutes of breathless toil up a zig-zagging path on the west bank of the Nant Cader. Bootsoles and drainage have scoured the soil away, undermining the knit of tree roots which now lie above ground in gnarled disarray; erosion control fences direct stomping feet away from the more sensitive parts. The sharp edge of a small conifer plantation marks the transition from woodland to mountain terrain. You can't yet see where you're going, but at least you know how to get there: by following the Nant Cader around the arm of the mountain to its source in the hidden cwm.

The expected view of Cwm Cau does not come. Instead, rising ground at the entrance conceals the lake and leaves the upper headwall of Craig Cau hanging unsupported. This is disappointing. But it's only a tease; as the path begins its ascent to the bounding ridge, Llyn Cau at last slides silkily into view. The path circling the rim of Cwm Cau flirts alternately with the precipitous inner edge and the gentle outer flank, from where you can gaze out over the rolling hills of Mid Wales and make plans for expeditions into a strange land. Cader Idris lies on the frontier between oneWales and another.

Near the summit of Mynydd Pencoed the ridge path passes close to the exit of Great Gully. In summer this is a rubble-filled cleft, overshadowed in every respect by the forbid-

Cyfrwy Arete in profile. The Table is the sunlit flat-topped tower at one third height. *Cyfrwy Arate o'r ochr. Gwelir y Bwrdd draean o'r Ffordd i Fyny, sef y tŵr pen-gwastad dan olau'r haul.*

ding prow of Pencoed Pillar on its south side, whereas a harsh winter transforms it into a snow-choked rift replete with adventure. Our ascent took place in marginal conditions, so that after struggling with ice spouts and chimneys of rotten rock we finally arrived at the steep exit only to find it snowless. The sun shone on the ridge above and we ached to escape the shivering uncertainty of the gully. So we swung the picks of our axes into soil frozen to the consistency of concrete and climbed on. The decision cost us dear in equipment (a £60 axe, ruined) but the memory has made us wealthy.

A collapsed fence litters the west side of Mynydd Pencoed, though neither hand of man nor hoof of sheep can interfere with the ecology of the eastern side which sweeps down to Llyn Cau at an untenable angle. The path continues its semi-circling of the cwm, first by dipping to a col, then by trudging over shattered rock towards Pen y Gadair. This final and uninspiring part of the ascent can be enlivened by contouring left to meet the Tourist Track—a popular if lacklustre ascent from the north—where it creeps around the lip of the impressive northern cwm. At its outer edge, beyond the scree slopes that slant down towards Llyn y Gadair, you will see the magnificent profile of Cyfrwy Arete, the prominent Table capping its lower third. Though barely more than a tough scramble, the rocks are worryingly loose; the pioneering skier Arnold Lunn, descending the arete in 1922, fell a hundred feet to serious injury after the huge block on which he stood detached itself from the mountain.

A short distance north of the rocky summit of Pen y Gadair lie the remains of a stone hut built in the early eighteen hundreds by Dolgellau guide Richard Pugh. Here walkers could buy refreshments "while waiting for the dispersion of misty clouds". It was used for this purpose for many years (the hut keeper was among those who helped Arnold Lunn after his fall), but unlike the Snowdon cafe did not have the regular influx of train-borne tourists to offset the diminishing demand from increasingly impecunious hill walkers. The misty clouds are still here, though the hut is now a dilapidated shelter and the refreshments do-it-yourself.

The traverse to Mynydd Moel takes you along the broad, stony back of the mountain. The path wanders cautiously across the middle, though by staying close to the edge you can peer down the northern ramparts and sustain the sense of elevation. Look north from Mynydd Moel and you will see the jumbled houses of Dolgellau, the gentle southern limb of the Rhinogs, and beyond that a grey strip of land rising above an ocean of haze: Snowdon, another long mountain in the distance.

Looking south towards Corris and Mid Wales from the ascent ridge to Mynydd Pencoed. *Golygfa tua'r de i gyfeiriad Corris a Chanolbarth Cymru o'r esgair sy'n codi at Fynydd Pencoed.*

106

Route summary: A secluded approach through remote valleys to rounded ridges and the highest summit in Mid Wales.

Difficulty: Class C.

Main summits: Pen Pumlumon Arwystli 741m/2430ft; Pen Pumlumon Llygad Bychan 727m/2385ft; Pen Pumlumon Fawr 752m/2468ft.

Duration: 14km/9miles; 600m/2000ft of ascent; allow 5hrs.

Terrain: Stony track; bridleway with frequent boggy sections; grass ridges (some of them pathless).

Special difficulties: Route-finding in mist on the cairned subsidiary shoulder of the main ridge.

Approach: Along the mountain road between Tal y Bont (on the A487 between Machynlleth and Aberystwyth) and Ponterwyd (on the A44 between Rhaeadr and Aberystwyth). Follow signs for Nant y Moch. At a bend in the road, about 1km east of the Nant y Moch dam, a surfaced track leads north-east along the side of the reservoir to a limited parking place for 2 cars at Maes Nant, almost at the end of the surfaced section (GR:774 879).

Route directions: Ignore the track leading down to the Maes Nant buildings and instead contour above the river on a track leading to a ruin at the confluence of the Afon Hengwm and Nant y Llyn. Fork right and ford the Nant y Llyn to follow a poor bridleway along the south bank of the Afon Hengwm to another ruin. Ascend by waterfalls to enter Cwm Gwarin. Cross the stream above a prominent switchback and ascend a grass spur to the right of crags to gain the cairn on the broad shoulder above (GR:808 897). Walk east to gain the main ridge at a saddle (in poor visibility it would be better to veer slightly

Looking back along the river approach from the crest of the cairned shoulder above Cwm Gwarin. Golygfa ar hyd yr afon o'r trum carneddog uwchlaw Cwm Gwarin.

north of east, entering a stream valley, and to follow a fence line up to the saddle).

Turn right and follow the fence line up the broad ridge to twin stone mounds at the summit of Pen Pumlumon Arwystli. (Note that the fence passes to the left of the actual summit; however, in bad visibility it can be followed throughout.)

Descend south-west to a saddle and continue along or near the fence line, over the summit of Pen Pumlumon Llygad Bychan and the saddle beyond, to the trig point and separate summit cairn of Pen Pumlumon Fawr.

Descend steeply north then turn north-west to flank or ascend the twin summits of Pumlumon Fach (the second top is the higher). Continue north-west down the spur until it steepens into a line of small outcrops. Trend left to follow a good path along the banks of the Maes Nant. Cross straight over a track and continue by the stream bank, avoiding the final ravine by steep grass further to its right.

Poor Plynlimon, highest hill in Mid Wales and barely anyone with a good word to say for it. So featureless is the southern slope that

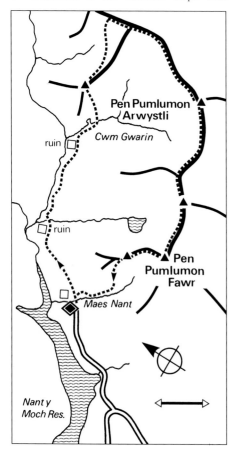

wooden stakes have been driven into the sodden ground to serve as marker posts in mist. In clear weather they help ease the monotony of the ascent. Beneath this slope passes the main road between Rhaeadr and Aberystwyth. It is a pleasant drive but few are tempted to leave their cars at Eisteddfa Gurig for the walk up Plynlimon, except perhaps for purgative purposes.

But Plynlimon also has a secret side, accessible only from the single-track mountain road between Tal y Bont and Ponterwyd. From the north-east shore of the Nant y Moch Reservoir, the valley of the Afon Hengwm penetrates deep into the uninhabited land north of Plynlimon: this route explores its ruins and waterfalls then escapes the lowlands for a high traverse of ridges where the wind blows unhindered. God has not forsaken Plynlimon, merely concentrated His attention on the northern side.

From Cader Idris I had seen the Mid Wales hills rippling the land into a wrinkled green skin. Because intervening valleys, roads and villages had been hidden, I assumed the region consisted entirely of sheep grazing and forestry. I came to Plynlimon expecting a green desert and found instead a new world of land and water. The narrow ribbon of the mountain road dipped and weaved into the heart of the range. In fifteen kilometres I passed no other car. I saw a lone angler at Llyn Nantycagl, and a birdwatcher at the Nant y Moch dam. In the next seven hours I would see no-one.

A surfaced track by the side of Nant y Moch Reservoir got me as far as Maes Nant, where the stream which drains the west slope of Pen Pumlumon Fawr (the Welsh spellings of individual summits have survived anglicisation of the collective name) topples down a ravine before entering the lake. Although there were glimpses of a summit high above, it was partially obscured by remnants of cloud from a morning of rain and I could not be sure. There would be time enough for that; high pressure

was forecast so the day could only improve. Already a speckling of blue hinted at a fine afternoon ahead.

The road degenerates to a stony track and contours the hillside above the Afon Hengwm to a ruin at the Nant y Llyn confluence. A corrugated iron lean-to suggests recent occupation, although the tree which has grown up inside the ruin, helping to prise away the walls from their foundations, is itself dying from old age. The surrounding fields are farmed by proxy.

Poor drainage leaves the Plynlimon valleys squelchy with bogs. The road which had become a track had now become a bridleway, and a scarcely used one at that. It flowed with streamlets so I resorted to following the drier riverbank, despite meanders. Nearby, a solitary and forlorn patch of sickly conifers marked a failed attempt at afforestation. It looked as though the sheep would have this place to themselves for some time yet. The bridleway came to an end at another ruin, this one more recently vacated. Mature trees overhung the building and although the roof had gone, the walls remained intact. Perched on the rubble of the collapsed ceiling was an iron bedstead, and on the river bank bloomed a solitary clump of daffodils. The place ached with emptiness.

A short distance upriver, where jagged rocks outcrop to left and right, the tributary stream issuing from Cwm Gwarin spills from a rock channel and slides into a pool. I had hoped this might be the beginning of a rugged mountain heartland, but above the falls the valley lay back again. The bogs were interminable, and there were no tracks or bridleways to ease my progress through the upper basin towards Pen Pumlumon Arwystli—the first objective. The time had come to quit the lowlands for open ridges; I leapt the stream at a narrowing and climbed a grass spur on to the high ground above the cwm.

Instead of the expected ridge I found a rolling moor with its own mounds and hollows. At an isolated cairn I sat back in the sunlight

Natural erosion on Plynlimon. Pen Pumlumon Arwystli in the background.
Erydu naturiol ar Bumlumon. Pen Pumlumon Arwystli yn y cefndir.

Bridleway on the approach from Maes Nant. *Llwybr troed ar y ffordd o Faes Nant.*

and let an hour go by. To the south, almost lost to the haze, I could see the shady hollow of crags and stream runnels where, had I kept to my original plan, I would now be stumbling and cursing. I could also see Pen Pumlumon Fawr, the highest summit of the group, peeping over the west side of the basin. It seemed a great distance away. Nevertheless, if all the ridges were as dry and firm as this one then I would reach it comfortably within a couple of hours.

First I would walk to the saddle at the source of the River Severn—an arbitrary objective if ever there was one. It goes like this: a water molecule evaporates from the Atlantic Ocean, crosses the coast in a cloud, condenses in a rain shower over Plynlimon, and then trickles through the mud into a slimy pool. This is the source of the River Severn. The river then flows through Wales and England, passing in and out of several animals and a few machines, and eventually re-enters the Atlantic Ocean where one day it will evaporate . . . .

At the saddle I put my foot in a bog. Maybe it was the celebrated source. To the left

stretched a land tortured by peat groughs and mires— thankfully not on my route. I turned to the right and followed the ridge over short, dry grass to the summit of Pen Pumlumon Arwystli. Here I found twin mounds of stones, each containing a circle shelter like a miniature volcano. The craters glowed with discarded orange peel. At a saddle beyond the summit most of the grass and soil had been stripped away by natural erosion, leaving a few clumps of vegetation isolated like glacier tables on mushroom mounds of peat. A rare red kite cruised overhead, adding to the strangeness.

The ridge passed over an unremarkable Pen Pumlumon Llygad Bychan, dipped to a third saddle and finally rose to the summit of Pen Pumlumon Fawr. Until now the views had been of empty hills—moody rather than memorable —but here was a gallery of classical pictorialism: Nant y Moch Reservoir glistening with evening reflections; Pumlumon Fach shapely under raking sunlight; Llyn Llygad Rheidol lost to purple shadows. It was too much to take in at one viewing so I crouched down in the lee of a boulder to eat what was

left of the food, intending afterwards to resume my adoration of nature. Then I got cold and aesthetic appreciation somehow lost its appeal. I turned away and hurried off down an uncharacteristically steep slope towards the north, hoping to cross the twin summits of Pumlumon Fach before the sun went down.

While descending from the second summit I came across a sheep guarding a dead lamb. The lamb seemed to have fallen over a crag and had been partially devoured. The sheep hissed me away. In an irony that escaped me at the time, I felt hurt that I should have been mistaken for a predator. Warped by loneliness, I had lost my grip on reality. The sun set on the mountain as I walked among the remainder of the herd on the lower slopes. Some of the more curious lambs bounced over the grass towards me. They looked good enough to eat.

THE BRECON BEACONS

Maps: The four sectors of the national park are shown at 1:50,000 scale on Landranger Sheet 160 (Brecon Beacons) and Sheet 161 (Abergavenney and The Black Mountains). The scale is adequate, though for little extra expense you can get 1:25,000 detail for the whole region in Outdoor Leisure 11, 12 & 13 (Brecon Beacons Central, Western and Eastern respectively).

Bases: Brecon itself is by far the most convenient base. All types of accommodation are available, including a campsite at the east side of town where the bypass rejoins the original A40 road. Although Brecon is accessible by public transport (the nearest rail stations are at Llandovery to the west and Abergavenny to the east, both on the A40 bus routes), approaches to the majority of walks are impractical without a car.

Drive south through Wales and it seems the entire country is folded into hills. Before dipping through the Valleys towards the coastal plain of industrial South Wales, it rears up one last time in the mountain waves of the Brecon Beacons. There are no high crags here, only high-angled scarps and gentle dip slopes, their rough edges worn away, their grass blankets smoothed by sheep.

The Brecon Beacons National Park comprises four hill groups, each separated by main roads. From west to east these are: the Black Mountain, Fforest Fawr, the Brecon Beacons, and (confusingly) the Black Mountains. Walks have been selected from each, and while four exploit the characteristic ridge structure—where an ascent to a summit is not an end in itself but a prelude to something greater—a fifth explores a concentration of waterfalls unique in Wales.

After the ascent from Llyn y Fan Fach. Picws Du (centre) and Fan Foel (left). Ar ôl dringo o Lyn y Fan Fach. Picws Du (canol) o Fan Foel (chwith).

31: THE BRECON BEACONS — Bannau Sir Gaer

Route Summary: A walk for Beacon enthusiasts with both mountain and moorland scenery. Ascends a track to a remote mountain lake, follows the edge of an escarpment, then descends over open moorland.

Difficulty: Class C.

Main summits: Bannau Sir Gaer (Picws Du) 749m/2457ft; Fan Brycheiniog 802m/2632ft.

Duration: 11km/7miles; 675m/2225ft of ascent; allow 4hrs.

Terrain: Stony track; grass and mud paths; trackless moor.

Special difficulties: Difficult route-finding in mist between Bwlch Blaen Twrch and Fan Brycheiniog, and throughout the descent (consider the emergency descent from Bwlch Blaen Twrch in these conditions).

Approach: From Llangadog (via Llandovery) or Brynamman on the A4069, or from Trecastle on the A40. Follow minor roads to Llanddeusant (signposted "Llanddeusant Church" and, in the later stages, "Llyn y Fan Fach"). Continue east from the church along the lane which gradually deteriorates into an unsurfaced track. Park on the riverbank (GR:799 238) near the beginning of the water authority track to Llyn y Fan Fach.

Route directions: Follow the track up the river bank to Llyn y Fan Fach. From the dam, ascend a grass path due west on to the ridge which descends from the west end of the escarpment. Swing left on to the escarpment crest and follow it eastwards, over a minor top, to the summit of Picws Du.

Descend steeply east to the distinctive col of Bwlch Blaen Twrch (emergency descent to the north from here, down a steep and winding path on the west bank of the stream). Ascend a pathless convex slope beyond the col, heading due east to the trig point at the summit of Fan Brycheiniog.

Follow a path north-east along the

The Black Mountain from Llanddeusant. Y Mynydd Du o Landdeusant.

escarpment edge to a small cairn on the promontory of Fan Foel (GR:822 223). Descend due north from the cairn to find the slight ramp which slants across the west flank of the spur. Follow it down to the right, gaining the crest of the spur below its steep section. Go north-west across the moor (sheep tracks but no continuous path) staying high up the north-east bank of the Nant Melyn. On reaching the far bank of the Sychnant (GR:808 243), follow a path curving down and across the hillside back to the parking place.

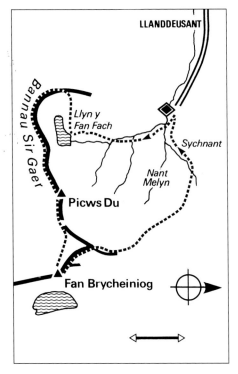

Llyn y Fan Fach below the Bannau Sir Gaer escarpment. The ascent path can be seen rising diagonally leftwards from the dam at the lake outflow. Llyn y Fan Fach islaw sgarp Bannau Sir Gaer. Gwelir y llwybr yn dringo'n groes i'r chwith o'r argae a'r llyn.

The Bannau Sir Gaer escarpment swells up beyond hedged pastures as a huge green wave, frozen in time the instant before breaking. This distinctive shape of northern escarpment and southern dip slope, so characteristic of the Beacons, has a convincing geological explanation. The underlying rocks are Old Red Sandstones from the Devonian period, having sedimentary origins in the gravel, sand and mud laid down in old river estuaries. Deposits accumulated to a depth of hundreds of metres, became compressed into a durable rock, and were then lifted up into a high plateau. All this took place several hundred million years ago. During the ice age which ended ten thousand years ago glaciers carved out the high cwms and long, U-shaped valleys. Shrinking glaciers then dumped mounds of gravel and clay in the valleys—natural dams for the formation of meltwater lakes.

Nowhere is this glacial history more apparent than at Llyn y Fan Fach, though admittedly the natural efficiency of the reservoir has been encouraged with a bit of concrete and stone. This route approaches the lake from the north, ascends to the crest of its western arm, circles on to Bannau Sir Gaer, and then follows the escarpment over Picws Du to Fan Brycheiniog, the highest summit of the group.

The lane from Llanddeusant gradually deteriorates into a track and effectively terminates at a riverside parking place where a Water Authority sign deters persistent motorists from pursuing things to the bitter end. Another sign reminds everyone to quit the land by 9pm or sunset, whichever is the sooner, though there's no indication of how this rule might be enforced. A narrow view of high hills barely compensates for some unpleasant walking up the knobbly track alongside the Afon Sychlwch, dammed and channelled with concrete into filter beds. Evidence of meddling gradually diminishes as the mountain influence builds, and not even the dammed waters of Llyn y Fan Fach can douse an imagination fired by the broad expanse of heathland now revealed below the curled headwall of Bannau Sir Gaer. Such a lonely place. Unchained winds shiver the greens, browns and yellows of the protective moor grass through tints and shades, while on the escarpment itself, natural erosion splits the underlying skin to reveal the flesh of ruddy soil and the protruding bones of scratty crags.

Out of the lake there once came a beautiful maiden who then presented herself to a young farm lad who happened to be grazing cattle near-by. This doesn't happen every day, even to a mythical farm lad, and the serendipity of the situation was not lost on him. He fell in love with her. She agreed to become his wife on the condition that should he strike her three times, or touch her with iron, (it depends which tale you hear), she would return to the lake along with the cattle she had

Picws Du seen from the ascent to Fan Brycheiniog. *Picws Du, fel y'i gwelir wrth ddringo Fan Brycheiniog.*

brought to the marriage. It was a trick, of course, and the lad—without any hint of malice—duly broke his vow, whereupon his wife stomped back to the lake, taking the cattle with her, and was never seen again. The moral of this tale is that you should read the small print of your marriage contract before the rot sets in.

A threadbare strip in the grass carpet indicates the direct line from lakeside to bounding ridge. It's a stiff pull, as they say, but after twenty minutes the worst is done. Only in the path's upper section, where it narrows and swings left to join the ridge route, has it worn through to the underlying sandy soil. The reward for this effort is a gloriously gentle stroll along the crest of the escarpment between dipping moorland and crumbling lip. It was somewhere along here that a group of teenage girls appeared as in a vision. They passed by without so much as a glance in my direction. Not that I could pass for an innocent young farm lad; nor, for that matter, could they pass for maidens, judging by the gossip about inter-dormitory activities the previous night. Gone are the days when you can find a wife by

hanging around lonely mountain tarns.

I had intended to return to Llyn y Fan Fach from Bwlch Blaen Twrch, the eastern col of Picws Du, but on arrival was deceived by the convex hillside above into embarking on what promised to be a short ascent to Fan Brycheiniog, the highest summit of the Black Mountain group. Initially the route followed a path along the escarpment edge, maintaining the character of the walk, but when it veered into a featureless bog I began to question my peak-bagging motivation.

An answer of sorts came when I emerged on the north-east escarpment, not far from the trig point and elaborate stone shelter of the summit. An orange sea glistened to the south: a purple land darkened to the north. Near-by the streams cut deep in the hillside and wriggled valleywards, their western banks shadowed into black zig-zags, while Llyn y Fan Fawr pooled bleak and dismal in the frosty shade far below. A solitary crow planed the updraughts, tracking this way and that, its call emphasising the chill.

I turned north and followed the edge on to the distinctive prow of Fan Foel at the eastern

extremity of the Bannau Sir Gaer escarpment. I sat for a while against the cairn, warming my face with the last of the sun and worrying about finding a suitable route down the prow. Although the map showed the dotted line of a path, the ground was hard with frost and I feared the steep grass would prove dangerously slippery. Nothing for it but to go and look. I aimed directly down the featureless convex slope and, just as I was becoming anxious about the gradient, came across a ramp slanting securely across the western flank of the prow. Within minutes I was trotting over the tufted moor, all obstacles behind. By now the sun had gone from the crest of the green wave and lit only the vapour trails scored by noiseless jets across the sky.

32: THE BRECON BEACONS: Waterfall Country

Route summary: A circular low-level walk visiting several impressive waterfalls. A delight at any time of year, but at its best after rain during autumn. Shorter alternatives are available.

Difficulty: Class B.

Duration: 16km/10miles; allow 5–6hrs.

Terrain: Muddy riverbank paths (boots or wellingtons essential), plus a short section of road walking.

Special difficulties: Young children must be closely supervised, especially near the waterfalls where the rocks can be dangerously slippery.

Approach: From Neath or Merthyr Tydfil along the A465. Turn off to Glyn-Neath then follow signs for Pont Nedd Fechan. Park adjacent to the Angel Inn (GR:901 076), just before bridging the Nedd.

Route directions: Turn left by the inn (signposted "Sgŵd Gwladys"), cross over a lane and go through a gate on to the riverbank trail of the Afon Nedd. Follow the path upstream for about 2km to a footbridge. Go up the left bank of the tributary to the viewing area for Sgŵd Gwladys. Either return directly to the footbridge, or continue to the fall, pass behind it using a narrow ledge and stepping stones, and return to the footbridge along the opposite bank. Continue up the bank of the Nedd, over a footbridge near a small fall and passing Sgŵd Ddwli, to the lane at Pont Melin Fach.

Cross the bridge, continue along the lane to a T-junction, then turn left. Turn right after about 1km on a stony track leading between fence-topped walls. Continue by a waymarked path, soon descending through woods to arrive in the valley of the Afon Mellte at Sgŵd Clun-gwyn. Cross by the footbridge a

Sgŵd Ddwli (in the distance), Afon Nedd. Sgŵd Ddwli (yn y pellter), Afon Nedd.

short distance upstream then turn right, returning downstream to the falls before forking left on the advised path away from the precipitous river bank. Continue along the forest edge, later merging with a path which arrives from low down on the right (optional detour down this path to view Lower Clun-gwyn). Curve left to enter the valley of the Afon Hepste then zig-zag steeply down steps to the river with a view upstream of Sgŵd yr Eira. Pass behind the veil of water and ascend the far bank to a T-junction of paths. Turn right and ascend steps to a large boulder on open ground. Follow the waymarked path south, finally descending a stony track to a parking area near a rock outcrop. Turn right and follow the road back to the Angel Inn.

Alternatives: (1) Follow the main route over Pont Melin Fach and along the lane to the T-junction. Turn right and walk back along the road to Pont Nedd Fechan. (2) Park on the road between Pont Nedd Fechan and Ystradfellte, near the stone track leading down to Sgŵd Clun-gwyn. Follow the main itinery as far as Sgŵd yr Eira, returning by the same route.

An aerial view of the Brecon Beacons National Park would show a land contoured with the smooth predictability of draped velvet. Sculpture on a grand scale. The medium is Old Red Sandstone: artistry courtesy of the ice age. This uniformity breaks down at the southern limit of the park boundary, where the old rock, dipping towards the industrialised lowlands, disappears beneath younger layers of limestone, grit and shale. Thus the Afon Nedd, Mellte and Hepste, after draining the southern slopes of Fforest Fawr, suddenly confront a bed of soluble Carboniferous Limestone. The outcome, resolved only after many thousands of years, is that the rivers now run through deep gorges, and in places through subterranean passageways. The next encounter is with a layer of Millstone Grit. Though an impermeable sandstone, faulting and other disturbances produced a river bed which alternated between hard grit and soft shale. With time the shale has worn away, leaving the rivers to fall abruptly over sharply defined shelves—the special attraction of Waterfall Country.

Further south another drastic change of scenery occurs. In this case due not to natural landscaping, but to widespread industrial exploitation of the Coal Measures. The village of Pont Nedd Fechan, at the start of the walk, lies on the boundary of this final transition. To the south we see a landscape created over a

Sgŵd yr Eira – Spout of Snow, Afon Hepste. *Sgŵd yr Eira, Afon Hepste.*

hundred years—raw, ugly and frenzied; and to the north, a landscape created over a hundred million years—mature, picturesque and calm. We go north.

Though none of the waterfalls lies very far from a road, to get the feel of the place it is best to link at least two or three by following one of the riverside paths up or down stream. However, this is not very practical unless you can arrange return transport. This walk solves that problem by taking a circular route and visiting almost all of the major waterfalls on the three rivers. The walk begins at the Angel Inn in Pont Nedd Fechan, a short distance upriver from the confluence of the Nedd and Mellte. Here the Nedd flows through the broadleaved woodland of a deep valley, the river overhung in places by jutting rocks—evidence of previous erosion. At this stage the path is some distance above the river, though in a couple of places steps lead down to where the water flows darkly through rock trenches.

I could have squandered the morning here, watching the armada of fallen leaves drift by, but I was eager to see Sgŵd Gwladys, the first of the waterfalls. This is found not on the Nedd but a couple of hundred metres upstream on its tributary the Afon Pyrddin. A platform at the end of the maintained section of path provides a view of the delicate spout which gushes over a shelf to fall seven or eight metres into a broad, shallow pool. Who was Gwladys? The name might refer to a daughter (one of twenty six) of Brychan, fifth century King of Brycheiniog. Curiosity took me beyond the viewpoint to the shallow cave behind the fall, its delicate swish now a thunderous roar. The water level in the pool was not too high and I found I could complete this unconventional crossing by balancing across stepping stones, returning to the Nedd along a path on the far bank.

Back at the main river the path strays high up the valley side, unwilling to get too close to the dangerous bank. It comes close to the river again to cross a small subsidiary stream by a footbridge, and to view a curious fall where the water sluices through a gap in a weir-like rock formation. From here I could see the bigger fall of Sgŵd Ddwli in the distance and was tricked into approaching it along plates of rock exposed in the river bed. Big mistake. After grovelling up a collapsing mud bank I ended up viewing the falls from the main path after all.

Gradually the valley opens out and the path crosses through a glade furnished with picnic tables. The stone bridge of Pont Melin-fach marks the end of the Nedd section and the start of a diversion by road to reach the Afon Mellte. This wasn't the boring trudge it promised to be.

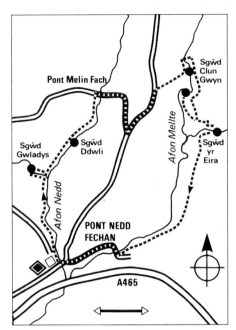

Sgŵd Clun Gwyn, Afon Mellte. Sgŵd Clun Gwyn, Afon Mellte.

At one point I surprised a grey squirrel foraging on the verge. It leapt into a tree and sprinted up the trunk, claws splayed, and disappeared into a camouflaged confusion of twigs. I hid for a few minutes behind a neighbouring tree to see if it would come down again, but it didn't show.

A stony track led between walls and over fields to the wooded valley of the Afon Mellte. Through the trees I could hear the muffled sound of tortured water. "TAKE CARE: VERY ROUGH STEEP SLIPPERY GROUND" said the sign. I took my hands out of my pockets and approached rock shelves at the top of Sgŵd

Clun-gwyn. Feeling adventurous I went down some 'very rough steep slippery ground' at the side and walked out at two-thirds height along a narrowing pavement to stand in the spray and reflect on the consequences of a slip.

To see the other falls of the Mellte entailed crossing to the far bank by an upstream footbridge and then re-visiting Clun-gwyn before heading off downstream towards Sgŵd Isaf Clun-gwyn. Here another sign raised the danger stakes another notch with the following exhortation: "DANGER: VERY STEEP ROUGH SLIPPERY GROUND. DEATHS HAVE OCCURRED. TAKE CARE." A diversion sign strongly advised me to use the detour path higher up on the valley side, and not wishing to occur my death, I turned to follow it. At that moment two elderly gentlemen and two ladies in town shoes wobbled past me on to the danger path above the ravine, clutching each other's arms for support. I did not expect to see them again.

The high path took me up to the forest edge and far away from the river, now a whisper in the valley base. Not wishing to miss anything, I continued past the falls and then back-tracked towards them on the stepped path of the safe southern approach. The path stopped short of the falls so I risked scrambling up a rocky slope to a ledge which I thought would bring a better view. A whippet belonging to a couple dithering further back had the same idea. It pushed past me and bounded up the slope, only to lose its footing on a pile of dead leaves. With a yelp it tumbled past me, legs flailing, and narrowly avoided plunging into the fast-flowing river. I was about to give up when who should I see coming towards me but the ashen-faced members of the pensioners party. I had counted them out and now I counted them back—one, two, three... four. Amazing!

Back on the high route I followed the path into the valley of the Afon Hepste. I had saved the most spectacular fall until last—Sgŵd yr Eira, the Spout of Snow. Here the Hepste comes to a semi-circular sill and drops eight metres in a glistening curtain. Incredibly the path crosses *behind* this wall of water, a route once used by shepherds when driving sheep across the river.

After dragging myself away from the mesmerising spectacle I climbed up the far bank to sit on a large boulder in the last of the evening sunlight. The lands of the industrial south were spread before me, grey from a premature dusk. Their proximity made this place seem all the more precious and fragile. It was great to be alive. Four senior citizens and one young whippet thought likewise.

33: THE BRECON BEACONS — The Brecon Beacons from the North

Route summary: A generally straightforward ridge walk, incorporating the highest summit of the Beacons. Momentarily exciting where the ridges steepen.
Difficulty: Class C.
Main summits: Cribyn 795m/2608ft; Pen y Fan 886m/2907ft.
Duration: 11km/7miles; 750m/2450ft of ascent; allow 4–5hrs.
Terrain: Grass paths to start and finish, with eroded sandy/muddy paths in the middle section. Some road walking.
Special difficulties: The upper sections of both the Bryn Teg and Cefn Cwm Llwch ridges may feel insecure to anyone unused to steep mountain terrain.
Approach: Leave the A40 Brecon by-pass at a roundabout on the west side of town. Take the road towards the town then turn right after about 500m on the Ffrwydgrech Road. Fork left after about 1km and continue for about 2km to where the lane turns sharp right. Go straight on, over a cattle grid, to a parking area at the end of the track (GR:024 247).
Route directions: Walk back down the

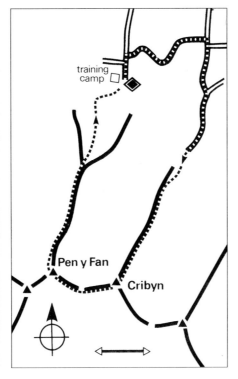

track on to the approach lane then turn right over a bridge. Continue for about 2km to a T-junction. Turn right and follow the lane for 1km to a second T-junction. Turn right again and go along the lane to its end in a little over 1km (GR:038 237). Continue by a stone bridleway and through a gate to open country. Leave the bridleway and ascend the Bryn Teg ridge by a grassy path, steepening in its upper reaches, to the summit of Cribyn.

Turn right and follow the worn path, descending to a col then rising steadily to the summit of Pen y Fan. Descend steeply northwards on to the Cefn Cwm Llwch ridge and follow the path over a cairned rise. Ignore paths to left and right where the ridge forks (GR:019 234) and descend the left side of the intervening valley to fields near the parking place (aim for the army huts if in doubt).

I imagined the Beacons to be boring green lumps stuck between the rural gentility of Brecon and the urban squalor of Merthyr. I had come by this opinion through a combination of northern chauvinism and the misplaced apologies of humble Beacon folk. Now I know different. I came, I saw, I capitulated. Now I must kneel before the altar of Pen y Fan and sing its praises.

The topography of the northern Brecon Beacons can be likened to a hand, its fingers spread into northern ridges, its knuckles raised into summits. My intention was to ascend the middle finger of Bryn Teg to Cribyn, circle the rim of Cwm Sere to Pen y Fan, and descend the index finger of Cefn Cwm Llwch. I could link the two fingertips using a series of lowland footpaths—or so the map promised.

The descent ridge of Cefn Cwm Llwch seen from the summit of Pen y Fan. The town of Brecon lies far below.
Trum Cefn Cwm Llwch o gopa Pen y Fan. Gwelir tref Aberhonddu yn bell i ffwrdd islaw.

Things looked very different from the ground. Having parked my car at a place convenient for the return, I had begun walking cross-country towards the base of Bryn Teg. I didn't doubt that route finding would be simple once I had reached the mountain proper, but right now I was balanced on a five-barred gate surrounded by a dozen geese with beaks like spring-loaded ring binders. I had green 'right-of-way' dashes on my side, but evidently the geese cared little for the niceties of Ordnance Survey maps. I sold them a dummy and escaped up a sunken lane choked with brambles. Then I spent a bloody, sweaty and tearful hour hacking a way through to open country. You will be relieved to note that in the summary I have described a less eventful approach along surfaced lanes.

This false start had cost me dearly in time. As I set off up the path which rose unswervingly up the ridge the frosty comfort of the morning had been superseded by an oppressive heat. Two soldiers, heavily burdened and menacingly fit, jogged past me on their way down. Following their example I put in a bit more effort, but it didn't agree with me. So it was back to plodding. There's not much more to say about this part of the ridge. No-one wants to read 'plod' written a thousand times. So let's take a mental leap to where the angle eases and a retrospective view of Brecon opens up (that's what I did, leaving my body to follow on in its own time).

Brecon has been a military base of one form or another since the Iron Age. The town remained strategically important throughout Roman and Norman times, and today retains its military connections thanks to the proximity of the Beacons—an ideal training ground for foot soldiers. And for aircraft. That morning I had stood on the bridge over the Usk and watched a pair of RAF trainers cruising low over the outskirts of the town. Not those nimble red jets that flick down the Ogwen Valley, but great lumbering things that looked ready to fall from the sky like a brace of shot grouse.

When the planes had gone I continued over the bridge into town, ostensibly to buy a map. Then I got distracted and spent an hour wandering the narrow streets. I went to the tourist information booth in the market square, but it was shut for the winter. A video tape played endlessly at the window, watched by a kid from one of the glitzy chrome homes of the fair people parked near-by. Exposed to daylight, the fairground rides had lost all their glamour. Last night, wide-eyed children from miles around had converged on the music and flashing lights. Later, while out looking for somewhere to eat, I had seen them walking away penniless and

At the summit of Cribyn. The ascent path along Bryn Teg is visible below. *Ar gopa Cribyn. Gellir gweld y llwybr ar hyd Fryn Teg islaw.*

bewildered, the sticky remnants of candy floss still on their cheeks.

Back on Bryn Teg I could now see the full length of both neighbouring ridges: to the left, Cefn Cyff rising in three steps to Fan y Big; and to the right, Cefn Cwm Llwch—my eventual route of descent—plunging from the summit of Pen y Fan to a gentle lower section. I approached the final intimidating rise of my ridge with suspicion. It reminded me of a small version of a bell-shaped snow peak in Switzerland which I had once climbed by repeating the same step-kicking movement five thousand times. The odd mixture of drudgery and insecurity, I remembered, had been sickening. Fortunately the steps in the ridge to Cribyn had already been cut—giant's steps kicked through the crisp turf into the underlying soil. Even so I would have turned back had the ground been frozen or lightly dusted with snow.

Cribyn summit lies exactly at the exit of Bryn Teg and thus at the apex of a triangular promontory—an ideal viewing platform for Pen y Fan and Fan y Big. I sat among the stones of its flattened cairn while several parties engaged on the southern circuit came and gasped and went. Having arrived first I felt that Cribyn was my property; I beamed with pride when they said it was much the best view they had seen that day. I offered to take pictures of them with their cameras while they posed self-consciously at the edge, the purple-brown escarpment for a backdrop.

Things were different on Pen y Fan. In spirit I shared my ascent with a hundred thousand predecessors (or a hundred times that number for all I know) who had trodden this way before me and worn the carpet through. Soil and gravel, and shelves of gritty sandstone piled one upon another, now lead to the table-top summit

of Pen y Fan. My arrival at the trig point coincided with that of two dozen supervised young people who had ascended from the Storey Arms. They stood at the lip of the western precipice and stuttered inadequate descriptions of the magnificent view to north and west. The more philosophical among them tried to hit the target with a few flightless darts of profundity, but many more were stunned into silence. Twenty minutes ago they would have been complaining about blisters and asking 'How much further, Miss?' For most of them this was their first summit. I wanted to shake them by the shoulders and say, 'This is what it's all about, this is why we wear silly hats and carry heavy bags and go up into the hills on Saturdays!' But I was silent too.

When the sun had turned red and the air become chilled I stepped on to the long slide of Cefn Cwm Llwch and came back to earth.

Pen y Fan (right) and Corn Du (centre, behind) seen from Cribyn. Note the severe erosion on the ascent path to Pen y Fan. *Pen y Fan (ar y dde) a Chorn Du (y tu ôl, yn y canol) o Gribyn. Sylwer ar yr erydu difrifol ar y llwybr i fyny at Ben y Fan.*

34: THE BRECON BEACONS — The Brecon Beacons from the South

Route summary: A long but uncomplicated circular walk over grass-topped escarpments linking all the highest summits of the Brecon Beacons.

Difficulty: Class C.

Main summits: Corn Du 873m/2863ft; Pen y Fan 886m/2907ft; Cribyn 795m/2608ft; Fan y Bîg 719m/2359ft; Waun Rydd 769m/2523ft.

Duration: 21km/13miles; 850m/2800ft of ascent; allow 7hrs.

Terrain: 4km of road and trail walking to start, otherwise generally good paths along gentle grass ridges (a few isolated boggy sections). Some short sections of rough ground on Corn Du and Pen y Fan.

Special difficulties: There are no route-finding difficulties except on Waun Rydd, which if necessary can be avoided. However, the whole route is exposed to bad weather and in those conditions would prove wearying and unpleasant.

Approach: From Talybont-on-Usk (via Brecon) or Pontsticill (via Merthyr Tydfil) along the minor road to a large parking place near its highest point (GR:056 175).

Route directions: Walk south-west down the road towards Pontsticill. Turn right after about 1km on to a track and fork right soon after (GR:049 168) to contour the forested hillside on a good bridleway, later merging with the lane leading to the Neuadd reservoirs. Follow the lane to the lower reservoir and cross the weir to the west shore (GR:029 180).

Ascend directly up the steepening hillside to the right of the forest block on to the ridge of Graig Fan Ddu. Follow the path along the crest of the escarpment to Bwlch Duwynt, cross over the main track from Storey Arms, and ascend a rock staircase to the summit of Corn Du. Descend the short east ridge and continue by an obvious path to the summit of Pen y Fan.

Descend the badly-eroded south-east ridge of Pen y Fan to a grass saddle. Ascend the obvious path steeply to the summit of Cribyn. Follow the escarpment path south, soon curving east, to The Gap of Bwlch ar y Fan at GR:032 205 (emergency descent to the right here along the bridleway). Ascend steeply eastwards on

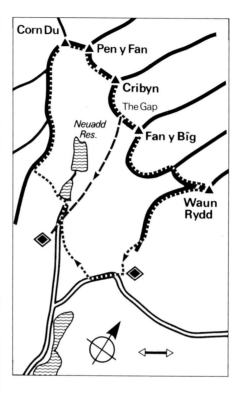

to the promontory of Fan y Bîg. Proceed south along the main escarpment path, curving east then north and passing a second promontory, to a shallow saddle at GR:058 206. Detour east over unpleasant tussocky grass to a small cairn at the indistinct summit of Waun Rydd (GR:062 206).

Return to the saddle and follow the path south-west along the Graig Fan Las escarpment (take care in mist to locate this path—it does not descend into the cwm from the saddle but rises slightly at first). Continue near the left edge by a good path then descend the final spur of Craig y Fan Ddu by a steep path on its right side. Follow the left bank of the stream down to the car park.

Alternatives: Park below the Neuadd reservoirs (GR:037 172), follow the main route as far as The Gap (GR:032 205), then turn right and return to the valley along the bridleway.

Something fundamental sets hill walking and lowland rambling apart—more than can be explained by the token objective of a summit. It's as if being physically raised up above the surrounding land gives impetus to the sense of spiritual elevation above earthly concerns. It hardly matters that the hill is a tiny one; what's important is the relative height difference and the absence of roads and fences. Nowhere is this sensation more evident than on the scarp edges of the Brecon Beacons.

I had been told the south side of the Beacons was boring: "Short walks up broad tracks over uneventful ground", they had said. And yet the map showed the possibility of a twenty kilometre ridge circuit around the Upper Neuadd Reservoir. On paper it looked terrific.

On the ground it didn't look anything. Hemmed in by forests, we saw no hint of a hill from the narrow road that skirts the Talybont reservoir. The day had started fine and warm, although clouds were already billowing up from the haze. It was Tony's first visit to the Beacons, and more than anything I wanted the day to stay clear long enough for him to see the northern escarpment in all its glory.

Some hill walkers like to step from the car, lace up their boots, and set off at once up a breath-snatching gradient. Others like to warm up gradually. The southern circuit of the Beacons will appeal to the latter group because it begins with a forty-minute stroll—part minor road, part bridleway—through the Taf Fechan Forest and into the valley of the Neuadd reservoirs. But you don't get owt for nowt; after crossing the weir of the lower reservoir we faced a two-hundred-metre grind straight up a concave hillside, and with nothing to ease the burden of effort except the certain knowledge that there would be no tougher task that day. Tony said we would crack it in twenty minutes; I said thirty. We made a bet. He raced on, I hung back. Our average was twenty five.

From the crest we could look down on the reservoirs (the lower one dry except for the wriggling Taf Fechan, heavy with sand), and also towards the head of the valley where the ups and downs of the main escarpment were profiled. We identified two more steep climbs—the ascents to Cribyn and to Fan y Bîg—but those were hours away. For the time being we could relax with a tasty path up the scarp edge

Rest stop on the promontory of Fan y Big. *Gorffwysfan ar benrhyn Fan y Big.*

to Corn Du. We set off at once, licking our lips.

As Beacon paths go, this one is little used. It might have taken the top of the ridge, broad and boring, but instead follows the very edge of the escarpment where shattered outcrops of gritstone support a quivering lip of grass. We had picked a good 'un, and knew it.

At the col beyond the slender Rhiw yr Ysgyfarnog we crossed the Storey Arms track (the word 'path' does not do it justice), which is so impatient for the summit of Pen y Fan that it can't even be bothered with a simple fifty-metre scramble up a rock staircase to the tabletop summit of Corn Du. We could.

Looking down from the summit on to the north-west ridge we saw the obelisk raised in memory of Tommy Jones, who died here in

August 1900, aged five. The story has lost none of its poignancy over the years. It was already six o'clock in the evening when Tommy and his father, a Rhondda miner, set off from Brecon railway station to visit the boy's grandparents at Cwm Llwch farm. Two hours later they stopped for refreshments at the soldiers' camp at the Login, just a few minutes from their destination. Here they met Tommy's grandfather and thirteen-year-old cousin. As evening came the two boys set off together up the valley towards the farmhouse, but halfway there Tommy got upset and turned back towards the Login to be with his father. He never arrived. Helped by the soldiers from the camp, the father and grandfather looked for Tommy until midnight without success. Three

hours later they resumed the search, now joined by police and public from Brecon. They found no trace of him. And so it went on, the next day and the next. Now they were looking for a body. Because of his age, no-one thought the little boy could have gone as far even as Llyn Cwm Llwch, so the search focused on the lowlands—the streams, woodland and bracken. The weeks went by. Perhaps he had been kidnapped by gypsies? Local gypsy camps were scoured by police to assuage the rumour-mongers, but without result. The mystery deepened. One month later, a Mrs Hamer from the Brecon district convinced her husband that she had dreamed of the place where Tommy would be found. Reluctantly he agreed to accompany her on to the Beacons. They found the body on the ridge above Cwm Llwch, just as predicted. It seems the boy had lost his way in gathering darkness and had probably come upon the path which climbs up Pen Milan. The path would have taken him on to the exposed ridge below Corn Du, where he eventually died of exposure. He wore a sailor suit and carried a whistle on a string around his neck. Perhaps he had blown the whistle while wandering aimlessly over the mountain in the hours of darkness before he finally lay down exhausted. But if he had, no-one had heard.

The clouds came and blotted out the sun; it was time to go. Within five minutes we stood on Pen y Fan, a chill north-easterly breeze sweeping up the faces of the escarpment towards us. We moved on, shuffling down the severely eroded south-east ridge. At the grass saddle beneath the ridge we were almost tempted to take a contouring path across the south flank of Cribyn to Bwlch ar y Fan, but I had already enthused about the superior view from Cribyn so we could hardly miss it out now. Once we had resigned ourselves to plodding up a hundred and thirty metres of high-angle grass and dirt we took a perverse pleasure in the execution, zig-zagging over to the left edge at intervals for a whiff of danger and a shot of cold air.

The last time I had stood on Cribyn the air had been crisp and clear, so our murky view of the four parallel fingers of the northern ridges was a little disappointing. I made up for it with a fulsome description of what we were missing. Tony gave me his 'leave it out' smile, glanced at his watch, and set off at a trot for The Gap of Bwlch ar y Fan.

The pony track which crosses the Beacons at The Gap is the continuation of the bridle-way we had followed earlier in the day. It was getting late and the thought of another 1:2 uphill grind made us hesitate. Perhaps we should cut our losses and follow the track down to the valley? In half an hour we could be safely down on the road. For a second time we put temptation behind us and within minutes sat smug on a natural rock seat on the promontory of Fan y Big. From now on, apart from a few gentle rises, it would be downhill all the way. According to the map we were little more than seven hundred metres above sea level. Spiritually, we were sky high.

On the descent from Pen y Fan, Cribyn rising ahead. *Wrth ddisgyn o Ben y Fan a Chribyn yn ymgodi o'n blaen.*

35: THE BRECON BEACONS —
Waun Fach and Pen y Gadair Fawr

Route Summary: Gentle walking over bleak moorland tops. Uses a track to reach high ground then follows windswept shallow ridges over the two highest peaks of the Black Mountains.

Difficulty: Class C.

Main summits: Waun Fach 810m/2658ft; Pen y Gadair Fawr 800m/2625ft.

Duration: 15km/9miles; 475m/1550ft of ascent; allow 5hrs.

Terrain: Stony track then paths over grass with frequent boggy sections.

Special difficulties: Very difficult route-finding in mist between the Cwm Cwnstab saddle and Waun Fach.

Approach: From Crickhowell on the A40 between Abergavenny and Brecon. Follow signs for Llanbedr then Grwyne Fawr Reservoir to a parking area near the end of the forest at GR:253 285.

Route directions: Continue along the lane for a short distance then fork right up a stony bridleway slanting up the east side of the valley to Grwyne Fawr Reservoir. The track deteriorates to a path before reaching a shallow saddle overlooking Cwm Cwnstab (GR:203 327). Turn left and follow the path along a broad ridge, over the false summit of Pen y Manllwyn and around the rim of Cwm Rhiangoll, to the summit of Waun Fach.

Follow the path south-east along a broad connecting ridge to the summit of Pen y Gadair Fawr. Either continue south-east along the ridge and turn left to descend a path along the forest edge to the river, or, better, descend north-east then east from the summit down open slopes of grass and bracken to the confluence of tributary and river (GR:248 291). Ford the river here, or a little way downstream, and turn right to return to the start (if the river is in flood and cannot be forded, walk about 600m upstream to where it is bridged by the dam access road).

The link ridge from Waun Fach to Pen y Gadair Fawr. Yr esgair gysylltiol o Waun Fach i Ben y Gadair Fawr.

At the eastern side of the Brecon Beacons National Park, close to the border with England, the high ground of the Black Mountains comes to an abrupt end and falls away in a north-west facing escarpment towards the Wye Valley. Four parallel ridges extend southeast from its trailing edge towards Crickhowell and Abergavenny, enclosing three valleys within. The topography is reminiscent of both the Brecon Beacons and the Black Mountain, with a scarp face, barren ridges and broad intervening valleys. The dramatic cutaways of Pen y Fan and Bannau Sir Gaer, however, are absent.

Of more than a dozen different routes along these ridges—including a day-long marathon which sweeps up every summit of note—this one involves the least effort for the greatest reward. A bridleway gets you out of the valley on to the scarp edge, from where a generally good path leads up the back of a rounded ridge, via the summit of Waun Fach, highest in the Black Mountains, to Pen y Gadair Fawr. Unfortunately the ridge holds water like a sponge, and during or after poor weather the going is grim to glutinous. If you can, wait for a week of dry weather or a night of frost.

Cameras do lie. A photographic record of a walk on the Black Mountains—this one included—will not be truly representative. The photographer seeks out features that might add depth to the composition, whereas an honest picture preserves the emptiness. This is not to say that the scenery is bland, merely that it does not transfer successfully on to film. It creates moods, not images.

I came to the Black Mountains one frosty midweek morning in November, having spent the previous week walking under cloudless skies in the Beacons. Now the high pressure system was finally slipping away, drawing in the first wisps of cirrus. This would have to be my final day. Sheep and ponies grazed among empty picnic tables at the end of the Grwyne Fawr lane. It was a lonely day in prospect.

Things began gently with a track slanting across the valley side. This was built in 1912 during construction of the Grwyne Fawr Reservoir dam, but is now designated a bridleway while Water Authority vehicles use the surfaced lane in the valley bottom. It provides a good view of the eventual descent from Pen y Gadair Fawr on the opposite side of the valley, and of potential sites for a river crossing at the bottom.

Streams draining the flanks of Waun Fach had eroded fan-shaped depressions in the hillside opposite, whereas on the track side of the valley the monotony was broken only by patches of bracken and the occasional bush heavily laden with berries. With not much else to see I looked forward to catching a first glimpse of the dam, which has been described as 'graceful'.

I've seen gasworks more graceful. In its pristine state I dare say the triangular structure of white stone blocks had a certain monumental appeal, but surely not now, its face stained black with the drainage from a battery of sluices. My admiration goes instead to the mathematical elegance of the bowed, concave geometry of the wall which gives it its strength.

Its original purpose fulfilled, the track quickly degenerates beyond the dam into a broad path. Nothing to see but clumps of moor grass; nothing to hear but the moaning wind. I felt cut off from the world, despite the evidence of last

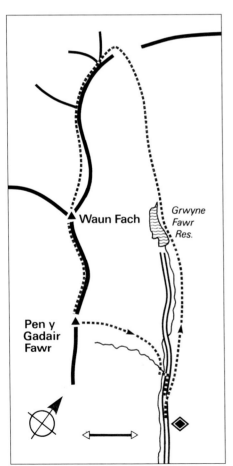

The dam at Grwyne Fawr Reservoir. *Argael Grwyne Fawr.*

The final rise to the summit of Pen y Gadair Fawr. Behind, the featureless dome of Waun Fach, highest summit of the Black Mountains. *Y codiad olaf at gopa Pen y Gadair Fawr. Y tu ôl, cryndo moel Waun Fach, copa uchaf y Mynydd Du.*

weekend's activity preserved as footprints in the mud. The path crests out at a plateau of bleached grass, disappointing in its emptiness. No sign of the escarpment. I huddled for shelter behind a peat hag and ate some revolting sandwiches, unsure if I could bear my own miserable company for the rest of the afternoon. I packed the rucksack and continued for another few minutes to where the bridleway crosses the exit of Cwm Cwnstab and dips down the escarpment. Everything changed. Now I could see the pastureland and villages of the Wye Valley, and above them a glider, silver white in the bright sunlight, flipping violently this way and that in search of thermals.

Three men appeared on the skyline to my right, their dogs zig-zagging in front, following the transverse path that I was about to take. They passed a hundred metres to the south and we raised our hands in greeting (midweek on the Black Mountains, this rates as a close encounter). Buttoned up against the wind, I then began the long haul up to Waun Fach. I thought I was moving well until a couple overtook me at speed, their windproofs thrashing like tent fabric in a storm.

Where the path levels and curves around the head of the Rhiangoll cwm, the three men and their dogs had found a superior windbreak and had stopped for lunch. I went off to take pictures of mountain ponies. When the animals realised I held nothing more appetising than a camera in my hands, they became irritable and trotted away, accompanied by a stifled tittering from the dog party. By the time I had given up hopes of becoming a wildlife photographer, dogs and men had topped Waun Fach and were already descending towards Pen Trumau. I was alone again.

Waun Fach is a ludicrous summit. Set within a circle of unfathomable slutch is a trig base—who knows how many have sunk without trace in the futile attempt to reach it?—while a few metres away stands a pathetic little cairn built from stones that could only have come up from the valley in the bottom of rucksacks. In geometric terms, the outlook is similar to that from the middle of a huge, upturned plate.

South-east of Waun Fach the nipple-like summit of Pen y Gadair Fawr protrudes into the skyline. A path down to the intervening saddle weaves among natural drainage ditches in an attempt to stay dry. It succeeds, more or less. The corresponding ascent is better drained, and in its final stages rises for fifteen metres at the unprecedented angle of twenty degrees—the only steep bit of uphill walking on the entire route. Pen y Gadair Fawr may be ten metres lower than Waun Fach, but it is superior in every other respect. There's even a wind shelter scooped out of the north side where you can prop a Thermos and spread a map.

The usual way down continues along the back of the ridge to the forest edge and then descends a steep path between streams and trees to Grwyne Fawr. A better alternative descends directly from the summit over the clumpy grass of an open shoulder. In its lower reaches the shoulder narrows to an arm (they usually do), where a grass path snakes through bracken to the confluence of stream and river.

I boulder-hopped across the river to the surfaced lane and walked back to the car, dry of foot and light of heart, my head full of undefined images. I knew words would be inadequate to describe the day. And they were. An empty page tells the story of the Black Mountains better.

SOUTH COAST

Maps: 1:50,000 mapping is adequate for all these walks. Landranger Sheet 157 (St David's & Haverfordwest) includes everything of interest in North Pembrokeshire. St Govan's appears on Sheet 158 (Tenby), although with a few notes extracted from the route description this is hardly necessary. The Gower is comprehensively mapped on Sheet 159 (Swansea & Gower). Inexpensive tide tables are sold in local newsagent's.

Bases: The entire coastal area of Pembrokeshire is so well served by hotel and bed & breakfast accommodation and campsites that it is pointless to list them. Youth Hostels are situated near Strumble Head, St David's Head, and Marloes. Port Eynon is the best base for the Gower walk, where in addition to the usual accommodation there are several campsites and a Youth Hostel. It can be reached by bus from Swansea.

Without exception, Pembrokeshire and the Gower Peninsula offer the finest coastal walking in Wales. A captivating mix of cliff, island and beach scenery will convert even the most sceptical 'mountain' walker, opening up a whole new realm of exploration.

Pembrokeshire supplies four of the five routes in this section. All are segments of the path which, with few deviations, follows the entire coastline of north and south peninsulas. Varied scenery was the main criterion for selection, though a strong secondary motive was the potential for contriving circular walks which involved as little inland walking as possible. The method failed on the Gower, where the section from Worms Head to Port Eynon—however inconvenient—could not be excluded.

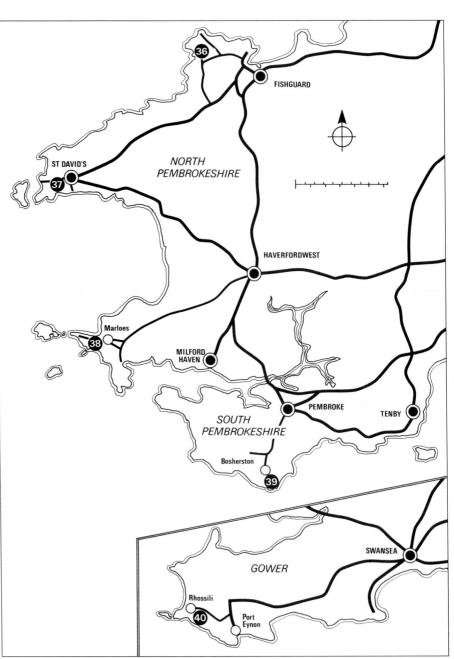

Strumble Head lighthouse at dusk. *Goleudy Pen Strwmbl rhwng dau olau.*

36: SOUTH COAST — Garn Fawr and Strumble Head

Route summary: Climbs a small hill for superb views of the rugged coastline then follows a cliff-top path to the lighthouse on Strumble Head.

Difficulty: Class B

Main summits: Garn Fawr 213m/700ft

Duration: 10km/6miles; 300m/1000ft of ascent; allow 3-4hrs.

Terrain: Generally good paths over grass, stones and heather (some boggy ground—boots advisable after wet weather). Some road walking to finish.

Special difficulties: Sections of the coastal path lie close to the cliff edge; young children must be closely supervised.

Approach: From Fishguard or St David's. A network of minor roads leaves the A487 between Goodwick and Mathry to serve the small villages on the headland to the north-west (the knobbly top of Garn Fawr is a distinctive landmark during the approach). One of these roads (shown on 1:50,000 maps and most road atlases) passes close beneath the east slope of Garn Fawr en route to Strumble Head.

Parking for several cars (GR:899 388).

Route directions: From the car park, take the signed path straight up the east slope of Garn Fawr. Leave it near the top to gain the summit and trig point with a simple scramble.

Return to the path and descend steeply westwards towards buildings and the start of a surfaced lane. After 100m on the lane, cross over a minor road on to the Youth Hostel track. Leave the track after just 10m for the signed coast path on the right. Follow the path downhill to

Looking across to Strumble Head from the summit of Garn Fawr. Golygfa i gyfeiriad Pen Strwmbl o Garn Fawr.

where it levels (possible detour down left on to a raised promontory above the sea) and continue along it for about 3km (obvious route-finding) to the road end above the lighthouse at Strumble Head.

Take the road east for about 400m to a sharp right bend. Go straight on and cross a stile to return to the coastal route. Where the path rounds the head of the second deep inlet (GR:905 407), turn right to follow a muddy path (marked "Public Footpath") leading inland between two streams to a stony track. Turn right along the track and follow it through a farmyard, bending left (surfaced now) to a junction with the Strumble Head road. Turn left then, after almost 1km, right at a T-junction to follow the rising road for 2km back to the car park.

Alternatives: If time is short then the final section of coast path can be omitted in favour of a direct return along the lane from Strumble Head.

The main road from St David's to Fishguard has no time for the ins and outs of the north Pembrokeshire coast, and gives few hints of what to expect there. Our attention is drawn instead towards a knobbly mound rising out of the surrounding pastureland like something nasty boiling up under the skin. This is Garn Fawr, up which the chosen walk begins. At 213m it hardly warrants the 'Fawr' appellation, and yet there are good reasons why it should have been chosen as the site of an Iron Age fort, one of them being that the summit provides unrestricted views in all directions.

The path to Garn Fawr begins from the lane which rises over its eastern flank, just fifty metres below the summit. A ten-minute bash up a grass slope followed by a little scramble brought me to the trig point a few seconds ahead of a trio of German lads who had climbed up from the west. Not that it was a race. While our cameras whirred and clicked, a fourth member appeared over a subsidiary top. The team leader shouted for him to pose on the 'spitz' for photographic purposes, which he did, grateful for the rest, and our cameras whirred and clicked some more. As soon as

the straggler arrived panting at the top, the lads zipped up their jackets and raced back down. For a second he looked at me with the weary expression of a dog with short legs, then he turned and hobbled off after them. I got the impression it had been like this the entire holiday. After they had gone I spent a few moments alone with the view, intrigued by the contrast between the mottled fabric of the land and the blue cloth of the sea. To the north the white needle of Strumble Head lighthouse appeared to be trying to stitch the two together.

A descent to seaward, rather steeper and rockier than that on the landward side, leads past fluted outcrops to where the coastal path emerges fresh from the Youth Hostel. Not far below is the proto-island of Dinas Mawr, the sea yet to eat through its connecting neck and cast it adrift. In the meantime it serves as a perfect viewing promontory for the cliff-lined bay of Pwll Deri, and for the neighbouring islands where fulmars wheel rigidly among the indents.

While rounding the next headland I saw what appeared to be a flight of steps hewn

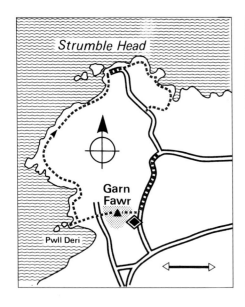

On the summit of Garn Fawr. *Ar gopa Garn Fawr.*

On Dinas Mawr, looking north across Ynys Ddu to the inlet of Porth Maenmelyn. *Ar Ddinas Mawr, golygfa ar draws Ynys Ddu hyd at gilfach Porth.*

from the vertical cliff face, leading down to the otherwise inaccessible shingle beach of Porth Maenmelyn. I would investigate. Short-cutting the path, I came to a deep fissure which ran parallel to the cliff edge, as if a slice of rock had begun to peel away from the land. Set within the confines of the fissure was an iron gate. I pushed and the gate creaked open, clearing a passage through to the staircase. The steps measured about a metre wide and made use of a natural ramp line slanting down the cliff face. In places they had been bolstered with concrete, though some of this had crumbled away and clearly the staircase was no longer used. The handrail appeared to have come away some time ago; it lay twisted and broken over the edge, leaving the exposed right-hand side of the steps unprotected. Slivers of shale littered each step, adding to the insecurity. To keep my footing I advanced with great caution pawing the rock for additional support and eyeing the drop with increasing unease. It was a reckless diversion, but I was gripped with curiosity.

I came to the impasse after eighty steps. A rockfall had collapsed the stairway, leaving nothing but shale inclined at an untenable angle. A slip here would be punished by a three-storey fall on to bone crunching rocks at the water's edge. It was suicide to go on. I looked for the bleached skeletons of my unsuccessful predecessors among the rocks below. I saw

none. Perhaps the bodies had been winched away by the coastguard, or taken by the sea. No-one knew I was here. I might lie in twisted agony on the rocks until nightfall, my weakening calls for help mistaken for the cries of seagulls. It would be a long, lingering and misunderstood death. No: I would go back. And did so, counting the steps to safety; ten, twenty, thirty, forty, fifty. I sweated at sixty, prayed at seventy, and laughed at eighty. Imagine if someone had locked the gate? There ought to be a warning.

There is. As I walked back up towards the main path I saw the reverse side of a large notice board. If I hadn't been so impatient I might have seen it earlier. It says: 'DANGER: DO NOT PROCEED BEYOND THIS POINT.' Good advice.

Although the path to Strumble Head weaves in and out of inlets in an attempt to follow the cliff edge, it regains its close association with the sea only at Carreg Onnen Bay—a bite of relative calm protected from the tide races off Strumble Head by the island which gives the bay its name. By now the sun was sinking, its fire doused. In comparison the pulse from the lighthouse seemed to grow in intensity with each cycle. Within the hour it would be sweeping across the water in a brilliant arc, looking for ships to save. A sailing dinghy drifted out of the sunset and homed in on the lamp like a moth. The light flashed its routine warning,

but the wind was offshore and there was no danger from the rocks. Then a squadron of journeying gulls flew overhead, arrow straight for home, too late for soaring antics above the headland.

Although the cliffs gradually diminish in height along the northern coast of Strumble Head, there are few places where you might safely bring in a dinghy, let alone land an army. So it is difficult to imagine that the ill-fated French invasion of 1797 took place at Carreg Wastad only a short distance along the coast. Twelve hundred men were landed, along with enough provisions to get them to Chester. Alas their copious stocks of brandy and wine ensured they got no further than Goodwick Sands where, two days later, they surrendered with minimal loss to Lord Cawdor of Stackpole.

A car park terminates the lane just above the Head; it was empty now, the day visitors long gone. Already they would be settling down in pubs and cafes, combing wind tangles from their hair and feeding seaside appetites. For my part I sat down on the lighthouse steps—a fine example of early twentieth-century Trinity House workmanship destined to be outlived only by brick-built Victorian public conveniences—and ate my way through a pile of rubbery sandwiches. The food was indifferent, the waiter uncouth, but the atmosphere was terrific. I had the table with a view.

37: SOUTH COAST — St David's and Ramsey Sound

Route summary: Magnificent coastal walking around rocky headlands and secluded inlets.

Difficulty: Class B.

Duration: 14km/9miles; allow 6hrs.

Terrain: Generally excellent cliff-top paths. 3km of road walking to finish.

Special difficulties: In places the path lies very close to cliff edges and so young children must be closely supervised.

Approach: From Fishguard or Haverfordwest along the A487 to St David's. Take the Haverfordwest road from the centre of St David's to a large car park at the edge of the built-up area (GR:757 252).

Route directions: Take the minor road signposted "Caerfai" from the car park to its terminus at a parking area above Caerfai Bay. Take the path leading down to the right (signposted "Coast Path") and follow it along the cliff-tops to St Non's Bay. Divert right to visit St Non's Chapel etc.

Return to the coast path and follow it into the deep inlet of Porth Clais. A choice of high or low paths on the far side of the inlet gains the next headland and a resumption of cliff-top walking to the promontory overlooking Carreg Frân. Continue around the indent of Porth Llysgu Bay and out on to the headland opposite Ramsey Island.

The path overlooking the sound leads eventually to the lifeboat station and harbour at St Justinian. From here follow the lane inland back to St David's, diverting left in the city to visit the cathedral and Bishop's Palace.

Alternatives: The sketch map shows several opportunities for short-cuts.

Pembrokeshire's special appeal is the sudden transfer from orderly pastureland to unruly sea that takes place so spectacularly at the cliff edge, a division to which this route clings with remarkable tenacity. Most walks have their dull interludes, but never this one. The day begins along quiet cliff-top paths and ends in the bustling streets of St David's. You won't miss

Porth Stinian and the lifeboat station, Ramsey Sound. *Porth Stinan a gorsaf y bad achub, swnd Ynys Dewi.*

a thing; from Caerfai to St Justinian, the path captures all the contrasts of this magnificent coastline.

Caerfai is one of the few places along the coast with a sandy beach; let yourself be tempted by a winding path down to the shore and you may get no further. The coast path, narrow but having a strong sense of its own identity and purpose, scorns this distraction and stays high, working its way a round the headland towards the rock-walled recess of St Non's Bay. Within the larger bay at St Non's are a number of narrower, inaccessible indents; ideal nesting grounds for fulmars. Far below, the sea rises and falls among boulders dark with slime.

Above the bay a large building houses the Christian retreat of St Non's. A tiny building adjacent to it is the Chapel of Our Lady and St Non, built in 1934 in the style of the old Pembrokeshire chapels and incorporating some of the stones from the fourteenth-century (or earlier) St Non's chapel—the ruins of which can still be seen in a near-by field. The old chapel was built on the site of a cottage in which St Non reputedly gave birth to David, who was to become the patron saint of Wales. On that night a great storm raged, and yet the birthplace "shone with so serene a light that it glistened as though the sun was visible and God had brought it in front of the clouds." A stone arch near-by protects the Holy Well of St Non, which supposedly appeared at the time

of St David's birth (500AD) with the property of healing diseases of the eye.

Holy places seem to have the power to move believers and agnostics alike—albeit the former to inner peace and the latter to inner turmoil. And yet for me the power of St Non's was soon overwhelmed by fundamental truths on returning to the cliff edge. No artefacts or incredible legends here; only the thick scent of gorse, a shag slapping the surface of the water in arduous preliminary flight, and a black-backed gull soaring on the updraughts with the merest corrective flick of its wing tips. Here, surely, is a church for everyone.

The path is forced to make a long detour inland to accommodate the deep inlet of Porth Clais, where a harbour wall—dating from the Middle Ages when Porth Clais was the port for St David's—calms the water at high tide. At low tide, when the inlet is empty apart from a trickling River Alun, the little boats lie at odd angles on the shingle, their mooring ropes tight to rings on the quay. Restored stone domes at the head of the inlet are the kilns in which limestone, brought in by coasters, would be calcined to make fertiliser. The kilns were built in the seventeenth century and fell into disuse only a hundred years ago. The coast path rises at once from the far side of the inlet. However, if instead you follow the low-level path, you will come to a secluded landing stage where you can stretch out on a suitably decrepit

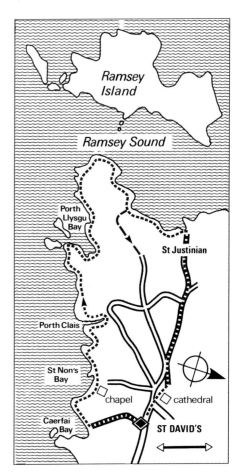

Below: St Non's Bay. The hump of Ramsey Island is visible in the distance.
Bae'r Santes Non gydag siâp gefngrwm Ynys Dewi i'w gweld yn y pellter.

Below: Fulmar, St Non's Bay. *Aderyn-drycin y Graig, Bae'r Santes Non.*

bench. Shielded from wind and tourists, there's no finer place to watch the day go by (through closed eyelids, of course).

At the Carreg Frân headland comes a view of fascinating intricacy; of the bird colony on Carreg yr Esgob, and of the cluster of islands off the southern tip of Ramsey. Forgetting itself, the path descends almost to the beach at the head of Porth Llysgu Bay. Here is a mixture of boulders, pebbles and sand, backed by cliffs of uncertain stability. Plastic rubbish brought in on the tide, and blown up from the beach on south-westerlies, lies snagged among the brambles, evidence of an unchallenged sin.

At Ramsey Sound the gorse thins and turns to grass while the path—the cliffs having been reduced to a few shelving rocks—descends close to the water's edge. The tide pumps through the gap at anything up to ten knots, inducing treacherous currents around the Bitches rocks which protrude into the sound from the Ramsey Island side. Sailing boats must wait for the turn before venturing into the sound, while motor boats engage maximum power and punch through regardless.

We are told that the Bitches are all that remain of a land bridge hacked away in the sixth century by St Justinian in an attempt to secure the solitude of his cell on Ramsey Island. Unmoved by this phenomenal display of strength, some of St Justinian's disgruntled followers settled a grudge by lopping off his head. In a remarkable show of dexterity, levity and grit, Justinian walked across the Sound, head in hand, so that both bits could be buried together in a grave overlooking the idyllic cove of Porthstinian.

Those less confident of their ability to walk on water can make the return trip to Ramsey from Porthstinian by boat; an especially worthwhile outing in late summer or early autumn when Atlantic grey seals breed in large numbers around the island. Nervous sailors will be reassured by the close proximity of St Justinian lifeboat station.

Leaving the coast, the final part of the walk follows a lane inland through fields towards St David's, its cathedral tower visible above the clutter of houses that comprise Britain's smallest city. Although St David founded a monastery at this site in the sixth century, construction of the grand cathedral which bears his name began only during the twelfth century, and that of the ostentatious Bishop's Palace in the fourteenth. What a splendid waste. I came away from St David's duly impressed by the cathedral and palace, but inspired only by the coastline.

Porth Clais. *Porth Clais.*

38: SOUTH COAST — *Marloes Peninsula*

Route summary: A conveniently circular walk around the varied coastline of a peninsula, visiting beaches and headlands and viewing cliffs, islands and inaccessible bays.

Difficulty: Class B

Duration: 13km/8miles; allow 4hrs.

Terrain: Sand and boulder beach; narrow cliff-top path (partly overgrown in places); short sections of track and road walking.

Special difficulties: The route across Marloes Sands is cut off at high water, though the normal coastal path is unaffected. In places the path passes close to the edge of unstable cliffs and young children must be closely supervised. The black cliffs above Musselwick Sands look inviting for adventurous scrambling but prove to be dangerously friable.

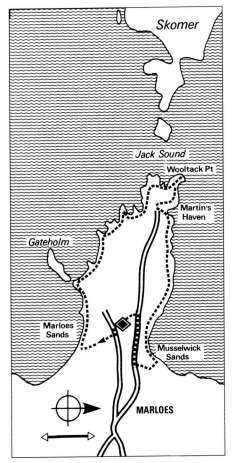

Approach: From the B4327 between Haverfordwest and Dale. Turn off (west) about 2km north of Dale for Marloes. Fork left for Marloes Sands just before entering the village. There is a large car park at the end of the road (GR:779 082).

Route directions: Go back down the approach road and turn right after 100m to follow a bridleway down to Marloes Sands. Either follow the rising coast path to the promontory overlooking Gateholm Island, or reach the same point over the sand and boulders of the beach, finally ascending by a grass recess at the west end of the bay.

Continue along the coast path, around Deadman's Bay and out on to the final head of the peninsula known as the Deer Park. Follow the path around the headland (signs may advise avoiding certain areas to protect rare birds) to Wooltack Point on its north-west tip.

Return from the point on to the coast path and follow it, via the lookout post, back to the neck. Cross a stile then turn left on to a track leading down to Martin's Haven. Bear right after 50m on

Jack Sound and Skomer Island from near Wooltack Point. Culfor Jack ac Ynys Skomer o Drwyn Wooltack.

to a narrow path leading around the north coast of the peninsula, finally descending into the recess leading down to Musselwick Sands.

Follow the recess inland, turn right (signposted "Public Footpath"), cross over a track, and go up the left side of a field. Cross the stile at the top of the field on to a surfaced road. Follow the road to the right for a little under 1km then turn left on to a track leading back to the car park.

Alternatives: The route can be shortened by following the short-cut across the 'neck' from Deadman's Bay to Martin's Haven, and then by returning to the start along a minor road.

Walking isn't about exercise and fine views, it's about emotion. No? Then stand above the cliffs of the Pembrokeshire coast, ears tingling from an on-shore breeze, eyes slitted against a low sun, and watch the gulls soar on upwelling air while the waves ritually kill themselves on the rocks beneath, and try telling me that it doesn't break your heart.

Childhood memories of the seaside are of crumbling sandcastles and gritty shrimps in paper cones. That's because those memories have word labels attached to them, unlike those of unspoken emotion, such as the sensation of dry sand escaping through your fingers, or of peering over a cliff edge at a hidden bay, or of standing on something wriggly beneath the waves. It could be that adult responses to the sea are mere revivals of those unspoken childhood memories. Or it could be envy. Perhaps all we really want in life is to fly like birds or swim like the fish, instead of pottering around our two-dimensional world encumbered with clothes and cars and houses. Don't you ever wish you could crawl back into that soothing, terrifying sea from whence we came?

The notable sights of the Pembrokeshire coast may be the villages, headlands, harbours and flowers; but make no mistake, the compulsion is the sea.

Let's be practical for a moment. Given that we can neither fly nor swim, a typical coastal journey on foot starts from A and ends at B, several inconvenient hours away. Which is why the untypical Marloes Peninsula walk—from the sandy curve of Marloes Sands, around the rocky protrusion of Wooltack Point, and back to the secluded bay of Musselwick, little more than twenty minutes from the start—is so attractive.

"A long, straggling, poor looking village," wrote Richard Fenton, describing early nineteenth-century Marloes in his *Historical Tour through Pembrokeshire*. If the village itself wasn't much to write home about, then its leeches certainly were; the Marloes Mere leech was highly thought of in Harley Street, where it was treasured for its superior blood-letting capabilities (to be fair, the mere had been partially drained by the time of Fenton's visit). Marloes eventually substituted tourists for leeches and now the village is a long, straggling, fair looking place. The oddest thing about Marloes is that it isn't on the coast. People who come here do so as a formality before travelling south to Marloes Sands, north to Musselwick Sands, or west to Martin's Haven. Best of all, of course, is to walk the coastline and visit all three, saving Marloes for evening relaxation. Its pubs are renowned for their curative powers.

Marloes Sands, "the most beautiful beach in Pembrokeshire", has escaped destructive inundation thanks to a ten-minute stroll down a bridleway. It might not seem much of a buffer zone to a walker, but it's enough to deter ice-cream vans and other 'essential' amenities. There's nothing here but golden sand, rock pools and a craggy headwall. At high water the bay gathers up the surf in its curved arms and slurps it over the teeth of its open jaw, sending the sunbathers scuttling back up the trail. I timed it late and arrived to find just one couple perched defiantly on an outcrop. I raced the incoming tide along what remained of the beach, jumping from boulder to boulder to escape the foam. With retreat cut off, and no possibility of an escape up the collapsing cliffs, I put all my hopes in finding an exit at the west end of the bay. Risky business, but it paid off.

The western headland of Marloes Sands overlooks the characteristically flat-topped island of Gateholm (accessible on foot at low tide), where there is evidence of more than a hundred Iron Age hut circles. The larger and similarly flat-topped island five kilometres south-west is the bird sanctuary of Skokholm, while the island an equal distance to the west is Skomer, its distinctive Mew Stone clearly visible at the southern tip. Beyond the headland the path resumes its familiar headland/bay sequence: cliffs to the left, fenced fields to the right, leaving the coast walker to balance the transitional knife-edge between land and sea. At one point, above the appropriately named Deadman's Bay, the edge is proving to be a

Gateholm Island and distant Skokholm Island seen from Marloes Sands. *Ynys Gatholm ac Ynys Skokholm yn y pellter, o Draeth Marloes.*

The south coast of Marloes Peninsula. *Glannau deheuol Penrhyn Marloes.*

little too sharp; the path creeps around the rim of a thirty-metre cliff which is in imminent danger of collapse. The warning notices are for real.

The official coast path short-cuts the tip of the peninsula by crossing the neck to Martin's Haven. In less of a hurry, we can continue on to the headland known as the Deer Park (the name is a reminder of a failed attempt by Lord Kensington to graze deer on this rather scrubby outpost). However, a notice urges walkers not to visit the south-west prominence where temperamental choughs are being encouraged to breed. After this diversion the path circles high above inaccessible shingle bays and out on to the craggy promontory of Wooltack Point, the southernmost tip of St Bride's Bay. The Point is romantically situated above Jack Sound, the strait between the mainland and Skomer, where the tide rushes through at up to six knots. The sound is partially choked by Midland Isle (traditionally 'Middleholm'),

where several ships have been wrecked. In 1837 the paddle steamer Albion, carrying fifty passengers and a hundred and eighty pigs on its delivery voyage from Dublin, struck a rock in the sound and limped as far as Gateholm, where the captain beached the ship on what became known as Albion Sands. The pigs escaped and got ashore, where they were given a lip-smacking welcome by the villagers of Marloes.

From Wooltack Point the path returns via the lookout post to the north side of the neck at Martin's Haven. During summer, small boats leave the haven for trips to Skomer, famous for its diverse bird population and wild flowers. Compared to that on the southern side, the path along the north side of the peninsula is rather more brambly, and the cliffs, though lower, less easily approached. At the far end the path enters an indent which leads down to Musselwick Sands—a secluded bathing area at low tide but otherwise unapproachable.

Intrigued by the unusual black rocks (a Black Middle Ordovician shale, I later discovered), I descended the rock trough and made a perilous crossing of a wave-washed scoop in the cliffs. Encouraged by the rubber-gripping flakes underfoot, I ventured further than I ought. The shale composition of the rock was treacherous, and I soon discovered that the flakes which at first gave such good support now crumbled beneath my fingers like cream crackers. If I fell I would slide down the scoop and into the heaving sea with no prospect of ever getting out again. Inch by inch I crept back along the rock, timing my moves with the surging of the waves. Suddenly I didn't want to fly in the sky or swim in the sea, I just wanted to return safe to dry land so I could potter around and do the things I was meant to do. The sea goddess said she would think it over.

Route summary: A short walk along the South Pembrokeshire coast, visiting lakes, a beautiful sandy beach and a remarkable chapel built into a recess in the cliffs. Can be extended to include more views of spectacular cliff scenery.

Difficulty: Class A.

Duration: 8km/5miles (13km/8miles); allow 3-4hrs.

Terrain: Good paths and tracks, sandy beach, and some road walking to finish. Scrambling over boulders when exploring Chapel Cove (optional).

Special difficulties: St Govan's Head, Chapel Cove and Huntsman's Leap areas are closed to the public during firing practice. Dates are posted in the village and are also available by phoning Castlemartin 321. Firing days are generally confined to midweek periods during the off-season. Bosherston Lakes, Broad Haven and Stackpole Head are not affected.

Approach: From Pembroke take the B4319 (signposted to Castlemartin), and turn left shortly after passing through St Petrox for Bosherston. Large car park near the church (GR:966 948).

Route directions: Take the path down to the lakes (signposted "Lily Pools"). Veer left on reaching the first lake to cross it by a footbridge. Walk along the far shore, following the main path over a second footbridge, and cross a third bridge of vehicle width soon after. Continue to the mouth of the lakes and bridge the outlet (GR:977 944) on to the sands of Broad Haven.

Exit the beach by steps rising from the west side on to the grass headland. If the red flag is flying then the route must be shortened here by returning to Bosherston along the lane from the car park. Otherwise enter the firing range and follow the marked track which cuts across the headland to the car park at St Govan's (a surfaced track can be followed out to St Govan's Head itself from the car park).

Steps leading down to the chapel will be found just south of the road-end. After visiting the chapel and exploring Chapel Cove, divert west along the coast path for views of Stennis Ford and Huntsman's

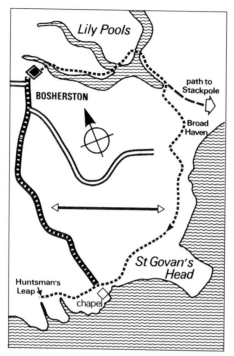

Bosherston Lily Pools. *Llynnoedd Lili Bosherston.*

Leap before returning to Bosherston along the road from the car park.

Alternatives: A detour to Stackpole Head is especially useful if firing practice prevents entry to the St Govan's area. From the stream outlet to Bosherston Lily Pools, take the coast path along the east side of Broad Haven and follow it for 2km or so, through Stackpole Warren and past the narrow headland of Mowing Word, on to the prominent Stackpole Head (GR:995 942). Return by the same route.

The South Pembrokeshire coastline has the other-worldly quality of a Mordillo cartoon; throughout its length, grey cliffs of carboniferous limestone plunge vertically into the sea from a level platform of green fields. Yet behind this overall simplicity lies a detailed complexity of promontories, bays, arches, islands, caves, beaches and stacks—evidence of preferential erosion by the waves on the bands of softer rock.

Fed by spring water percolating upwards through the rock, the lime-rich and unpolluted Bosherston Lily Pools sustain an unusual variety of aquatic plants and animals, including otters. The most prolific plants are the water lilies, which in summer rise and spread across the surface in a floating carpet of white blooms. At one time the lakes also provided fresh water for Bosherston, and the pump which filled the water cart still stands on the shore.

I had the lakes almost to myself, sharing the early morning sunshine only with a gull, a pair of coots, and a few hundred thousand assorted flying, crawling and swimming insects. As yet the lilies were submerged, although the surface of the water had assumed a solidity of its own in the still air.

Laid across the joint of the first fingery lake is a footbridge-cum-causeway of stone and wood, a half-metre wide and guarded on one side by a wooden rail. It reminded me of the ornamental pool at a park where I was taken as a child, in which shoals of gaudy coloured carp with pop eyes and gaping mouths would glide beneath the lilies. I leaned over the rail, peering into my shadow and my past, and was delighted to see a dozen small fish cruising through the water, among them a perch with its distinctive spiny dorsal fin and zebra stripes.

St Govan's Chapel. The steps and doorway right of centre lead to the rock cleft in which St Govan reputedly hid from the Lundy pirates. *Capel Sant Gofan. Y mae'r grisiau a'r drws ychydig i'r dde yn arwain at yr hollt yn y graig y credir i'r sant ymguddio ynddo rhag môr-ladron Lundy.*

A second bridged causeway, structurally similar but longer than the first, spans the knuckle of the middle-finger inlet. While crossing I disturbed a predatory bird which had been toying with something on the far shore. I hurried over and discovered a small furry animal lying on the path, legs in the air. It was a mouse, its head bitten clean off.

After crossing the rubble of the dam (not obvious as such), the path bridges the trickling outflow then follows the stream past hairy dunes and out on to the sands of Broad Haven, a beautifully proportioned south-facing beach flanked by cliffs. Here and there, spidery trails recorded the frantic scurrying of animals landlocked by an ebbing tide. Otherwise the sand surface was as smooth as drying plaster, my own erratic trail the only human footprints. Seduced by lethargy, I sat on a piece of driftwood to watch the retreating wavelets collapse with hypnotic regularity at the shore.

I must have fallen asleep because when I opened my eyes again the waves were more distant, their sound muted. I looked out beyond

the jaws of the bay to the silhouetted Church Rock. Its spire pricked my conscience; I was meant to be visiting St Govan's Chapel. I moved on reluctantly, ascending the steps on to the high ground above the bay where a high fence delineates the perimeter of the MOD firing range. As if to emphasise the transition from playing to killing fields, a formation of army helicopters droned low overhead, ploughing the air.

A flight of stone steps, traditionally uncountable by mortal beings (but no problem at all to little smart-Alecs in short trousers), leads down to the tiny St Govan's Chapel tucked halfway down the recess in the cliffs below the car park. The roof is intact, and there are few windows, so after entering through the arched doorway it takes a few minutes for eyes to adjust to the light. The chapel, possibly of sixth century origin, measures about six metres by four and is empty except for a covered well in the floor, now dry, and an altar at the east end. Steps next to the altar lead up into a recess in the natural rock of the cliff. The recess

is St Govan's original cell, and the scene of a miraculous escape. Govan came to Pembrokeshire from Ireland, where he was Abbot of the Dairinis monastery. It is said that on arrival he was chased by pirates from Lundy Island, and that he sought refuge in the cliffs below the headland. When all seemed lost, a fissure opened up in the rocks to hide him from view until the pirates had passed. The interior of the fissure is said to show the imprint made by his ribs. Overcome by shame at his cowardice, he vowed to stay in Pembrokeshire and make amends by attempting to convert the pirates.

From a doorway at the east end of the chapel, more steps lead down to a covered well, also now dry. A modest affair, it is regularly mistaken for a rubbish container or outside toilet. The cove below the well is choked with huge boulders, although the agile will find a way through and down to sea level. On days of storm, waves driven by south-westerly gales smash themselves into froth on the rocks, whereas at low tide during calm weather there are opportunities to explore the coastline. To the east, beyond a natural arch, boulders lead down to rock pools at the entrance to a deep cave with a low ceiling and floor of pebbles. To the west, a ledge leads through another natural archway and out on to the shelving platform below the cliffs. At low water the platform can be followed around to a deep cave; take great care, because the incoming tide soon cuts off any possibility of retreat. Mindful of this, and still smarting from recent misadventures, I entered the western cave with trepidation. Unlike the friendly eastern cave, this slurping, sucking orifice dripped water from its roof of yellow rock and wrapped me in its chilly breath. Huge boulders, green with slime, had been tossed into the base, so that in my attempts to penetrate the depths I risked an ankle-breaking slip into a man-trap from which I would never emerge. I imagined an amphibious sea monster to be watching me from the shadows at the back of the cave, salivating at the approach of this unexpected titbit.

Back above the chapel, it is worth diverting west for a few minutes along the coast path to view the awesome rift of Huntsman's Leap—favourite venue among intrepid rock climbers and popular final destination for the annual outing of the South Wales branch of the Voluntary Euthanasia Society.

The lane from St Govan's car park leads straight back to Bosherston village, an odd mixture of old and new, tasteful and tacky. Passing Ye Olde Worlde Cafe (I am not joking), I came to the squat church of St Michael and All Angels. Inside it was cool and quiet, and I was alone except for the caretaker in an adjoining storeroom, sharpening his gardening tools in readiness for summer. Comments in the visitors book described the atmosphere it conveyed, ranging from the expected "peaceful", "tranquil" and "restful", through to one from Rolf von Khulmann from Germany who, perhaps under some kind of linguistic misapprehension, thought the experience "cute". The final entry was from Gaymor of Mars who records that he left 66p in the collection box and found the place "muddy".

Broad Haven sands and Church Rock.
Traeth Aber Llydan a Church Rock.

The coastline of Stackpole Warren seen from the Mowing Word headland. *Glanna môr Stackpole Warren o benrhyn Mowing Word.*

Route summary: An adventurous walk along the finest stretch of coast on the Gower Peninsula.

Difficulty: Class C.

Duration: 16km/10miles; allow 6-7hrs.

Terrain: Narrow cliff-top paths. Simple boulder scrambling to reach Worms Head.

Special difficulties: The causeway to Worms Head is exposed only for about two-and-a-half hours either side of low water. Times are posted outside the information office in Rhossili and at the Coastguard lookout above the causeway (or phone Rhossili 202). Aim to leave the Worm at least half an hour before cut-off time, or face the consequences . . . Though rough going, the causeway is time consuming rather than problematic. However, the rock neck between Inner and Middle Head is unsuitable for young children or nervous scramblers. The same applies to optional low-level paths on the route to Port Eynon; if in doubt take the high path away from the cliff edge (and even then young children must be closely supervised). Paviland Cave is accessible only at low water during spring tides (the non-tidal approach is dangerous). The Culver Hole is accessible from below for several hours either side of low water.

Approach: From Swansea take the A4118 to Port Eynon, where there is a large car park convenient for the return (GR:468 852). The walk starts from Rhossili, 7km further west at the end of the B4247. Buses to Rhossili are infrequent, and there may be no alternative but to walk (note the short-cut along the bridleway from Moor Corner Farm at GR:464 865).

Route directions: From the large car park at Rhossili (GR:415 881), take the cliff-top track westwards to the Coastguard lookout. Tides permitting, descend the winding path on to the causeway and cross it to the Worm. Flank the Inner Head on the

Worms Head from Rhossili. The natural causeway linking the Worm to the mainland is passable only for a few hours at low tide. *Pen Pyrod o Rosili. Ni ellir cerdded y sarn naturiol sy'n cysylltu Pen Pyrod â'r tir mawr ond am ychydig oriau'r dydd, adeg y trai.*

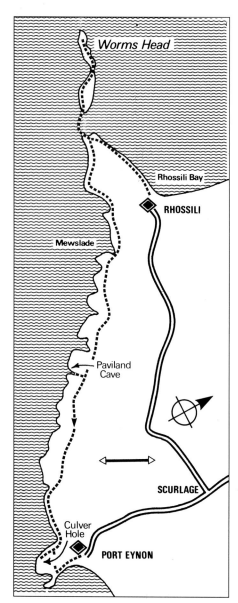

south side and scramble across the rock neck on to Middle Head. Passage to the Outer Head is restricted during the nesting season (15th March to 15th July). Return by the same route to the mainland.

Either re-ascend to the lookout and follow the cliff-top path eastwards to Fall Bay, or take a narrow low-level path to the same place (includes some scrambling). Follow a rising path (NOT the climbers' path which leads horizontally rightwards between high cliffs) on to the next promontory. Continue along the path above cliffs, detouring inland where necessary to avoid inlets. The inlet leading down towards Paviland Cave (GR:437 858) is identified by the drystone wall in its base.

Shortly before arriving at the end of a track from Overton (GR:455 853), turn right to descend a twisting narrow valley. Cross a stile on the left and follow the coast path around the bay of Overton Mere on to Port Eynon Point. Stay on the low-level path around the point to find the Culver Hole, which is accessible for several hours either side of low water. Ascend to the memorial stone on the Point and then descend the east side of the headland, through old quarries, to the ruins of The Salt House. Turn left and follow the signed footpath back to Port Eynon.

Alternatives: (1) The walk out to Worms Head is worthwhile in itself for a short day. (2) The coast walk can be extended eastwards to Oxwich Bay and beyond.

The Gower Peninsula, famous for its cliffs and golden sands, is extremely popular with day trippers from the towns of South Wales. Nevertheless, you need not stray far from the sunbathing hot-spots to escape the crowds, even on summer Sundays. This route takes a day-sized chunk out of the Gower coast path, following it from Rhossili to Port Eynon. Although there are similarities between this stretch and some sections of the Pembrokeshire coast, the path here is less intent on following the cliff edge, and in places you will find yourself wandering across fields, temporarily out of sight of the sea. Even so, this is a superb outing, with plenty of opportunities for unscheduled adventure.

In my naivety I parked at Port Eynon with the intention of catching a bus to Rhossili. Defeated by a timetable at the bus stop, I enquired at the general store opposite. The shopkeeper sniggered: "If you want to get to Rhossili today," he said, "you'd better start walking."

The car park at Rhossili is five times the size of the village. Thousands come here daily during the season to laze on the beach or stroll out to the point overlooking Worms Head, that unlikely strip of land which lurks off the coast like some gigantic, petrified sea serpent. Today I was more interested in the Worm than the beach. Unfortunately there was a problem with the tides. According to the Coastguard notice board, I had just half-an-hour to explore the Worm before the sea flooded the natural causeway that links it to the mainland. Nevertheless, I felt sure that the quoted cut-off time would incorporate a leeway of at least fifteen minutes to cater for the idiots who might overstay their welcome on the Worm. I reckoned I could safely give myself an extra ten or fifteen minutes on the deadline.

The word 'causeway' does not adequately describe the raised platform of jagged rocks leading out to the Worm. With time to spare it provides a pleasant scramble over encrusted boulders and among teeming rock pools, but when you're in a hurry it becomes a maze of ankle-snapping fissures. Leaping recklessly from rock to rock, I passed a nature class, nets and jam-jars in hand, working their way slowly back to the mainland. The teacher gave me a withering look but said nothing.

I followed the path around the south side of Inner Head and across the rock neck on to the Middle Head, pausing to take pictures of the Devil's Bridge, an archway eroded by waves that threaten to bite the beast in two. An RSPB restriction prevented me from visiting Outer Head so I used up my time allowance exploring the rocks and bays. The sounds of waves and bird cries filled my head and I entered another world. How lucky I was to be alone here on such a fine afternoon! ("Yes", murmured an inner voice, "but why are you alone?")

During this time the causeway remained hidden from view by the Inner Head, but I had no reason for concern; the deadline had only just passed, and by my own worst estimate I still had ten minutes before I ought to begin the crossing. As I strolled back I amused myself by working out the consequences of being cut off by the incoming tide. It would be a six hour wait until the water level dropped sufficiently for a crossing, by which time it would be dark. I carried no torch, and unless there was a moon, which there wasn't, I would have to wait until daybreak. However, my brother would become worried long before that (we had arranged to meet at seven o'clock); he would alert the Coastguard who would then come swarming across to the Worm, torches flashing, and drag me off squirming with embarrassment to safety. What a lark! It didn't bear thinking about.

I turned the flank of the Inner Head and the causeway came into view. Oh shit. Already there was a fifty metre gap in the land bridge, and what remained was rapidly disappearing under the waves. I sat down on the edge of the grass, put my head in my hands, and prayed for a parting of the waters. I felt a warm glow inside, as if my soul had been touched by an almighty power. I opened my eyes and looked up. As usual it hadn't worked.

Dammit, I would rather drown than suffer the indignity of a rescue. I rolled up my trouser legs and, cameras swinging wildly around my neck, starter running towards the narrowest section of the water-filled gap. At first I could run over shingle and wade across shallow pools, then I came to where even the rock teeth were submerged. I began jumping from one to the next. They were difficult to see under the foam and

I took several false trails, each time halted by a deep channel. Exasperated, I contemplated swimming for it, but with a thousand pounds worth of camera gear at stake it was out of the question. I retraced my route once more and tried again, by now forced to wait for the troughs between waves so I could see the next landing place.

It was at this point that I noticed a battery of birdwatchers sitting on the headland below the Coastguard lookout, binoculars raised in high expectation. "Come on sucker, make my day," they would be saying to themselves. That did it; in a frantic burst of underwater hopscotch I solved the final sequence and reached a continuous string of dry rocks leading to the shore. I was wet to the crotch. Not having the shame to pass the birdwatchers, I crept round the corner and hid in a recess among the rocks to dry off.

But you can't hide from yourself; I nearly packed it in and went home. Then an inner voice said: "There, there, it needn't happen again if you're sensible." So I went on.

By the time I reached the valley leading down towards Paviland Cave it was precisely high water. From my rucksack lid I pulled out one of two booklets I had bought from the information centre at Rhossili. Under the Paviland Cave entry it said: "Access is reasonably easy and safe only at low water. The rising tide soon isolates the cave." A pity, I did so want to see it. I thought I would go down anyway; I might at least be able to see the opening from the opposite headland.

As predicted, the gulch was flooded, cutting off access to the cave. The only alternative approach lay across a bank of shale at the head of the gulch, followed by some rock climbing to get on to the headland. It did not look inviting. Parts of the shale bank had already collapsed, and a fall from there would probably be fatal. But there was no harm in looking; I could always back off. I edged across the bank, got on to the rocks at the far side, and descended to a ledge. This was as far as my precious cameras were going. I left them in an expensive pile and began traversing the ledge out across the cliff. Then I heard a strange sound, like the wheezing of a chronic consumptive. It seemed to be coming from a hole in the rocks. Nerves already taut, I peered into the darkness. Nothing. Silence. Then as I turned to leave, the wheezing began again. How curious. I stuck my head in the hole and listened. The wheezing changed to a whistle and a gust of

The Culver Hole, Port Eynon Point.
Twll Culver, Trwyn Porth Einon.

stale air hit my face. Instinctively I jerked my head back and a second later a foaming spout of water gushed out. Blow hole!

Ten minutes later I decided that the trembling in my limbs had subsided sufficiently for me to complete the rock climb across the wall to enter the cave, a tapering thirty-metre hole in the cliff face.

Paviland Cave has long since been scoured of the archaeological finds that made it famous. The bones of an ice-age human occupant, probably a nomadic hunter, were excavated here in 1823. Other finds include an ivory pendant carved from a mammoth tusk, and bone needles which were probably used to sew clothing from animal skins. (In case you wondered why cave dwellers should choose a home plagued by acute access problems and penetrating damp, I ought to remind you that 20,000 years ago the Bristol Channel was dry and the cave overlooked a plain roamed by mammoth and reindeer. Yes, I read it in the booklet).

On regaining the safety of the coast path— I'll spare you a blow-by-blow account of the return trip—I consulted the second, more detailed booklet on the Gower caves: ". . . because of difficulty in crossing the gully, access is really only practicable on about 8 days in the month . . . (entry by) the right-hand side of the valley is steep and dangerous and should only be attempted by experienced rock climbers. Several young people have been killed here." It seems strange that I should have lived long enough to become too old and experienced to die on reckless adventures.

The light was already failing as I followed the coast path on to Port Eynon Point and came to that other famous cave, the Culver Hole. This is not a cave at all, but a deep fissure in the rock that has been partially blocked off by a man-made wall of limestone blocks. Apertures in the wall look like windows, and the structure has been mistaken for a smugglers' hideout. However, the interior staircase accesses only a series of small recesses in the wall and it is more likely that the Culver Hole was built to breed pigeons as a source of food. A rope hung down from the lowest aperture in the wall, but there was no way of reaching it from my side of the fissure, and the high tide prevented the normal low-level approach. Perhaps if I climbed over the cliff to the far side, traversed out above the sea, and then jumped the gap in the ledge, I might just be able to make a grab for the rope and climb up before the next wave rushed into the inlet . . .

Fall Bay. *Fall Bay.*

142

APPENDIX: Glossary of Welsh Place Names

Pronunciation

In General:
−voice the vowel sounds in a pure rather than shaped fashion
−stress the penultimate syllable
−assume spelling is phonetic

Vowel Sounds:

short	long
a − as in rat	a − as in barb
e − as in pen	e − as in dale
i − as in pin	i − as in seen
o − as in top	o − as in shore
u − as in swim	u − as in bean
w − as in foot	w − as in tool
y − as in rim	y − as in mean

y − as in nurse (the words y and yr also use this sound)

Consonants:

b
c − as in cap
ch − as in the German nacht
d
dd − as in the
f − as in of
ff − as in off
g − as in go
ng − as in sing
h, l
ll − as hissed l sound
m, n, p, ph
r − as in English, but trilled
rh − as in English, but with a stronger emission of breath
s − as in sit
si − as in shop
t
th − as in thought

Commonly Used Place Names

aber	river mouth
afon	river
aran	high place
bach	small, little
bont	bridge
bryn	hill
bwlch	col
cae	field
capel	chapel
carn/carnedd	cairn/heap
castell	castle
cau	hollow
clogwyn	cliff
coch	red
coed	trees, wood
craig	crag
crib	comb (sharp ridge)
cribin	rake (rocky ridge)
cwm	hollow, valley, cirque
dau, dwy	two
drws	door
du, ddu	black
dwr	water
dyffryn	valley
esgair	ridge
fach	small, little
fawr	large, big, great
ffordd	road
ffynnon	spring, well
foel	rounded/bare hill
garn/garnedd	cairn/heap
glas	blue (green)
goch	red
glyn	valley
gwyn, gwen	white
gwynt	wind
hafod	summer dwelling
hendre	winter dwelling
isaf	lower, lowest
llan	church, village
llwybr	path
llyn	lake
maen	stone, block
maes	field, meadow
main	narrow
mawr	large, big, great
moch	pigs
moel	rounded/bare hill
mynydd	mountain
nant	brook
newydd	new
ogof	cave
pen	head, top
pont	bridge
pwll	pool
rhaeadr	waterfall
rhiw	hill, slope
rhos	moor
rhyd	ford
tal	front, end
tri	three
trum	ridge, summit
twll	hole
ty	house
tyddyn	small farm, cottage
uchaf	upper, highest
un	one
wen	white
y, yr	the
yn	in

143